SAMUEL JOHNSON AND THE THEME OF HOPE

SAMUEL JOHNSON AND THE THEME OF HOPE

T. F. Wharton

MACMILLAN PRESS
LONDON

© T. F. Wharton 1984
Softcover reprint of the hardcover 1st edition 1984

All rights reserved. No part of this publication may be reproduced or transmitted, in any form or by any means, without permission

First published 1984 by
THE MACMILLAN PRESS LTD
London and Basingstoke
Companies and representatives
throughout the world

ISBN 978-1-349-17405-8   ISBN 978-1-349-17403-4 (eBook)
DOI 10.1007/978-1-349-17403-4

To Arthur Humphreys

Contents

Acknowledgements		viii
List of Abbreviations		ix
1	Life: 'vain imaginations'	1
2	Work: the 'scheme of life'	11
3	*Irene*: 'gleams of reason' and 'clouds of passion'	20
4	*London*: 'surly virtue' and 'pleasing dream'	29
5	*The Vanity of Human Wishes*	43
6	*The Rambler*: 'those that aspire to the name of authors'	57
7	*The Idler*: the 'voluntary dream'	74
8	*Rasselas*: the 'phantoms of hope'	89
9	*A Journey to the Western Islands*: 'imagination' and 'idea'	119
10	The Literary Criticism: 'propriety of thought'	139
11	Levet: 'hope's delusive mine'	157
Appendix		165
Notes		173
Select Bibliography		183
Index		186

Acknowledgements

I should like to record my thanks for the encouragement given to me by my friend Rosemary De Paolo, fellow-Johnsonian.

List of Abbreviations

Anecdotes	Hester Lynch Piozzi, *Anecdotes of the late Samuel Johnson, LL.D.*, published in *Johnsonian Miscellanies*, ed. G. B. Hill, 2 vols (Oxford, 1897)
EIC	*Essays in Criticism*
ELH	*A Journal of English Literary History*
ES	*Essays and Studies*
Hawkins	Sir John Hawkins, *The Life of Samuel Johnson, LL.D.* (London, 1787)
JEGPh	*Journal of English and Germanic Philology*
Letters	*The Letters of Samuel Johnson*, ed. R. W. Chapman, 3 vols (Oxford, 1952)
Life	James Boswell, *The Life of Samuel Johnson, LL.D.*, ed. G. B. Hill, rev. L. F. Powell, 6 vols (Oxford, 1934–50; 2nd rev. edns of vols V–VI, 1964)
PQ	*Philological Quarterly*
SEL	*Studies in English Literature*
Thraliana	*Thraliana: The Diary of Mrs Hester Lynch Thrale (later Mrs Piozzi) ... 1776–1809*, ed. K. C. Balderston, 2 vols (Oxford, 1942)
Works	*The Yale Edition of the Works of Samuel Johnson*, gen. ed., vols I, II and VI, A. T. Hazen; subsequently J. H. Middendorf (New Haven, Conn., 1958–)

1 Life: 'vain imaginations'

Bertrand Bronson some years ago remarked that there are two Johnsons:[1] the caricature of a rugged eccentric, transmitted by Macaulay's *Encyclopaedia Britannica Life of Johnson* (1856), and the thoughtful moralist revealed in his works. Two Johnsons still exist, although they have slightly shifted their ground. The 'popular' Johnson, generally known as *Doctor* Johnson, is now located in the *Oxford Dictionary of Quotations*, six of whose nine 'Johnson' pages are devoted to his conversation, and to the most epigrammatic remarks that Boswell can yield. Journalists, politicians and after-dinner speakers raid these pages in search of second-hand brilliance, and perpetuate 'Doctor' Johnson to audiences who know nothing more of him than that he said 'patriotism is the last refuge of a scoundrel', or 'when a man is to be hanged in a fortnight, it concentrates his mind wonderfully', or 'a woman's preaching is like a dog's walking on his hind legs. It is not done well, but you are surprised to find it done at all.' The market for this Johnson has always been good, even in his own lifetime. Boswell amusingly records that Goldsmith – always jealous of Johnson's reputation as a speaker – was 'mortified, when talking in a company with fluent vivacity, and, as he flattered himself, to the admiration of all who were present; a German, who sat next to him, and perceived Johnson rolling himself, as if about to speak, suddenly stopped him, saying, "Stay, stay – Toctor Shonson is going to say something".'[2]

The 'other' Johnson has now become what Bronson himself called 'Johnson Agonistes', his neuroses painfully laid bare.[3] It would be fair to say that this Johnson is much less popular in every sense; particularly with his admirers. Of course, serious biographers have carefully explained the connection between the first Johnson, an ardent and aggressive believer in the aim of a reasonable life, and the second. There is sometimes detectable, nevertheless, the wish to play down the evidence of the second Johnson. Johnson has always been a much-loved man, capable of inspiring devotion, and there is a temptation to present his extraordinariness in the most palatable terms.

To do so is to blur the important fact that 'everything about his character and manners was forcible and violent'.[4] The fullest truth about his character may be represented by extremes and contradictions. Certainly, his passion for reason and truth – he is said to have 'fought for truth as the drunkard fights for the bottle'[5] – is best seen in the context of his full acquaintance with fantasy and delusion. More significant in terms of literary study, the sanity of moral pronouncement which is the most distinctive mark of his work may be inseparable from an equally vital concern, within the same work, with fantasy and delusion.

It is well known that Johnson was deeply interested in mental illness. Burton's *Anatomy of Melancholy* 'was the only book that ever took him out of bed two hours sooner than he wished to rise'.[6] In part, of course, the interest was self-concern. Mrs Thrale tells us that he 'had studied medicine diligently in all its branches; but had given particular attention to the diseases of the imagination, which he watched in himself with a solicitude destructive of his own peace, and intolerable to those he trusted'.[7] Mrs Thrale's case was admittedly a special one, but others speak with similar disquiet of this side of Johnson. In his Highland tour, Johnson informed Lady McLeod of Skye, virtually a stranger to him, 'I inherited ... a vile melancholy from my father which has made me mad all my life, at least not sober.' Lady McLeod was moved to 'wonder he should tell this'.[8]

In his literary work, this near-obsession with the irrational took productive form. It constitutes his single most persistent theme. More than any of his other familiar and recurring ideas – the moral theme of envy, the idea of the 'choice of life', his theory of the 'vacuity of life' and the filling up of time – the theme of fantasy, vain hope, and the power of the imagination actually shape his creative work, frequently focussing on the imaginative act itself. As Johnson entered the great decade which produced most of his best-known work, the theme became increasingly a conscious and central one; one which he approached with increasing confidence and candour and which culminated in *The Idler*. *Rasselas* reveals a much more fearful handling of the theme, an attitude which is reflected in his later attitude to the imagination in his critical work; but marked much more pronouncedly in his own subsequent silence as a creative writer. While 'creative 'work admittedly forms only a small fraction of Johnson's published achievement, Johnson the encyclopaedist is also intriguingly related to the theme of the 'phantoms of hope'. The entire course of Johnson's life of writing may be seen to be shaped by his theme.

If delusion was his abiding interest, clarification was his conscious aim; not only of his own thoughts, but of those of others. As Reynolds once said, 'no man had like him the faculty of teaching inferior minds to think',[9] and his age accepted him as its teacher. Indeed, one friend, the Rev. Dr Maxwell records that 'he seemed ... to be considered as a kind of publick oracle, whom everybody thought they had a right to visit and consult'.[10] Yet, it must be doubted whether Johnson ever seriously resented the role. He loved to win. As he confessed, this included 'talk[ing] for victory'.[11] He succeeded in dominating even the 'Literary Club', which included the best minds of his generation. The great usefulness of such eminence was that he would be heard with respect, even when what he had to say displeased.

This was less a matter of Johnson teaching a specific body of difficult truths than of him contesting all thoughtless opinion. The startling and quotable nature of much of his most famous conversation is the direct result of his deliberate provocation of assumption and dogma. Slogans and prejudices were his repeated targets. Here, he meant to shock. When he proposed, to an elderly company at Oxford, a toast to the 'next insurrection of the negroes in the West Indies' he undoubtedly succeeded.[12] Able, as Boswell knew to 'talk upon any side of a question',[13] he was willing to do so, to provoke thought in others. He constantly delighted in the company of those capable of the same kind of penetration as himself. His first acquaintance with Reynolds reveals the instant liking for each other of two men who delighted in penetrating cant. The meeting occurred at the house of the respectable Misses Cotterell:

> The ladies were regretting the death of a friend, to whom they owed great obligations; upon which Reynolds observed, 'You have, however, the comfort of being relieved from a burthen of gratitude.' They were shocked a little at this alleviating suggestion, as too selfish; but Johnson defended it in his clear and forcible manner, and was much pleased with the *mind*, the fair

view of human nature which it exhibited.... The consequence was, that he went home with Reynolds, and supped with him.[14]

With lesser men, Johnson's legendary rudeness may largely be explained by his impatience with their incapacity to think for themselves. Young John Lade was unfortunate enough to ask a silly question, 'Mr Johnson, would you advise me to marry?' and was told, 'I would advise no man to marry, Sir, who is not likely to propagate understanding.'[15] Johnson was in every sense a charitable man, and very often took pity on the feeble-minded; but usually *after* their humiliation was complete. Belligerence was part and parcel of the struggle for clear thinking. On an occasion when Johnson pronounced himself satisfied with the quality of the previous night's conversation ('we had good talk'), Boswell replied, 'Yes, Sir; you tossed and gored several persons.'[16] However, clear thinking was the essential aim. It is not as the testy pedant but as the insistent definer of the qualities of things that he should be regarded, when we see him, typically, quibbling that 'No man was born a miser, because no man was born to possession.'[17]

Such an insistence demanded great clarity of colloquial style, and this was something which Johnson trained to achieve. He 'used to say that he made it a constant rule to talk as well as he could both as to sentiment and expression, by which means, what had been originally effort became familiar and easy. The consequence of this was ... that his common conversation in all companies was such as to secure him universal attention, as something above the usual colloquial style was expected.'[18] His friends in their various ways testify to the extraordinary nature of his talk. Mrs Thrale apologises that she 'cannot give each expression of Dr Johnson with all its force or all its neatness'.[19] Boswell, citing a comment of a friend, triumphs that his conversation could be 'all printed without any correction'.[20] This great sanity and clarity were, however, quite clearly artefacts, and Johnson was the subject of a biography which commemorated above all the part of him which was artefact. Biographer and subject were ideally adapted to each other. Indeed, Boswell did his part in creating 'Doctor' Johnson. Boswell was responsible for assembling conversational opponents to meet the champion. If the opponents were enemies, so much the better: 'I knew Lord Monboddo and Dr Johnson did not love each other: yet I was unwilling not to visit his lordship; and was also curious to see them together.'[21] On another occasion, Boswell conceived the desire 'to obtain an introduction [of] Dr Johnson [and] John Wilkes, Esq. Two men more different could perhaps not be selected out of all mankind. They had even attacked one another with some asperity in their writings.'[22] In addition to obtaining opponents, Boswell was often responsible for selecting the ground on which any contest would be fought. Since Johnson was 'like a ghost: you never speak till you are spoken to',[23] his biographer had to develop the skills of 'leading the conversation ... starting topicks and making him pursue them. He appears to me like a great mill, into which a subject is thrown to be ground.'[24] Accordingly, 'I introduced Aristotle's doctrine in his "Art of Poetry" of the ... "purging of the passions", as the purpose of tragedy. "But how are the passions to be purged by terrour and pity?" said I, with an assumed air of ignorance, to incite him to talk, for which it was often necessary to employ some address',[25] or, far more ludicrously, 'If, Sir, you were shut up in a castle, and a new-born child with you, what would you do?'[26] In creating this artefact, Johnson willingly collaborated; occasionally turning the narrative to its best advantage. When the two men spoke about the comical mystery of what Johnson did with the orange-peel he invariably pocketed, Boswell pronounced, '(with a mock solemnity,) "he scraped them and let them dry, but what he did with them next he could never be prevailed on to tell", JOHNSON: "Nay, Sir you should say it more emphatically: – he could not be prevailed upon, even by his dearest friends to tell." '[27] When Boswell wrote his account of Johnson in the Highlands, he had the benefit of his friend's constant interest in the project. In London, it was more than friendship that made Johnson insist on Boswell's admission to the Literary Club, despite sharp opposition. His disciple's presence meant that he was sure of a prompter and a witness when he tussled for truth and clarity, with his 'deliberate and strong utterance'.[28]

It comes as something of a surprise that the man who said 'when a man is tired of London, he is tired of life', said it with a strong Midlands accent. 'Garrick sometimes used to take him off, squeezing a lemon into a punch-bowl, with uncouth gesticulations, looking round the company, and calling out, "Who's for *poonsh?*" '[29] On the page, the words he spoke or wrote belong to 'that great CHAM of literature, Samuel Johnson'.³⁰ When fleshed out into life, they seem immensely incongruous with their author. Those who met Johnson, having first known his works, registered something approaching shock. Murphy found him covered in soot from a chemical experiment. Bennet Langton, ardent *Rambler*-reader, was 'exceedingly surprised when the sage first appeared. ... From perusing his writings, he fancied he should see a decent, well-drest, in short a remarkably decorous philosopher. Instead of which, down from his bedchamber, about noon, came, as newly risen, a huge uncouth figure, with a little dark wig which scarcely covered his head, and his clothes hanging loose about him.'³¹ Facially, the scrofula he caught in infancy scarred him, left him blind in one eye, short-sighted in the other, and partly deaf. However, what above all earned him the contemporary nickname of 'the great oddity' was less his appearance than the peculiarities of his manner.

> Talking to himself was, indeed, one of his singularities ever since I knew him. I was certain that he was frequently uttering pious ejaculations; for fragments of the Lord's Prayer have been distinctly overheard. ... He had another particularity, of which none of his friends ever ventured to ask an explanation. ... This was his anxious care to go out or in at a door or passage, by a certain number of steps from a certain point, or at least so that either his right or his left foot (I am not certain which,) should constantly make the first actual movement when he came close to the door or passage. Thus I conjecture: for I have, upon innumerable occasions, observed him suddenly stop, and then seem to count his steps with a deep earnestness; and when he had neglected or gone wrong in this sort of magical movement, I have seen him go back again, put himself in a proper posture to begin the ceremony, and having gone through it, break from his abstraction, walk briskly on, and join his companion.

Boswell also concedes it

> requisite to mention, that while talking or even musing as he sat in his chair, he commonly held his head to one side towards his right shoulder, and shook it in a tremulous manner, moving his body backwards and forwards, and rubbing his left knee in

the same direction, with the palm of his hand. In the intervals of articulating, he made various sounds with his mouth; sometimes as of ruminating, or what is called chewing the cud, sometimes making his tongue play backwards from the roof of his mouth, as if chuckling like a hen, and sometimes protruding it against his upper gums in front, as if pronouncing quickly under his breath, *too, too, too.*[32]

Strangers were not at all sure what to make of him. Sir Joshua Reynolds recalls that

> when he and I took a journey together into the West, we visited the late Mr Banks, of Dorsetshire; the conversation turning upon pictures, which Johnson could not well see, he retired to a corner of the room, stretching out his right leg as far as he could reach before him, then bringing up his left leg, and stretching his right still further on. The old gentleman observing him, went up to him, and in a very courteous manner assured him, that though it was not a new house, the flooring was perfectly safe. The Doctor started from his reverie, like a person waked out of his sleep, but spoke not a word. (Quoted in *Life*, vol. I, p. 145)

Another anecdote follows, in which Johnson, visiting Richardson the novelist, was present when Hogarth arrived. The newcomer began a conversation on the aftermath of the '45 rebellion and the conduct of the king.

> While he was talking, he perceived a person standing at a window of the room, shaking his head, and rolling himself about in a strange ridiculous manner. He concluded that he was an ideot whom his relations had put under the care of Mr Richardson, as a very good man. To his great surprize, however, this figure stalked forwards to where he and Mr Richardson were sitting, and all at once took up the argument, and burst into an invective against George the Second.... In short he displayed such a power of eloquence, that Hogarth looked at him with astonishment, and actually imagined that this ideot had been at the moment inspired.[33]

It is not clear whether Johnson was aware that his behaviour was unusual. Poor Miss Reynolds, who was on one occasion his companion when, in the street, 'he began his antics with his feet and hands ... like a jockey at full speed' and 'men, women and children gathered round him laughing', commented that he was 'seeming[ly] totally unconscious of having committed any impropriety'.[34] What is abundantly plain is that he feared for the balance of his mind. There can have been no more terrible fear for one who lived so cerebral an existence, but then Johnson was a believer in guilt and punishment.

> The solemn text, 'of him to whom much is given, much will be required', seems to have been ever present ... in a rigorous sense, and to have made him dissatisfied with his labours and acts of goodness, however comparatively great; so that the unavoidable consciousness of his superiority was, in that respect, a cause of disquiet. He suffered so much from this, and from the gloom which perpetually haunted him, and made solitude frightfull, that it may be said of him, 'If in this life only he had hope, he was of all men most miserable.'[35]

Unfortunately, even his hope of another life was far from secure. Johnson's memory of his own faults could be relentlessly long. In the last year of his life, he could still dwell on a youthful misdemeanour, and its sequel, perhaps fifty years later:

> Once indeed ... I was disobedient; I refused to attend my father to Uttoxeter market. Pride was the source of that refusal, and the remembrance of it was painful. A few years ago I desired to atone for this fault; I went to Uttoxeter in very bad weather, and stood for a considerable time bareheaded in the rain, on the spot where my father's stall used to stand.[36]

On this occasion, propitiation was successful, but guilt was not always so simply laid. The main burden of it fell on his work, where no act of expiation could diminish his sense of a sacred duty wilfully neglected. The full record of his self-reproach is to be found in the *Annals*; his collected prayers, diaries and meditations. To read them is to understand the force of Boswell's remark about the parable of the talents: the prayer 'when I shall render up at the last day an account of the talent committed to me I may receive pardon for the sake of Jesus Christ. Amen.' is comparatively hopeful. Others record something which can only be called despair: 'I have done nothing: the need of doing is pressing, since the time of doing is short.' Thirteen years later, his life still seems 'a barren waste of time with some disorders of body, and disturbances of the mind very near to madness'.[37]

Johnson's morbid melancholia became common knowledge shortly after his death, as rival biographers scrambled to make their disclosures. As early as 1787, Hawkins could refer to 'that melancholy which the public now too well knows was the disease of his mind'.[38] But as Hawkins and the rest heaped their indignation on Mrs Thrale, for deserting Johnson in his hour of greatest need, she held the most sensational secret of all, undisclosed until her own diaries, the *Thraliana*, were published in our own century.[39] She held the key to this in more senses than one. Item 649 in the sale catalogue of Mrs Thrale/Piozzi's library and effects was 'a padlock, with a manuscript note attached – "Johnson's padlock committed to my care in the year 1768" '.[40] The rest of the evidence fits all too well: the cryptic line in Johnson's diary, 'De pedicis et manicis insana cogitatio';[41] Mrs Thrale's reference to the 'Secret far dearer to him than his Life' with which 'our stern Philosopher Johnson trusted me about the years 1767 or 1768';[42] the letters between them in which he begs 'que vous me tienne dans l'esclavage que vous scavez si bien rendre heureuse', and she replies 'If we go on together your Confinement shall be as strict as possible ... do not quarrel with your Governess for not using the Rod enough.'[43] The evidence is incontestable. The only problem is how literally to interpret it. Possibly not too much weight should be placed, here, on a comment of Mrs Thrale's (though the italics are her own). Pointedly referring to Johnson's opinion that 'a Woman has *such* power between the ages of twenty five and forty five, that She may tye a Man to a post and whip him if She will', she notes, 'This he knew of himself was *literally* and *strictly* true I am sure.'[44] A far more attractive interpretation is provided by John Wain. While stressing that personal experience may have formed Johnson's very clear perception that 'madmen are all sensual in the lower stages of the distemper ... but when they grow very ill, pleasure is too weak for them, and they seek for pain', he nevertheless interprets the relationship between Mrs Thrale and Johnson in terms of fixation rather than enactment. Johnson suffered 'desires of which he was ashamed but which he felt impelled to confess to her. He felt so impelled ... because to confess his strange cravings to the woman who had become the object of them was in itself a kind of relief. ... By laying himself open to her – and thus, as they both well knew, giving her the power to inflict mortal hurt on him by betraying his confidence ... he acted out, blamelessly, part of his fantasy of total surrender.'[45]

Some knowledge of these distressing aspects of a life he himself described as 'radically wretched'[46] may help us to understand the power over him exercised by the whole idea of fantasy. His moral sanity was formed in response to it. It dominates all his work as a theme.

2 Work: the 'scheme of life'

One of the challenges Johnson makes to the reader is the resistance his work puts up to any attempt to interpret its overall purpose and direction. The *shape* of his writing career is easy enough to perceive. Nearly all his notable work is crammed into one decade of his middle life. Till then, a journalist, he seemed 'a great genius, quite lost ... to the world'. Later came his life as the great conversationalist. Interpretation is harder. Why did his creative period come so late? What prompted it? Why did it finish so abruptly? Perhaps the key question is the first. If it is possible to define the reason why the impulse to create was so tardy, the other questions may answer themselves.

The word 'create' of course needs to be handled carefully. Paul Fussell's book, *Samuel Johnson and the Life of Writing*, carefully explains the eighteenth century's very wide understanding of what constituted acceptable literary genres. He argues forcefully for an understanding of writing, in the eighteenth century, as the craft of persuasion rather than the medium of self-expression. He points out that 'the pattern of the literary career conceivable in Johnson's time does not imply development and change – it implies intensification'.[1] Yet even in this book, another kind of terminology and an untrained set of expectations unavoidably sidle in. *Irene*, if bad, is still 'original writing'. Johnson's career in the late 1740s takes a notable turn for the better when he 'moves away from the inherited tones of the Augustans to disclose his own'.[2] It is probably inevitable that we should search Johnson's early years for some signs of the powers he possessed as a creative writer; which might well include poetic imitation or adaptation, not just 'original composition'. We find only *London*, and even that is hardly the work of a young man. It is difficult to talk about the 'intensification' of the non-existent.

Yet, from the meagre scraps of school exercises and university translations, Johnsonians have been able to perceive clear signs from his earliest years of the style and preoccupations of his best work.³ The gifts were latent, but unused. Certainly, in terms of powers of mind, Johnson's youth was extraordinary. In the *Annals*, Johnson recalls an incident indicating that, even at the age of eight, he knew himself to be wiser than his mother. Speaking of his studies at Lichfield grammar school, he said, 'Of the parts of Corderius or Aesop, which we learned to repeat, I have not the least recollection, except of a passage in the Morals, where it is said of some man, that, when he hated another, he made him rich; this I repeated emphatically in my mother's hearing, who could never conceive that riches could bring any evil. She remarked [on] it as I expected.'⁴ His exceptional gifts were recognised even by his schoolfellows. 'Such was the submission and deference with which he was treated, such the desire to obtain his regard, that three of the boys, of whom Mr Hector was sometimes one, used to come in the morning as his humble attendants, and carry him to school.'⁵ When Johnson went to Oxford, 'Dr Adams, now Master of Pembroke College, told me, I was the best qualified for the University he had ever known there.'⁶ Under the encouragement of friends and allies such as Adams, or his cousin Cornelius Ford, or his Lichfield mentor Gilbert Walmesley, Johnson's self-confidence was developed. It grew, indeed, to somewhat contemptuous proportions. Of his headmaster at Stourbridge where in 1726 he was taken on as a kind of pupil-teacher Johnson said, 'he saw I did not reverence him'.⁷ At Oxford he soon began to 'cut' any lectures he considered substandard; and, when fined for this, told his tutor William Jorden, 'Sir, you have sconced me two-pence for non-attendance at a lecture not worth a penny.'⁸ Strongly competitive, Johnson began to develop the habit of seizing 'the wrong side of a debate, because most ingenious, that is to say, most new things could be said upon it'.⁹ He determined, as an undergraduate, 'to fight my way by my literature and my wit'.¹⁰ Yet we are told that it was diffidence alone which retarded his literary career: 'before he could be sure of his own powers, he needed to see what he could do as a writer for the periodicals, as a translator and as a political pamphleteer'.¹¹ While Johnson was far from immune from lack of confidence, and suffered a particularly severe crisis of this nature when forced, by poverty, to leave Oxford, such an account fails entirely to satisfy.

Another explanation may be possible. The principal sense in which the eighteenth century understood the word 'literature' was 'learning'. It was this sense of the word which Johnson promoted to the primary sense when he came to define it in his *Dictionary*. When, therefore, he speaks of thinking to fight his way 'by my literature', what he means is by scholarship, rather than by, say, poetry. When Gilbert Walmesley provided him with a reference to take to London in his first search for literary work, he recommended him as a 'very good scholar and poet'.[12] The scholar came first and it is notable that Johnson's first offerings to the world of journalism were essentially bookish in nature: a translation, of Father Jerome Lobo's book *A Voyage to Abyssinia*, and an offer to translate Father Sarpi's *History of the Council of Trent*.

It is interesting, too, that any plans he had for a career in the world of letters seemed to alternate at regular intervals with other ideas; notably of becoming a simple pedagogue. His first job was as a school 'usher' at Market Bosworth. It did not last long, and his old schoolfriend Hector procured him a little journalistic work, and encouraged him in the Lobo translation. On the strength of this came his first approach to Edmund Cave of the *Gentleman's Magazine* in London; offering more or less to revolutionise the *Magazine's* literary section. When, within a year, however, Johnson married 'Tetty' Porter, his thoughts turned again to schoolteaching, and he applied for a job in Solihull. His application failed: the school governors had heard that he was 'a very haughty, ill-natured gent., and that he has a way of distorting his Face (which though he can't help) the gent. think it may affect some lads'.[13] Undaunted, Johnson used some of his wife's money to found his own school at Edial: a catastrophic venture, attracting only three pupils (one of whom, however, was David Garrick). Only when this failed did Johnson turn again to writing: beginning work on his tragedy, *Irene*, and again approaching Cave with the Sarpi project. Eventually Cave took him on, and Johnson began to show signs of a definite bid for literary recognition. Besides *Irene* there was *London*, a 'poetic imitation' of Juvenal in the manner of Pope; and two prose pamphlets in the Swiftian mode, *Marmor Norfolciense* and *A Complete Vindication of Licensers of the Stage*. Yet, in the same year, 1739, he made another attempt to return to schoolteaching. It failed, this time because Johnson lacked a university degree.

Even when working as a journalist in the succeeding years, Johnson was drawn to projects concerned with scholars and scholarship. Possibly what had attracted him to Father Sarpi had been Sarpi's immense intellectual range: 'he frequently convers'd upon Astronomy with mathematicians, upon Anatomy with Surgeons, upon Medicine with Physicians, and with Chemists upon the Analysis of metals, not as a superficial Enquirer, but as a complete Master'.[14] Consistent with this are the biographical subjects he chose to write on, for the *Gentleman's Magazine*: Boerhaave, the Dutch physician and scientist, who had died in 1738; Morin, the seventeenth-century French physician and botanist; Barretier, the prodigious German linguist, astronomer, mathematician and philosopher, who had died in 1740, aged nineteen.

Not surprisingly, therefore, Johnson's own 'literary' projects are notably more scholarly than creative. Boswell reproduces, towards the end of the *Life of Johnson*, the *'Adversaria'*; a list of projects compiled at some indeterminate date by Johnson. These include numerous schemes to edit poems or translate treatises; to write histories − of criticism, of mythology, of Venice, of the revival of learning in Europe; to make collections − of the letters of English authors, of proverbs, of travel works; to write dictionaries − of geography, of Common Prayer, of ancient history, of English poetry. These projects reveal not only Johnson's own claims to polymathy but an interesting tendency to pursue these interests into encyclopaedic undertakings If none of these particular schemes ever came to fruition, Johnson did accept, from his early years in journalism onwards, commissions for analogous work. For instance, there were his contributions of biographies to his friend Dr James's *Medicinal Dictionary* in 1742. Then came a much more extensive project for the publisher Osborne whom he met through James. This was to provide a descriptive catalogue of the 'Harleian' collection of books − about 50,000 books, 350,000 pamphlets and over 7000 volumes of manuscripts − which Osborne had bought and wanted to advertise for re-sale. It was an immense task which stretched to the full Johnson's capacity to 'grapple with whole libraries',[15] and it strains belief that it was only a part-time job. Johnson's period of writing, single-handed, the Parliamentary Debates for the *Gentleman's Magazine* in fact almost exactly coincides with his time with the Harleian.

Finally, after a gap of ten months, he embarked on a great encyclopaedic project of his own. He had recently made one more attempt to leave writing for another profession, this time law. He had failed, again because of the lack of a degree. Now, at the age of thirty-six, he made his deal with the publishers and began work on the *Dictionary of the English Language*, an idea which had 'grown up in his mind insensibly'.[16]

The massive task he set himself and accomplished, was to produce, in eight years, with only six amanuenses, the kind of great national dictionary never seen before in Britain. He set out to match the achievements of France and Italy, which were written by academies over decades. Apart from anything else, he set himself to read through English literature from Elizabethan to Augustan times; noting usage, isolating the 40,000 words he selected for definition in their various senses, in passages which illustrated their meaning (about 114,000 quotations in all). The result has been described as 'one of the greatest single achievements of scholarship, and probably the greatest ever performed by one individual who labored under anything like the disadvantages in a comparable length of time'.[17] His enlightened principles, of description rather than prescription, of illustrative quotation, of precise definition, became the model for all future dictionaries. Only in etymology and historical principle were further improvements to be made, and the *New English Dictionary*, which made them, was not even to begin for another century.

But if Johnson did not, in our accepted sense of the word, even want to be a 'writer' but a scholar, the fascinating thing is that the *Dictionary*, his great scholarly achievement, released in him all his latent creative talent as a by-product. He wrote his second Juvenal 'imitation', *The Vanity of Human Wishes*, as his work on the *Dictionary* began. This, and the *Plan of a Dictionary of the English Language*, were the first published works to which he had put his name. There followed a decade of assured moral writing, in *The Rambler*, *The Idler* and *Rasselas*; and, with them, national celebrity, an honorary doctorate and a Royal pension.

Without the *Dictionary*, however, it is doubtful whether any of these works – which for him were secondary – would have been undertaken. Walter Jackson Bate writes persuasively of Johnson's work-conscience: of the excessive burdens of self-demand he imposed; of his simultaneous rigid resistance to these and any other demands on his abilities; of the consequent paralysis of guilt in his most tormented periods.[18] The importance of the *Dictionary* was that Johnson was finally able to satisfy the demands he made on himself; and to release the tensions and conflicts which blocked his creative gifts. Intriguingly, Johnson apparently told Tom Tyers that the two hundred or so *Rambler* essays were written 'by way of relief' from the *Dictionary*; and Hawkins speculates that the *Idler* essays were written as a diversion during the later work on the Shakespeare edition.[19]

No lesser achievement would have had the same power of appeasement. Professor Bate is far less convincing when he implies an inevitable connection between Johnson's rapid personal maturity at this period, and a new literary career, 'turning now ... to the human condition and the central problems of living'.[20] Without the *Dictionary*, there could be no such inevitability.

Certainly, creative writing on its own was quite inadequate to satisfy Johnson's idea of a fitting achievement in 'literature'; to evoke the kind of dignified pride which resounds in the Preface, announcing how the *Dictionary* was 'written with little assistance of the learned, and without the patronage of the great; not in the soft obscurities of retirement, or under the shelter of academick bowers, but amidst inconvenience and distraction, in sickness and in sorrow'.

This is perhaps best understood if we consider the extreme ease with which Johnson could compose 'creative' work. Once this is seen, it will be evident that nothing that came so easily to him could have satisfied his self-demands. Certainly, as a poet, Johnson enjoyed an extraordinary extempore facility; to such an extent that his lesser English verse was usually not in writing at all, but composed and recited on the instant, simply to amuse, or to oblige, or to quell. In 1777, the gift was still intact. He recited an eighteen-line poem on the occasion of Mrs Thrale's birthday, which lines she 'wrote down from his mouth as he made them'. Johnson then pointed out to her, 'you may see what it is to come for poetry to a Dictionary-maker; you may observe that the rhymes run in alphabetical order exactly'.[21] There are numerous other instances of Johnson rattling out verses as a kind of social gesture; to rise to a challenge, to squash an opponent, or to help a friend go courting! That such pieces survive at all we have to thank the eager copyists. For Johnson himself, their existence was merely conversational. Even with his more serious pieces, there is the same method, and some of the same apparent indifference. *The Vanity of Human Wishes*, by far the most serious and sustained poem Johnson ever wrote, was 'begun as he walked on Hampstead Heath'. Boswell records with awe the 'fervid rapidity with which it was produced ... I have heard him say that he composed seventy lines of it in one day, without putting one of them on paper till they were finished'.²² If there is more than a touch of Johnsonian pride about this story, his indifference is equally clearly revealed on the occasion when Boswell asked him whether he would give the world any more of his Juvenal imitations. 'He said he probably should give more, for he had them all in his head.'²³ Unfortunately, he never bothered to write them down. When, in the early 1750s, Johnson actually renounced versifying, in a poem to Baretti (untitled), it is the same note of indifference or even contempt which can be heard. The poem begins with a boast:

> I too can feel the rapture, fierce and strong;
> I too can pour the extemporary song,

but then comes the confession,

> But though the numbers for a moment please,
> Though musick thrills, or sudden sallies seize,
> Yet, lay the sonnet for an hour aside,
> Its charms are fled and all its powers destroyed.

This poem was the last Johnson composed in any form for a decade. It is clear that his very facility in verse was counterproductive.

Compare this, though, with translation, and a quite different picture emerges. In fact, a great deal of Johnson's verse output actually consists of translation: from Latin into English; from Greek into English; and occasionally from French, Italian or Spanish into English. Alternatively, there are translations into Latin: his undergraduate translation of Pope's *Messiah*, or his one hundred or so translations from the Greek anthology with which, Boswell tells us, late in life 'during his sleepless nights he amused himself'.²⁴ There are, in addition, a sizeable number of original compositions in Latin. Unlike his English verse, Johnson was evidently in the habit of writing his translations down. Occasionally, he published them.

Of course, Johnson was an able linguist. Nevertheless, translation was sometimes of a higher order of difficulty as a test; and this was an important criterion. It was as a rigorous test that he regarded languages. This was his motive for adding Dutch, in his seventies, to a collection which already included Latin, Greek, French, Italian and Spanish: 'I feared that I had neglected God, and that then I had not a *mind* to give him: on which I set out to read Thomas a Kempis in Low Dutch, which I accomplished, and thence I judged that my mind was not impaired, Low Dutch having no affinity with any of the languages I knew.'[25] Again, when on 19 June 1783 he sent Mrs Thrale a copy of his *Prayer on Losing the Power of Speech*, following a paralytic stroke, he explained that he had composed the prayer in Latin verse, 'that I might try the integrity of my faculties. . . . The lines were not very good, but I knew them not to be very good; I made them easily, and concluded myself to be unimpaired in my faculties.'[26]

I translate, therefore I am. Alternatively, I translate, therefore I am saved:

> Almighty God, giver of all knowledge, enable me so to persue the study of tongues, that I may promote thy glory and my own salvation. Bless my endeavours, as shall seem best unto Thee; and if it shall please Thee to grant me the attainment of my purpose, preserve me from sinful pride; take not thy Holy Spirit from me, but give me a pure heart and humble mind, through Jesus Christ. Amen.[27]

Here, translation ranks, because of its comparative difficulty, on the same theological level as the *Dictionary*, which is also commemorated and marked by prayer:

> I began the 2d vol of my Dictionary. . . . O God who hast hitherto supported me enable me to proceed in this labour & in the Whole task of my present state that when I shall render up at the last day an account of the talent committed to me I may receive pardon for the sake of Jesus Christ. Amen.[28]

Again, there is the reference to the parable of the talents, with its reminder of work as a sacred duty. If translation could here rank alongside the *Dictionary*, by comparison the casual labour of English verse-composition could not compete.

However, as already seen, when the sense of duty was at last assuaged by a great scholarly task, Johnson's greatest English poem could be evoked and published. In fact, there is an uncanny coincidence in Johnson's output between the ebb and flow of the two types of work. With the *Dictionary* came *The Vanity of Human Wishes* and *The Rambler*. When, a decade later, he embarked on his next scholarly work, the edition of Shakespeare, there was *The Idler* and *Rasselas*. As work on the Shakespeare petered out, the creative output disappeared. When his next compilation was begun, *The Lives of the Poets*, there is an (admittedly slight) trickle of English verse once again. There seems to be more to this than just a matter of Johnson getting his pension, and not writing any more.

The other interesting feature of the pattern is that the creative work not only coincides with the academic endeavours, but also provides a commentary on it. At the same time that he achieves real contributions to human learning, he writes also of the dream of immortality as the principal dream of human existence, and records the various ways in which the dream not only stimulates but threatens achievement. He writes – in *The Vanity of Human Wishes* – of how, even when the dream is apparently achieved, the achievement turns out to destroy the dreamer. Time and again, Johnson turns specifically to the dream of literary greatness. This is the dominant motif of the *The Rambler*. The Johnson whose drive to greatness creates his achievements in the fields of learning, therefore himself becomes the central subject-matter of the parallel creative work. The 'phantoms of hope' are concretely realised in his scholarship, and minutely examined in his poetry and prose. And of course, once released, the creative work was even capable, if sufficiently ambitious, of attaining to a theological status of its own. On *The Rambler*, Johnson composed a prayer very like the other two: that

> in this my undertaking thy Holy Spirit may not be withheld from me, but that I may promote thy glory and the Salvation both of myself and others. Grant this O Lord for the sake of Jesus Christ. Amen.[29]

3 *Irene*: 'gleams of reason' and 'clouds of passion'

The theme of fantasy and phantom appears prominently in Johnson's earliest work, the tragedy *Irene*. From the earliest draft versions of the play's speeches, Johnson had a clear idea to convey. He was at pains to spell it out when he eventually wrote a Prologue for its first performance, many years later. The message is not (though the Epilogue lends some support to this idea) that it is not a good idea to marry a Turk. Nor is it simply an exhortation to be virtuous and true to one's religion. Its message concerns states of mind. The virtuous and true are rewarded with decisiveness and steadiness: by contrast the vicious are condemned to torment themselves with guilt, longing and disappointment. The Prologue clearly links the ideas of morality and calm, immorality and torment:

> Learn here how Heav'n supports the virtuous mind,
> Daring, tho' calm; and vigorous, tho' resign'd.
> Learn here what anguish racks the guilty breast,
> In pow'r dependent, in success deprest.
>
> (ll. 9–12)

Even the audience is linked in to the idea of phantoms of the mind, with Johnson making clear to which camp, virtuous or vicious, he suspects they belong:

> Ye glitt'ring train! whom lace and velvet bless,
> Suspend the soft sollicitudes of dress;
> From grov'ling business and superfluous care,
> Ye sons of avarice! a moment spare:
> Vot'ries of fame and worshippers of pow'r!
> Dismiss the pleasing phantoms for an hour.

> Our daring bard with spirit unconfin'd,
> Spreads wide the mighty moral for mankind.
>
> (ll. 1–8)

The mighty moral is of course not quite original, but neither is it entirely without interest, thanks to Johnson's insistence on depicting 'vice' as a state of mind in which fantasy prevails: an idea which is not quite as familiar a formulation in the eighteenth century as its converse, that virtue consists of the most reasonable line of conduct. In his later writings, Johnson was to move far away from this highly moral and schematic view of fantasy, but already the idea is pursued with such persistence in this early play as to indicate that the mind's fantasies formed one of Johnson's central preoccupations.

The 'fantasy' theme gets underway as soon as we meet Irene for the first time, at the beginning of Act II. We find her trying in vain to imbibe some of her friend Aspasia's virtuous resolution, to withstand the suit of the Turkish emperor Mahomet. Both the Greek girls are captives in a conquered country, and the strain is beginning to tell on Irene. In the presence of Aspasia, who has successfully withstood Mahomet's advances, she feels that 'the glitt'ring vanities of empty greatness, / The hopes and fears, the joys and pains of life, / Dissolve in air, and vanish into nothing'. However,

> when thou art absent,
> Death rises to my view, with all his terrors;
> Then visions horrid as a murd'rer's dreams
> Chill my resolves, and blast my blooming virtue:
> Stern Torture shakes his bloody scourge before me,
> And Anguish gnashes on the fatal wheel.
>
> (II. i. 11–16)

Aspasia has little time for this kind of stuff, and is quick to point out that fantasies are largely self-made: 'The weakness we lament, our selves create . . .

> We learn to shudder at the rustling breeze,
> Start at the light, and tremble in the dark,
> Till Affectation, rip'ning to belief,
> And folly, frighted at her own chimeras,
> Habitual cowardice usurps the soul.
>
> (ll. 26–33)

Aspasia will go so far as to confess the imagined presence of a phantom of her own, the ghost of her own true love, Demetrius, lost in the battle against the Turks, 'whose soul, perhaps, yet mindful of Aspasia, / Now hovers o'er this melancholy shade', but she scorns Irene's suggestion (which we already know to be true) that he might still be alive, as a 'delusive dream' and refuses to entertain it.

In fact, Demetrius is not only alive, but has been recruited with his friends and followers in a counter-plot against Mahomet. The counter-plot has been conceived by Cali Bassa, a discontented Grand Vizier. In the past, he had acted against Mahomet, inviting Mahomet's father Amurath to resume his abdicated empire. Now, after Amurath's death, he fears Mahomet's revenge. Here, Johnson makes a detectable change to his sources. His own early manuscript notes on the story confirm the standard version; that, indeed, 'Cali Bassa was hated by Mahomet'. However, by the time the final version of the play was written, Johnson had decided otherwise, and when Mahomet is told of Cali's plot, his reaction in the play is one of incredulous horror, that a man he had respected and trusted should prove a traitor:

> Was it for this, that sick'ning in Epirus,
> My father call'd me to his couch of death,
> Join'd Cali's hand to mine, and falt'ring cry'd,
> Restrain the fervour of impetuous youth
> With venerable Cali's faithful counsels?
> Are these the counsels? This the faith of Cali?
> Were all our favours lavish'd on a villain?
>
> (II. vi. 6–12)

The effect of the change is to establish that Cali's fears of Mahomet's revenge are all a delusion of his own making. As if to make the point clearer, Johnson makes Cali rather baldly confess his own inclination to fantasy. He meditates on the vulnerability of the dreamer to mishap:

> While with incessant thought laborious man
> Extends his mighty schemes of wealth and pow'r,
> And tow'rs and triumphs in ideal greatness;
> Some accidental gust of opposition
> Blasts all the beauties of his new creation,

O'erturns the fabrick of presumptuous reason,
And whelms the swelling architect beneath it.
(II. iii. 3–9)

The idea of Cali's 'dreams' is later confirmed by a fellow Turk and co-conspirator, Abdalla, who becomes disgruntled at Cali's reluctance (understandable, in view of Demetrius's place in the conspiracy) to promise him the possession of Aspasia as his reward for services rendered:

Dar'st thou thus dally with Abdalla's passion?
Henceforward hope no more my slighted friendship,
Wake from thy dream of pow'r to death and tortures,
And bid thy visionary throne farewell.
(IV. iv. 8–11)

The other main 'vision' with which the play deals is 'passion' itself. The Turks naturally specialise in the illicit version, and the play's chief victim is Mahomet. Again, the confession of fantasy is made baldly. In the play's first scene of courtship between Mahomet and Irene, there is actually little to choose between the infatuations of each. In terms of cunning, however, Mahomet wins on points, arguing cleverly that she should forget her pangs of conscience, since God could never take seriously the failings of a sex made for weakness and for ornament. This clever piece of provocation reveals Irene as a champion of women's rights, and when she adduces, as proof of women's powers, their capacity to enslave men, Mahomet is almost home.

IRENE
Mean as we are, this tyrant of the world
Implores our smiles, and trembles at our feet:
Whence flow the hopes and fears, despair and rapture,
Whence all the bliss and agonies of love?

Mahomet tells her whence, with remarkable candour:

Why, when the balm of sleep descends on man,
Do gay delusions, wand'ring o'er the brain,
Sooth the delighted soul with empty bliss?
To want give affluence? and to slav'ry freedom?

> Such are love's joys, the lenitives of life,
> A fancy'd treasure, and a waking dream.
>
> (II. vii. 39–48)

However, if Mahomet can name his own malady, and describe it clearly, he is unable to cast it off until the very end. Johnson, with another change of mind, deleted an early jotting which suggested that 'attention rouses from the dream of love'[1] when Mahomet heard of Cali's treason. In the finished version of the play, he preferred to keep Mahomet asleep, until Irene is apparently implicated in the plot against his life. The intelligence is actually false, and Irene dies for a treachery she did not even contemplate, but the rumour is enough to turn love to loathing; and Mahomet finally realises the immense superiority of virtue and Aspasia over Irene and dreams:

> If thou art more than the gay dream of fancy,
> More than a pleasing sound without a meaning,
> O happiness! sure thou art all Aspasia's.
>
> (IV. vii. 12–14)

The nature of Mahomet's success in persuading Irene makes it clear that the delusion which assails *her* is not of passion, but of power. Aspasia insists that the dream is a delusion – 'Dream not of pow'r thou never can'st attain' (III. viii. 69) – but Irene is too far gone for good counsel. No sooner has she urged the powers of her sex to Mahomet – 'Beats not the female breast with gen'rous passions, / The thirst of empire, and the love of glory?' (II. vii. 57–8) – than her own imagination is entirely captivated by the thought of power. Admittedly, it begins as a desire for the power to do good, 'charm'd with the thought of blessing human kind' (II. vii. 73). It is of this that she tries to persuade Aspasia in Act III, scene viii, in somewhat ambitious terms:

> O! did Irene shine the Queen of Turkey,
> No more should Greece lament those prayers rejected.
> Again should golden splendour grace her cities,
> Again her prostrate palaces should rise,
> Again her temples sound with holy musick:
> No more should danger fright, or want distress
> The smiling widows, and protected orphans.
>
> (ll. 51–7)

Provoked, however, by Aspasia's lofty distaste and frank incredulity, Irene quickly goes on to reveal her ambitious dreams in their true light:

> Go, languish on in dull obscurity;
> Thy dazzled soul with all its boasted greatness
> Shrinks at the o'erpow'ring gleams of regal state,
> Stoops from the blaze like a degenerate eagle,
> And flies for shelter to the shades of life. . . .
> Ambition is the stamp, impress'd by Heav'n
> To mark the noblest minds, with active heat
> Inform'd they mount the precipice of pow'r,
> Grasp at command, and tow'r in quest of empire;
> While vulgar souls compassionate their cares,
> Gaze at their height and tremble at their danger.
> (ll. 98–116)

From this point in the play, Irene takes to wearing Turkish costume! At the end of the play, as Aspasia and Demetrius escape to freedom, Irene undergoes one final tussle between ambition and conscience, but the conflict is decided in an instant, when Demetrius attempts to pull her to the waiting boat:

> Forbear this rudeness,
> And learn the rev'rence due to Turkey's Queen.
> Fly, slaves, and call the Sultan to my rescue.
> (V. v. 54–6)

Johnson, in these speeches, applies his theme of fantasy with more energy than dramatic skill, but certainly there is no escaping the insistent theme. The terminology of dreams is tossed casually about, throughout the play. When Irene is arrested on suspicion of treason, she haughtily asks her accuser, 'What dream of sudden power / Has taught my slave the language of command! / Henceforth be wise, nor hope a second pardon' (V. vii. 1–3). When, earlier, Mahomet contemplates the conquest of Rome, he thinks with satisfaction of papists ripening for the kill, 'Till angry Heav'n shall mark them out for ruin, / And war o'erwhelm them in their dream of vice' (IV. v. 36–7). Johnson also makes sure to include the *torments* of the guilty mind, where fantasies become phantoms. Irene's death-speech provides the best example:

> Unutterable anguish!
> Guilt and Despair! pale spectres, grin around me,
> And stun me with the yellings of damnation!
>
> (v. ix. 49–51)

He also tries to make sure that the distinction between the states of mind which characterise and befall the good and wicked are sharply delineated. The good abjure fantasies, appealing instead to reason. Aspasia repeatedly tries to set Irene right by 'set[ting] the glitt'ring fallacy to view' (III. viii. 128). She is equally quick to proclaim her own contentment at the loss of all 'glitt'ring trifles' (IV. i. 108); and her fears for the conspiracy are soon quelled: 'Enough – resistless reason calms my soul –' (IV. i. 1). In detail, too, Johnson tries to keep the distinction clear. While the wicked only dream, the good exhort themselves and each other to 'awake'. Demetrius, indeed, is urged by his friend Leontius to awake from 'this dismal dream' (I. i. 83), namely his grief over what he supposes to be the death of Aspasia. Demetrius duly responds.

Yet, his response is not immediately to awake, but to replace a dismal dream with a happier one:

> From those bright regions of eternal day,
> Where now thou shin'st among thy fellow-saints,
> Array'd in purer light, look down on me:
> In pleasing visions and assuasive dreams;
> O! sooth my soul, and teach me how to lose thee.
>
> (ll. 99–103)

It is fair to say that the attempt at an absolute differentiation does break down, either by design or inadvertently. The four driving forces of the imagination are, in this play, as always in Johnson, 'hope and fear, desire and hate'.[2] If the last two are fairly efficiently expunged from the minds of the virtuous, the first two clearly remain, to generate dreams. As to hope, the best illustration of the process comes from Demetrius in Act III, scene ii, impatiently demanding action from Cali:

> When will occasion smile upon our wishes,
> And give the tortures of suspence a period?
> Still must we linger in uncertain hope?
> Still languish in our chains, and dream of freedom

Like thirsty sailors gazing on the clouds,
Till burning death shoots through their wither'd limbs?

As to fears, and even spectres, Aspasia surprisingly confesses her anxieties about the conspiracy, in terms markedly similar to Irene's fears for her life:

> Nor end my terrors with the Sultan's death;
> Far as futurity's untravell'd waste
> Lies open to conjecture's dubious ken,
> On ev'ry side confusion, rage and death,
> Perhaps the phantoms of a woman's fear,
> Beset the treacherous way with fatal ambush.
> (IV. i. 67–72)

She elaborates her fears at some length.

At one stage, even religion is depicted as merely an alternative area of fantasy, competing with dreams of earthly ambition:

> Those pow'rful tyrants of the female breast
> Fear and ambition, urge her to compliance;
> Dress'd in each charm of gay magnificence,
> Alluring grandeur courts her to his arms,
> Religion calls her from the wish'd embrace,
> Paints future joys, and points to distant glories.
> (I. iii. 12–17)

However, the speaker, here, is a Turk, and his subject is Irene. Johnson decided in his final version of the play to delete from earlier notes a similar subversive passage from a soliloquy of Aspasia at the opening of Act V:

> Whence rise these restless cares? these strong emotions?
> These chilling doubts, and agonizing horrours?
> From generous piety, or abject fear?[3]

In a play where action is suspended into anticipation, the phantoms of hope and fear entirely dominate the speeches. They are the whole preoccupation of the play. In a fascinating passage in draft, which Johnson felt unable to fit in to the finished work, he saw God looking down pityingly on human 'ignorance and error', and anticipating the endless multiplication of human delusion. He 'Beholds the birth of infant Indias yet unexpanded into thought / Unknown to hope and fear and fraud and falshood'.[4] Even if the play fails as drama, it promises much for the future, especially where it finds itself conceding the fantasies of hope and fear in even the virtuous mind.

4 *London*: 'surly virtue' and 'pleasing dream'

For who would leave, unbrib'd, Hibernia's land,
Or change the rocks of Scotland for the Strand?

is the first of many rhetorical questions asked by Johnson's poem *London* (ll. 9–10), in its indictment of the city. The problem with rhetorical questions is the answers they sometimes provoke. To this one, T. S. Eliot dryly remarked, 'the answer is, Samuel Johnson, if anybody'.[1] Eliot is by no means the only critic who has remarked on the immense disparity between the detestation of city life declared in the poem, and Johnson's well known love of London, so forcefully declared in his later days: 'When a man is tired of London, he is tired of life.'[2] But then, perhaps, the critics suggest, Johnson was merely adopting a modish position, because his literary career seemed to demand it: 'Actually, Johnson adored London and was exhilarated no end by its racy surface. ... His "real" relation to the views of which *London* is constructed is perhaps best illuminated by Donald Greene's remark: "Satire is a *genre*, and if you are going to write satire, you must find something to satirize ... every budding poet, whatever his politics, wrote satire and found the state of England deplorable." '[3]

Certainly, Johnson was making a bid for recognition in his choice of a highly popular form, the classical imitation, which he later described as 'a kind of middle composition between translation and original design, which pleases when the thoughts are unexpectedly applicable and the parallels lucky'.[4] The description is of a kind of literary game between writer and reader; and in his own *London*, Johnson challenged comparison between his own skill in playing the game, and that of the form's acknowledged master, Alexander Pope. Johnson insisted that the footnotes in the first edition should give quotations from the original Latin text,

Juvenal's Third Satire, 'part of the beauty of the performance (if beauty be allowed it) consisting in adapting Juvenal's sentiments to modern facts and persons'.[5] In doing so, he was mimicking Pope's printing of corresponding passages of Horace opposite his own imitations of them. As it happened, Johnson's bold claim to be compared with the greatest living poet was favoured by the coincidence that in the very week *London* was published, there appeared another imitation from Pope; *One Thousand Seven Hundred and Thirty Eight, a Dialogue something like Horace*. As Boswell says, 'The first buzz of the literary circle was, "Here is an unknown poet, greater even than Pope." '[6] *London* was a great success. A second edition was called for within a week, and a third within a month. It ran to five separate editions of its own, and was included in various eighteenth-century poetic anthologies.

If part of the success was due to the chosen form, and the skill with which it was deployed, another part was due to the specifically political commentary into which Juvenal's social satire is converted. Here, especially, Johnson was aiming for majority appeal. His ammunition consists of the common stock of Opposition propaganda against the Walpole administration. As Hawkins pointed out, it can all be found in the Opposition paper, *The Craftsman*: 'that the Minister was [the country's] greatest enemy, and that his opponents, only, meant its welfare ... that science was unrewarded, and the arts neglected; that the objects of our politics were peace and the extension of commerce; that the wealth of the nation was unequally divided; ... that restraints were laid on the stage; that the land was plundered, and the nation cheated; our senators hirelings, and our nobility venal; and lastly, that in his visits to his native country, the king drained this of its wealth'.[7] These are exactly the charges echoed by Johnson's poem; and echoed with the diction of party slang. Probably the key cant word of the period was the word 'patriot'. It is the focal word of Opposition. Whether that Opposition consisted of Bolingbrokean Tories; or disaffected Whigs such as Pulteney or Carteret or Chesterfield; or the City interest under Barnard; or the Young Patriots, such as Pitt, grouped under the protective eye of Lord Cobham; the diverse groups could at least agree on one thing. Walpole's peace policies – pursued in the face of blatant foreign iniquity and opportunism – were selling out the national interest. To be an opponent of Walpole, therefore, was to be a 'patriot', and indignation could not but be fed by the recent revival of the affair of

Jenkins' Ear in a House of Commons Investigating Commitee in March 1738; when all the old resentment at the powers Spain exercised to police her trade routes was again whipped up. In *London*, the incident is specifically alluded to, in the accusation that Government spokesmen 'plead for pirates in the face of day' (l. 54) – the 'pirates' are the Spanish *guarda costa*. With all the uninhibited simple-mindedness of the propagandist, *London* represents a 'patriot' as white, a courtier (Queen Caroline and King George supported Walpole) black (l. 52).

There is evidence, then, in Johnson's choice of material and of form, that his first thought was to achieve popular acclaim by saying what people wanted to hear; a clever game, fitting the hits of modern party propaganda into the framework of the ancient poem. However, other interpretations are possible; in particular, the ghost of Savage continues to haunt interpretations of the poem, and the figure of 'Thales' in the poem is commonly thought to represent him. Some time in this period, Johnson met, at Cave's shop, that most plausible and entertaining of malcontents, Richard Savage; *soi-disant* but unacknowledged bastard son of the Countess of Macclesfield, and an eternally impecunious hanger-on of London society. The significance of the meeting to the poem is that Savage, once a supporter of Walpole, was now committed to opposition, and had recently written a poem in that cause, *Of Public Spirit in Regard to Public Works*. The two men evidently formed a bond of common penury and common political extremism: 'one night in particular, when Savage and he walked round St James's-Square for want of a lodging, they were not at all depressed by their situation; but in high spirits and brimful of patriotism, traversed the square for several hours, inveighed against the minister, and "resolved they would *stand by their country*" '.[8] The date of this period of intimacy is by no means clear. Boswell transmits the testimony of the Rev. John Hussey that Johnson said 'he was not so much as acquainted with Savage when he wrote his *London*',[9] yet in April 1738 *The Gentleman's Magazine* published Johnson's epigram, '*Ad Ricardum Savage*', framed in terms of such passionate concern as to suggest an existing acquaintance. It seems, also, rather to be stretching coincidence to suggest that, quite without knowledge of Savage's ultimate retreat from London to Wales, Johnson's Thales, should 'Give to St. David one true Briton more'. Of course, Savage was not to leave for Wales until 1739; but then he may have planned to do so much earlier, and spoken of that intention to Johnson.

This, of course, is speculation, and not even strong speculation, but the speculation is not merely idle. The interest of the Savage connection is that it may well provide a second kind of motive for Johnson's writing of *London*; not, this time, a conventional or a commercial motive, but a personal one. Donald Greene's account of this kind of motive goes as follows:

> One must imagine the young Johnson newly arrived in London, sore at the neglect of the world, repelled by the ugliness of city life, and homesick for the gentler scenes of the Midlands. Through the instrumentality of Savage, or Hervey, or Guthrie, or *The Craftsman*, there is revealed to Johnson the appalling wickedness of Walpole's regime, which is responsible for the sad state of the world in which 'slow rises worth'. The young man's eyes are opened. He eagerly seizes on the Walpolian iniquities and uses them as pegs on which to hang his own griefs: bribery and castrati and masquerades become projections and symbols of the Johnsonian dissatisfaction with the world. . . . This is to make out Johnson to be a rather naive young man; yet, after all, until he arrived in London he had lived on the whole a bookish and academic life. . . . There would have been nothing in his earlier experience to cause Johnson to doubt *prima facie*, the horrendous picture of a vast Walpolian conspiracy to subvert the liberties and virtues of England.[10]

By this account, Walpole is not a conventional figure of rebuke, but is Johnson's legitimate personal target, on which all his personal disappointment may be vented. If Opposition slang, and the small change of Opposition propaganda may be found in the poem, so too may be found there some traces of a real personal involvement. Many have commented on the intensity of the famous passage on poverty, a subject on which Johnson was well qualified to speak as an authority. There is no mistaking the heartfelt vehemence with which this section erupts into the poem, and the almost paranoid sense of victimisation and humiliation that it conveys. This, the poem's clearest conviction, is spelled out in couplets stiff with anger:

> This, only this, the rigid law pursues,
> This, only this, provokes the snarling muse.
>
> (ll. 160–1)

The lines invite a personal interpretation; the thought that Johnson has been, probably, the victim of both these ills.

The existence of two possible motives for the poem, the conventional/commercial and the personal, may go a long way to explain some of the confusions and difficulties the poem poses to its alert readers. The first impression it makes is of a scathing, almost swaggering certainty about both the nature and the cause of the country's troubles. The closer the reading, however, the more the inconsistencies emerge. It may well be that the inconsistencies derive from a not-quite-successful attempt to force a diffuse, intelligent personal discontent into the unthinking mould of faction.

As far as certainty goes, the poem does its best to speak in absolutes, the absolutes of right and wrong ('While I, whose rustick tongue / Ne'er knew to puzzle right, or varnish wrong', ll. 79–80) and of black and white ('Here let those reign, whom pensions can incite / To vote a patriot black, a courtier white', ll. 51–2). Johnson later on came to have his doubts about 'patriotism'. *Marmor Norfolciense*, a year later, acknowledged that breed which is 'made a patriot by disappointment or disgust'. The *Dictionary* was to give as its secondary definition of 'patriot', 'a factious disturber of the government'. Twenty years later came his most famous pronouncement on the subject: 'Patriotism is the last refuge of a scoundrel.'[11] However, for the moment, Johnson subscribes to the theory that Opposition is patriotism, and patriotism is virtue. These comforting certainties, and the accompanying luxuries of xenophobia, are indulged to the full. Foreigners are contemptibly effeminate. Witness the 'warbling eunuchs' (l.59) of Italian opera, or the mincing parasites – 'Obsequious, artful, voluble and gay' (l. 111) – of France. Foreigners are all liars; they 'lye without a blush, without a smile' (l. 147). They threaten to infect our country, since, now, even some natives can 'lend a lye the confidence of truth' (l. 56); and with the lie threatens to come the whole habit of moral compromise, of 'Ways and Means' (l. 245). Probity and masculinity are, then, the chosen British virtues enshrined in the poem, virtues whose very essence is inflexibility and stubborn defiance. It may be recalled that the song *Rule Britannia*, in which 'Britons never will be slaves', dates from this period; and just as Thomson's song is from the masque, *Alfred*, so Johnson's poem draws on a heroic past of 'Alfred's golden reign' (l. 248), and boasts of freedom as a national heritage: 'from slav'ry far, / I drew the breath of life in English air' (ll. 117–18).

These inflexible virtues are duly enacted in the sort of verse Johnson writes. Rarely can the heroic couplet have sounded quite so assertive. The balance, native to all heroic couplets, will always give an impression – however spurious – of judiciousness. Here, the balance is not merely between line and line, but between half-line and half-line. Phrase answers phrase, on either side of the strong cesura. A few lines will serve as illustration:

> Illustrious Edward! from the realms of day,
> The land of heroes and of saints survey;
> Nor hope the British lineaments to trace,
> The rustick grandeur, or the surly grace,
> But lost in thoughtless ease, and empty show,
> Behold the warrior dwindled to a beau;
> Sense, freedom, piety, refin'd away,
> Of France the mimick, and of Spain the prey.
> (ll. 99–106)

It can easily be seen how the cesura, strongly pointed by punctuation, matches 'rustick grandeur' with 'surly grace'; 'thoughtless ease' with 'empty show'; 'of France the mimick' with 'of Spain the prey'. For reinforcement, or for opposition, the technique is the same: 'heroes' with 'saints'; or 'warrior' against 'beau'. In the early parts of the poem, the parts most clearly dedicated to a political theme, concentrated sections of this kind continually occur, amounting, on average, to one line in four. Johnson, in militant mood, positively drills up and down the line.

Another sign of stylistic bullying is the deliberate withholding of detail. In place of the profusion of Juvenal, Johnson rations his evidence to what he believes he can control. Admittedly, there is a certain amount of the detailed parallel-hunting which is essential to the 'imitation'. So, where Juvenal speculates that, if one could tear oneself away from the delights of the Roman circus, one might buy, for less than a year's rent of a gloomy town garret, an excellent country house at Sora or Fabrateria or Frusino; Johnson provides the appropriate translation of contexts:

> Could'st thou resign the park and play content,
> For the fair banks of Severn or of Trent,
> There might'st thou find some elegant retreat,

> Some hireling senator's deserted seat;
> And stretch thy prospects o'er the smiling land,
> For less than rent the dungeons of the Strand.
>
> (ll. 210–15)

Elsewhere, the search for parallels is much less assiduous. Johnson's use of contemporary detail is on the whole brief and allusive. The poem does refer to particular horrors such as the notorious excise tax; the defence in Parliament of Spain's right to stop and search ships; or the daily Government 'news' sheet, the *Gazetteer*. But these more precise details are carefully rationed, and confined mostly to the first third of the poem. The later sections, on the French parasites, or the miseries of the poor, are hardly specific at all. Juvenal describes in detail all the latest fashions his parasite-Greeks have brought with them; from slanting harp-strings, to the shape of a sandal. The impression is of real detail forcing itself into the poem. With Johnson, it is the other way round. Detail is controlled for brevity and dismissal: 'They sing, they dance, clean shoes, or cure a clap' (l. 114). As a result, his tone is fairly straightforward. In Juvenal, self-righteousness and scorn are likely at any time to turn suddenly into self-mockery and complicity. Exuberance and fascination are never far away, and the exuberance is always spilling into detail. In Johnson, by contrast, there is a kind of aloofness and command. Once the first third of the poem is over, and the theme of national decline stated with a proper sense of random allusiveness, he can settle down and locate, from the Juvenal poem, just three instances of that decline. In Juvenal, these three features – parasites, the fire, city bullies – are merely details on a broad canvas. Johnson makes each a separate tableau. From his stock of iniquities, these are the three he will consent to show us.

However, part of the fascination of the poem is the way all these apparent certainties evaporate under any kind of close scrutiny. This can hardly have been Johnson's intention, but it is entirely to his credit. There is, after all, no discredit in not quite succeeding in writing a poem of jejune political prejudice. To this extent, uncertainty becomes an asset.

As good a starting point as any is Johnson's handling of the figure of Thales. Thales is the speaker for the bulk of the poem. The first-person narrator, after briefly setting the scene of Thales' departure, thereafter merely listens to Thales' tirade, and reports it for us. He is, of course, a friend and sympathiser: as Johnson was to Savage, so, here, the narrator is to Thales. Moreover, Johnson has given Thales a persona of rugged surliness – 'surly virtue' (l. 145) – which fits more closely what we know of Johnson himself than what we know of Savage. It is as if he wished to give a sense of a complete identity of views.

Yet, intriguing differences still appear. There is, for instance, the different treatment of the idea of the pastoral retreat by the narrator and by Thales. The difference is a matter of some significance, since, as John Hardy's study of the poem points out, the pastoral ideal is the one positive of the poem (far more seriously handled than in Juvenal, where the idea of a humble pastoral existence reduces Thales to a fit of giggles about the glories of owning a solitary lizard). In *London*, highlighted by constant contrasts with the venal life of cities, the pastoral comes to represent the ideal of virtuous simplicity and the possibility of national rejuvenation.[12] But, while Thales' pastoral vision is one of such abundant fertility that his labours will primarily be to improve the garden as a place of repose ('There prune thy walks, support thy drooping flow'rs, / Direct thy rivulets, and twine thy bow'rs', ll. 216–17), the narrator's version of pastoral is far 'harder'. The lines about Hibernia's land, the rocks of Scotland, and a possible exchange for the Strand have already been quoted. It is Professor Hardy's colleague, Ian Donaldson, who points out that 'the way his question is framed is significant: he does not say, as we might expect him to say, who would not leave London for Scotland? but rather: who would ever leave Scotland for London? Scotland's rocks, London's Strand: Johnson's word-play sets up a subtly antithetical effect, reminding us gently of a possible similarity between Scotland and London, neither of which is without its hardships'.[13] At the very outset of the poem, then, within only thirty lines of the first of Thales' many pastoral sketches – 'Some pleasing bank where verdant osiers play, / Some peaceful vale with nature's painting gay' (ll. 45–6) – the narrator sets himself at a sceptical remove from the views of his friend.

This is no real surprise. One central Johnsonian theme is the evil of envy,[14] but Thales emerges quite clearly as 'the satirist as loser. His wealth has been "dissipated" (l. 20), he regards the French as "competitors" (l. 144), his chief complaint is that "unrewarded science toils *in vain*" (l. 39). His sole concern, in other words, is not with the social evil, but with his personal failure.'[15] This makes his 'peaceful slumber, self-approving day, / Unsullied fame, and conscience ever gay' (ll. 89–90) sound more than a little hollow. Admittedly, self-betrayal is not nearly so obvious in Thales as with Juvenal's Umbricius, whose loudest complaint is his lack of success in competing with the rich for the best whores. Nevertheless, he is still caught in the uncomfortable posture so familiar to satiric personae: rigid 'surly virtue', writhing with envy.

Accordingly, when the narrator, at the beginning of the poem, dutifully introduces his speaker with a few words of keen support, before handing over the platform, his words inevitably reflect doubt rather than conviction.

These opening lines are important to Thales' theme. His flail stretches far and wide. Like most impecunious extremists, its general tenor is of the degeneracy of modern times, and of the inferior race which is sapping the country's strength. To give some vestige of intellectual coherence to the racist rantings, a conspiracy theory is necessary, and the narrator tries his best:

> Here malice, rapine, accident conspire,
> And now a rabble rages, now a fire;
> Their ambush here relentless ruffians lay,
> And here the fell attorney prowls for prey;
> Here falling houses thunder on your head,
> And here a female atheist talks you dead.
> (ll. 13–18)

The conspiracy-theory is necessary because, while it is one thing to suggest – as Thales does – a connection between corruption in political life, and suspicious private goings-on; it is quite another, *unless* you have a conspiracy, to suggest that the politician-in-office is somehow responsible for the entire range of the country's ills. Accordingly, the narrator tells us that there is a plot. He names its three agents – malice, rapine, accident. He demonstrates carefully the way they operate in permutation: rapine and accident (rabble and fire); rapine and malice (ruffians and attorneys); accident and malice (falling houses and female atheists). The trouble is that the narrator quite clearly cannot take seriously his own theme. He 'seems to assure us, winkingly, from behind his hand, that these are witty exaggerations'.[16] The give-away is undoubtedly the preposterous 'female atheist'.

However, the poem's self-doubt does not consist merely of discrepancies between the views of Thales and the more intelligent narrator, hardly noticeable in a long poem. Through Thales' own voice, another kind of mind and a much wider set of preoccupations are heard to emerge. This happens very notably with the human theme. In a propagandist poem, compassion (except to the very select group of supporters) is the last emotion one expects to see invoked. Yet repeatedly, the poem, in Thales' hands, seems to turn to melancholy themes of man's perennial, pitiable unhappiness. The poem's most celebrated line, capitalised in the text and advertised in advance ('This mournful truth is ev'rywhere confess'd'), is,

> SLOW RISES WORTH, BY POVERTY DEPRESS'D
> (l. 177)

But this is a general, a universal truth. The local political application ('But here more slow') is a very lame afterthought. The same happens with such highly condensed moments of human comprehension as this one: 'For what but social guilt the friend endears?' (l. 83). The line is pregnant with understanding, but its compassion is disastrous to the need to fix blame. Likewise, as D. V. Boyd notes, 'the midnight murd'rer' is not only 'cruel with guilt', but also 'daring with despair' (ll. 238–9). He is 'both the instrument and the victim of social evil'.[17]

Far and away the most significant area of such intelligent reservations emerging is the theme of dreams and ambitions which insistently intrudes into the poem; so powerfully as to create an entire counter-theme. The counter-theme is of a common humanity, a shared failing, experienced alike by the poem's villains and victims.

A convenient starting-point here is with the poem's bitterest theme, the theme of poverty. This surely is the last place to find broad charitable impulses in Thales. Yet this is what emerges in the portrait of the 'sober trader'.

> The sober trader at a tatter'd cloak,
> Wakes from his dream, and labours for a joke.
> (ll. 162–3)

This diminutive two-line portrait is of an enemy of promise, yet it achieves detailed comprehension. Though a trader, he labours only for a joke (for which he *has* to 'labour', since he is evidently not very bright!). Though sober, he still has his dreams. It is here, in acknowledging the fantasies and aspirations of even the dullest respectability, the most oppressive jiber at promise, that Johnson's submerged theme emerges in the middle of Thales' indignation. The trader is at one in his pitiable dreams with far 'worthier' figures in the poem. He shares his dreams even with the righteous poor:

> But hark! th'affrighted crowd's tumultuous cries
> Roll thro' the streets, and thunder to the skies;
> Rais'd from some pleasing dream of wealth and pow'r,
> Some pompous palace, or some blissful bow'r,
> Aghast you start, and scarce with aking sight
> Sustain th' approaching fire's tremendous light.
> (ll. 182–7)

What is evidently shared with the sober trader here is the pleasing dream. No doubt the trader's dream, too, was of 'wealth and power' – they often are. The shared dream is in striking contrast to what is otherwise a wide disparity of mind between the dull trader, and the able 'starving merit'. In both cases there is also a shared gap between dream and reality; whether the reality be the 'little all' of 'starving merit' or the scarcely better idle dullness of the trader.

Needless to say, the idea of the dream also comes to embrace Thales himself, particularly with regard to his pastoral fantasies. Just a few lines before this, Thales was longing for a 'secret island in the boundless main' (l. 172), but his fantasies are usually closer to home; for instance, 'Some pleasing bank where verdant osiers play, / Some peaceful vale with nature's paintings gay' (ll. 45–6). Shortly, his vision is to take a rather more practical form, in which cash calculations are made, however optimistically:

> There might'st thou find some elegant retreat,
> Some hireling senator's deserted seat;
> And stretch thy prospects o'er the smiling land,
> For less than rent the dungeons of the Strand;
> There prune thy walks, support thy drooping flow'rs,
> Direct thy rivulets, and twine thy bow'rs;
> And, while thy grounds a cheap repast afford,
> Despise the dainties of a venal lord:

> There ev'ry bush with nature's musick rings,
> There ev'ry breeze bears health upon its wings;
> On all thy hours security shall smile,
> And bless thine evening walk and morning toil.
>
> (ll. 212–23)

The dream is not exactly modest. Indeed the elegant retreat is very much akin to the 'pompous palace' dreamed by starving merit. It is equally fantastic. Geographical inexactitude (*some* elegant retreat, *some* deserted seat) combines here with airy expectation (*ev'ry* bush, *ev'ry* breeze) and with the smiling landscape of eighteenth-century pastoral cliché. The only work done in this landscape is fantasy-work: a little pruning here and there, and the vast landscape is shaped into bower and prospect. Yet miraculously, this landscape of graceful leisure also provides Thales with complete nutritional self-sufficiency. But then, Thales is after all something of a wastrel. Johnson's *Dictionary* quotes the lines from *London* about the 'small remains' of Thales' 'dissipated wealth', to illustrate the tertiary sense of 'dissipate': 'To spend a fortune'. His dreams are fundamentally of 'repose' (l. 47) rather than activity.

Here, he is at one with a kind of national torpor. The only active figure is the French parasite, 'studious to please' (l. 123). 'Slumber' (ll. 72, 89) pervades the poem. This is a 'thoughtless age' (l. 60), lost in 'thoughtless ease' (l. 103). Almost every life we glimpse is lived in obedience to fantasy. The sober trader; the parasite's patron forming 'ev'ry wild absurdity' (l. 138); even the bully. The 'fiery fop, with new commission vain, / Who sleeps on brambles till he kills his man' (ll. 226–7) is a figure with his own fantasies of manhood, to be fulfilled at the expense of the defenceless ('Their prudent insults to the poor confine' – l. 233).

Where activity does emerge, it is dedicated to the realisation of fantasy; as, for instance, where the parasite obediently labours to incarnate his master's whims:

> Practis'd their master's notions to embrace,
> Repeat his maxims, and reflect his face;
> With ev'ry wild absurdity comply,
> And view each object with another's eye;
> To shake with laughter ere the jest they hear,
> To pour at will the counterfeited tear,
> And as their patron hints the cold or hert,

To shake in dog-days, in December sweat.

(ll. 136–43)

In effect, these collaborators-in-fantasy are the only advantage the rich enjoy over the poor. Thales has only his own imagination to bend 'ev'ry bush' to his desire. With the patron, 'ev'ry wild absurdity' and 'each object' are moulded into being, by the 'mimick art' of his followers.

With so strong a theme of fantasy running through the poem, all its apparent masculine certainty evaporates. How, when all is fantasy, can a sense of right and wrong, particularly of the specific political nature Thales would suggest, still survive? While a great deal of pleasure may be gained from Thales' scorn for his inferiors, and for the masterly lowering of tone he uses to convey it – 'Can Balbo's eloquence applaud, and swear / He gropes his breeches with a monarch's air' – satiric distance tends to shade into compassionate affinity. Even the standards by which both Thales and the narrator allege to form their sense of national pride, the vision of a greater and more heroic past, is acknowledged to be itself a fantasy:

> Struck with the seat that gave Eliza birth,
> We kneel, and kiss the consecrated earth;
> In *pleasing dreams* the blissful age renew,
> And call Britannia's glories back to view.
>
> (ll. 23–6, my italics)

Donald Greene has noted dream-imagery in those Parliamentary Debates for which Johnson alone was responsible; particularly in Walpole's long closing speech in the 1741 censure debate. In this speech, he accuses his opponents of creating national alarms of a quite invented kind; a fiction of tyranny in which they possibly by now believe. 'If their dream has really produced in them the terrors which they express... compassion would direct us to awaken them from so painful a delusion.' Professor Greene's view is that this signifies Johnson's recantation of the delusions of his own political extremism of 1738 and 1739, the extremism particularly of *London*.[18] In fact, *London* itself carries its own doubts and, effectively, its own recantation. In its hesitancy, its indecision as to cause and effect, villain or victim, *London* is a better poem than its theme. In the development of its persistent imagery of dream and delusion, shared by all, the poem actually develops a counter-theme of compassion for the universal unfulfilled longings of man.

It is to be doubted whether, this being the case, *London* is quite the poem he intended to write. Interestingly, the suggestive medium in which he works produces in Johnson as writer an imaginative seduction parallel to the poem's own dream-theme. To this extent, poetry, however easily it came to Johnson, provided a far less controllable medium than prose. Two of the three poems which are acknowledged to be 'great', work subversively contrary to the declared theme.

George Fraser wrote suggestively of the independent power words develop in Johnson's poetry: 'one's attention in reading Johnson . . . should not be on a core of similar meaning in successive words, but on sharp differences at the edge of that core'.[19] The phenomenon is what brings *London* to intelligent life. The true fulfilment of Johnson's poetic power had to wait another decade, for *The Vanity of Human Wishes*.

5 *The Vanity of Human Wishes*

The key image of *The Vanity of Human Wishes* is the image of the portrait in the golden frame. It comes in the section which concerns itself with the vain wish for political success (ll. 73–120). The section includes a description of the rise and fall of a generalised 'statesman'; and then a brief narrative of the career of Wolsey; the historical narrative closely echoing the pattern of the general, fictitious one.

This technique, of giving the general fate of one area of vain human wish, and following it with one or more specific historical examples illustrating the general fate, is commonly used in the poem. For the fate of the scholar, the example is Laud. For the fate of the warrior, there are three examples: Charles XII of Sweden, Xerxes and Charles Albert of Bavaria. There is a constant interplay of statement and illustration. Detail is constantly compelled into pattern. The individual is constantly described in terms of the general law. If the poem is, in a sense, a portrait gallery of great historical figures, it is also so organised as to minimise the significance of each individual face.

This is the importance of the metaphor of the picture-frame and the portrait of lines 83–90. With the statesman's fall,

> From every room descends the painted face,
> That hung the bright Palladium of the place,
> And smoak'd in kitchens, or in auctions sold,
> To better features yields the frame of gold;
> For now no more we trace in ev'ry line
> Heroic worth, benevolence divine:
> The form distorted justifies the fall,
> And detestation rids th'indignant wall.

The ancient tragic pattern of rise and fall is deftly alluded to, in the idea of the 'fall' of the portrait from its prominent, admired position, now that the subject of the portrait is disgraced. The idea of the portrait is so handled, however, as to submerge the individual tragic fate within a general momentum. The 'frame of gold' represents the brilliant political career. It is a career which is briefly occupied in turn by a succession of apparently famous men; all eventually disgraced, or even forgotten; all succeeded by others, who are forgotten in their turn. The frame of gold 'yields' to 'better features' in an incessant process. The human wish for success survives: each successful man is obliterated. Down the perspective of centuries, the frame mocks the portrait. The mockery strikes deep, since the portrait is so closely tied up with concepts not only of individual worth, but of the individual's identity. In Johnson's handling of the metaphor, these concepts disintegrate. The 'painted face' economically suggests not only portraiture, but cosmetics. The beauty, the very shape of the face becomes a matter of adjustment and interpretation. The meretricious 'bright[ness]' becomes 'the form distorted', succeeded by 'better features'.

Johnson uses a technique he had used in *London*, the technique of near-quotation. The invisible inverted commas effectively throw doubt on modish hyperbole. In *London*, he used the technique to 'place' the effusiveness of the French parasite: 'In ev'ry face *a thousand graces shine*, / From ev'ry tongue *flows harmony divine*' (ll. 127–8, my italics). Here, the 'speakers' are the onlookers of the political career:

> For now no more we trace in ev'ry line
> *Heroic worth, benevolence divine.*
>
> (ll. 87–8, my italics)

In an existence which becomes terrifyingly subjective, beauty is transformed, by failure, into ugliness; and ugliness then 'justifies' failure. It is a mocking, unanimous travesty, even shared by 'th'indignant wall'.

The whole idea, encapsulated in the portrait-image, of the individual career trapped in the universal logic of defeat, is then driven home by the way the portrait of Wolsey follows the general pattern of the 'sinking statesman'. In the latter, 'Unnumber'd suppliants croud Preferment's gate, / Athirst for wealth, and burning to be great' (ll. 73–4). The image is of the gateway to a stately house. The gateway is crowded with clamouring hopefuls. From their number, a few are selected, and, once admitted through the gate, are launched to success like rockets: 'Delusive fortune hears th'incessant call, / They mount, they shine, evaporate, and fall' (ll. 74-5). The human rocket idea always promises entertainment. One remembers Marvell's superb comic use of it in describing the destruction of the enemy in the Dutch Wars: 'Monsieurs like rockets mount aloft and crack.'[1] Johnson's unique contribution to the destructive image, as D. V. Boyd points out,[2] is in the word 'evaporate' with its Johnsonian implication of the evanescence of life.

Rise, glitter, evaporate, fall. The career is a brief one. However, there is still time for a dream-like transformation to take place. Those who are launched to success become a kind of Preferment-house for others, who clamour at the gates of the new statesman. This is alluded to negatively, in his decline, when we are told that 'the sinking statesman's door' (l. 79) is no longer thronged with 'the morning worshiper', the 'dedicator', the 'weekly scribbler'.

One of those launched is Wolsey. He too rockets to power: 'Still to new heights his restless wishes tow'r' (l.105). Like the generalised 'statesman', he becomes the gate of Preferment for others: the word 'suppliant' in 'His suppliants scorn him, and his followers fly' (l. 112) is an unmistakeable link with the 'unnumber'd suppliants' who 'croud Preferment's gate' earlier on. Like the sinking statesman he too is deserted. His suppliants 'scorn him, and his followers fly', and Wolsey even echoes the suggestion of evaporation in the statesman. For all Wolsey's 'full-blown dignity', there is the suggestion of transparency in the line 'Thro' him the rays of regal bounty shine' (l. 102).[3]

The essential point is the way the individual portrait inescapably follows the general fate. Without labouring the point, it is worth mentioning that his 'full-blown dignity', and the 'power in his voice and fortune in his hand' – the puns are very suggestive – also echo earlier and less glamorous figures in the poem. These are the 'new-made mayor' with his 'unwieldy state' (l. 58); and the 'hireling judge' who 'For gold ... distorts the laws' (l.26).[4] The ensnaring echoes here are very demeaning, and mock Wolsey's ambition to tower over the rest of mankind.

Notable in this section is a sense of nightmarish transitions and landscapes. This is in fact present from the outset:

> Let observation with extensive view,
> Survey mankind, from China to Peru;

> Remark each anxious toil, each eager strife,
> And watch the busy scenes of crouded life;
> Then say how hope and fear, desire and hate,
> O'erspread with snares the clouded maze of fate,
> Where wav'ring man, betrayed by vent'rous pride,
> To tread the dreary paths without a guide,
> As treach'rous phantoms in the mist delude,
> Shuns fancied ills, or chases airy good.

The first two lines were once tartly paraphrased by Coleridge; 'Let observation with extensive observation, observe mankind extensively.' The other lines here are *less* susceptible to parody or even to paraphrase. The location created in these opening lines is rapidly transformed from the familiar school atlas ('China to Peru'), or the familiar urban scene ('the busy scenes of crouded life'), to a nightmarish amorphous landscape. In it, man the social being is suddenly left groping, alone, without a guide, to find his way through a clouded maze, deluded by misty apparitions, his way set about by traps. If, in any sense, the idea of the Pilgrim's quest lies behind these lines, one can only feel that the landscape created for Johnson's secular pilgrims is the more nightmarish of the two. The 'bold hand' is seen, the 'suppliant voice' is heard; but both are oddly disembodied, and set in a context of sinking ('How nations sink', l. 13) or choking ('Impeachment stops the speaker's pow'rful breath', l. 19) or falling headlong ('And restless fire precipitates on death', l. 20). The idea of mankind perched perilously on the edge of a void is twice more referred to in the poem: in the picture of Wolsey climbing upward 'near the steeps of fate', only to fall 'With louder ruin to the gulphs below' (ll. 125, 128); and with the portrait of the virtuous elderly, whose rather dubious reward is to 'set unclouded in the gulphs of fate' (l. 312). The sense of vertigo that these opening lines create is promptly developed in the next paragraph, where, under the influence of the 'wide-ranging pest' of money (which, like the ruffian, two lines later, 'rages unconfin'd'), the landscape starts to move and become active. The 'madded land' 'shakes', as with a fever. Bushes and trees 'rustle' and 'quiver'. The gales are 'tainted' (l. 46). Vultures 'hover' (l. 36). The activity is felt in the personifications Johnson uses. Far from inert, they spread snares, listen maliciously, wing the afflictive dart, stop the breath, shake and seize. And, in collaboration with the malicious activity of hope, fear, vengeance and the rest, the human figures are gradually introduced. The hireling judge and ruffian, the rival kings, 'Th'insidious rival and the gaping heir' (l. 48). Far more effectively than in the opening of *London*, they seem to 'conspire' with the personifications and the landscape. The 'insidious rival' recalls, since it contains a Latin pun (*insidior* =ambush), the ambush feared by the traveller with his new riches. The 'gaping' heir gapes not only with vacuity, but with rapacity, recalling 'confiscation's vultures' of a few lines earlier.

The opening lines therefore create the sensations of giddiness, enclosure and threat. The sense of enclosure seems particularly strong, thanks to Johnson's handling of the couplet. Once again, Johnson makes a point of producing a sense of balance within the single line:

'Shuns fancied ills, or chases airy good' (l. 10), or
'Rules the bold hand, or prompts the suppliant voice' (l.12), or
'Each gift of nature, and each grace of art' (l. 16), or
'Wealth heap'd on wealth, nor truth nor safety buys' (l. 27), or
'Increase his riches and his peace destroy' (l. 40).

Here, the structure becomes not only balanced, but antithetical. The lines separate the natural opposites: hope and fear, desire and hate (l. 5); the anxious and the eager (l. 3); shunning and chasing (l. 10); nature and art (l. 17); enhancing and destroying (l. 40). It is a metrical technique used to cover and hold all the options. It gives a sense of mortal life, lived according to inexorable behavioural laws, propelled into extremes, and crushed into pattern.

The technique is of some interest to the poem at large, because Johnson inherits from Juvenal, and develops with enthusiasm, the rhythm of wild oscillation from victory to defeat. This is especially Juvenal's theme when he deals with the fate of the warrior. Hannibal, the man for whom Africa was too small, and half Europe not enough, ends his life as a plaintive exile. Xerxes, whose armies drank rivers dry, who paved the sea with ships and commanded the winds, returned, defeated, from Salamis in a single ship. These are collapses inherited and developed by Johnson.

Charles XII of Sweden, who replaces, in Johnson's version, the portrait of Hannibal, begins his career with an illusory control over the antitheses of human nature which we encountered at the start of the poem, with his 'frame of adamant, a soul of fire'. 'No dangers fright him, and no labours tire; / O'er love, o'er fear extends his wide domain' (ll. 193–5). He is 'unconquer'd lord of pleasure and of pain' (l. 196). Of course, what we have is another Johnsonian half-quotation. Johnson quotes the *belief* – of Charles or his admirers – that he has conquered the laws of human nature. And with equal presumption, he proceeds to extend the conquest outward; to make the world reflect his omnipotence.

Neatly, Johnson suggests the hopelessness of his ambition. His blustering speech, 'Think nothing gain'd, he cries, till nought remain, / On Moscow's walls till Gothic standards fly, / And all be mine beneath the polar sky' is dropped into an eerie silence, in which, suddenly, Charles seems to be utterly 'solitary', though watched by millions, and by the elements themselves:

> The march begins in military state,
> And nations on his eye suspended wait.
> Stern Famine guards the solitary coast,
> And Winter barricades the realms of Frost.
>
> (ll. 205–8)

But, in another half-quotation, Charles again underestimates his task, and overestimates his powers. The threatening personifications of Stern Famine and Winter become, in his view, mere 'want' and 'cold': 'He comes, not want and cold his course delay' (l. 209). And then comes disgrace, with no interim: 'Hide, blushing Glory, hide Pultowa's day' (l. 210). Now, the anticipated desertion and solitariness are enacted against him, as his punishment:

> Did rival monarchs give the fatal wound?
> Or hostile millions press him to the ground?
> His fall was destin'd to a barren strand,
> A petty fortress, and a dubious hand.
>
> (ll. 217–20)

The immortality he craved is achieved only ironically: in the 'everlasting debt' (l.188) of his bankrupted nation; and in the capacity of his story to 'point a moral or adorn a tale' (l.222). This is the fate of every conqueror: 'To rust on medals, or on stones decay' (l. 190). It is a fate shared by Charles of Bavaria, 'His foes derision, and his subjects blame' (l.253).

Markedly, Johnson concentrates the force of these reductions, of all into nothing, into tiny detail. It is a kind of zooming-in technique, focusing on one symbolic incidental of defeat. In the narrative of the statesman, the downfall is picked out in the detail of the portrait removed from the wall. In the fall of Xerxes, Johnson concentrates the full force of overthrow into the oar of a boat:

> Th'insulted sea with humbler thoughts he gains,
> A single skiff to speed his flight remains;
> Th'incumber'd oar scarce leaves the dreaded coast
> Through purple billows and a floating host.
>
> (ll. 237–40)

Everything here works to mock the conqueror. The heroic commonplace of 'purple billows' here take on a double extra force. Their colour is the colour of the blood of Xerxes' army; and is the answer to that army's earlier appearance as the 'gaudy foe' (l. 236). The invasion fleet now becomes a 'floating host' only in the sense of bobbing corpses. The 'incumber'd oar' can scarcely push a way through them.

It is reported that these were Johnson's own favourite lines in the poem and this reinforces our sense that the whole task Johnson has set himself, composing in his head, 'on the stretch', and then carefully revising the text, was, to create as dense a texture as possible of verbal suggestion. Apparently, Boswell objected that, in the 'scholar' section in the 1755 edition,

> the fever of renown
> Spreads from the strong contagion of the gown;
> O'er Bodley's dome his future labours spread,
>
> (ll. 137–9)

'spread' occurs too soon after 'Spreads'. Johnson told him to change 'spreads' to 'burns', and Boswell noted with satisfaction that the change was actually 'more poetical, as it might carry an allusion to the shirt by which Hercules was inflamed'.[5] In Johnson's various revisions of the poem – in the manuscript itself, for the projected second edition in 1749 and finally for inclusion in Dodsely's *Collection of Poems* in 1755 – Johnson made numerous careful detailed changes, well over a hundred in all. Only a relatively small number of these changes are corrections. The rest are improvements, made in the direction of extra nuance.

In nothing is Johnson's preoccupation with double-meaning more obvious than in his use of the pun. In the *Dictionary*, he defined 'metaphor' as a 'simile comprised in a word'. When the word is a pun, figurative meaning burgeons from the line. The section which best illustrates Johnson's use of pun is the one on old age.

Johnson describes how, in his old age, the miser is surrounded by his grasping, legacy-hunting relatives:

> The still returning tale, and ling'ring jest,
> Perplex the fawning niece and pamper'd guest,
> While growing hopes scarce awe the gath'ring sneer,
> And scarce a legacy can bribe to hear;
> The watchful guests still hint the last offence,
> The daughter's petulance, the son's expence,
> Improve his heady rage with treach'rous skill,
> And mould his passions till they make his will.
>
> (ll. 275–82)

The most obvious pun here is the one in the last line, 'will', where pun becomes an '*oxymoron* comprised in a word'. There is one other straightforward pun in the passage, and two other instances of multiple meaning in a word. The first line contains examples of the latter. Here, the 'still returning tale, and ling'ring jest' refer, primarily, to the dotard's senile repetition, time and again, of the same small stock of stories; and to the protracted tedium of his old jokes. They also suggest, however, the 'still-returning' persistence of his would-be heirs, and their regret that the old man's life is still 'ling'ring' on. Two lines later, we have one of Johnson's best puns, in the 'gath'ring sneer'. Its primary suggestion is of a sneer taking shape on the relatives' faces; but the pun also suggests that their sneer is related to the expectation of 'gath'ring' the old man's wealth; and there is a third suggestion, too, of a collective 'gath'ring' of predators.

In this last suggestion, the portrait of old age, as the portrait of Wolsey had done, draws in suggestions from other parts of the poem. Once again, the 'inherited' metaphors suggest a universal pattern and logic, common to every part of life, from which no individual life can escape. The 'unnumber'd maladies' which 'invade' the joints of the miser, and 'press the dire blockade', recall two earlier figures. The idea of multitude, siege and blockade recalls the myriads and barricades in the portraits of warriors. They also bring back to mind the figure of Wolsey, with his 'unnumber'd suppliants', and his wretched death, 'with maladies oppress'd' (l. 117). As to the idea of predation, it has been there since the beginning of the poem and 'confiscation's vultures'. In one intervening section, again the section on Wolsey, Johnson had also introduced the idea of the ruined man, surrounded by an alert audience:

> At length his sov'reign frowns – the train of state
> Mark the keen glance, and watch the sign to hate.
> (ll. 109–10)

In the portrait of the miser, the two ideas – of predation, and of a keen audience – join hands. The idea of the predator, pure and simple, is first introduced, as it were to prepare us, in the line, 'Time hovers o'er, impatient to destroy'. Gradually, we are given the picture of the ancient sensualist, once himself an eager feeder, but now incapable of enjoying the 'tasteless meats and joyless wines'. He is a near-carcase, waiting to be dismembered. His blunted senses are sharply contrasted with the preternatural alertness of the 'gath'ring' of 'watchful' relatives. Once again, the echoes stretch wide. Here, they stretch back to the 'gaping heir' of line 48. Once again there is a sense of an enveloping pattern of defeat.

Johnson's attitude to that pattern is still a matter of debate. The poem retains some of the crushing dismissal of mankind which it inherits from Juvenal. The reductions of heroism to derision still survive in Johnson's poem. At the same time, there is none of Juvenal's glee at the fall of famous idiots, of his sense of rich satisfaction in the crushing of *hubris*. Johnson's poem is not without a sense of pathos for the innocent naivety of Charles's military pride; for the 'blushing' humiliation of Charles (l. 210) or of a now 'humbler' Xerxes (l. 237); or for the poor uncomprehending Bavarian, the 'baffled prince' (l. 251). The hesitant uncertainty of *London* as to whether a nation was more villain or victim, here becomes a far more central compassionate ambiguity. Nearly all the coarser elements of Juvenal's derision are stripped away – the old man's toothless jaws and dripping nose, and so on. In their place comes a humane comprehension of human needs and human mechanisms; in particular, Johnson understands well that the human wish, however vain, is necessary and central to the human condition. His theory of the vacuity of life is not yet central to *The Vanity of Human Wishes*, as it was to become in *Rasselas*, but it is anticipated in his metaphors of the void and the gulph. Once again, it is the portrait of Wolsey which proves to be central. It provides the key moment of comprehension of the human need for a wish, an aim, an ambition:

> Claim leads to claim, and pow'r advances pow'r;
> Till conquest unresisted ceas'd to please,
> And rights submitted, left him none to seize.
>
> (ll. 106–8)

Wolsey's 'fall' in a sense predates his disgrace. Already, his life had palled, having achieved all its targets (the aftermath of the *Dictionary* was to prove in Johnson's own life the soundness of this perception). It is here that his life disintegrates. Recalling the image of the rocket, his true demise is not that he should 'fall', but that he should 'evaporate'.

Yet, Johnson still retained from Juvenal the invocation to Democritus, and the spirit of laughter. What is more, the laughter is, in theory, more radical here. In Juvenal, Democritus is affectionately recalled as a man to whom the spectacle of human folly was unfailingly comic. Johnson's Democritus is rather different, and more omnivorous is his sense of humour. He laughs equally at the 'robes of pleasure and the veils of woe' (l. 66). 'All aid the farce, and all thy mirth maintain' (l. 67).

When Fanny Burney had produced her novel *Evelina*, the literary world, and even some of her own circle of friends – the circle included Johnson and the Thrales – tried to persuade her to follow up her success with a comedy. At the Thrales' house in Streatham one morning, Mrs Thrale once again raised the subject, only to see Johnson

> see-sawing in his chair . . . laughing . . . so heartily as to almost shake his seat as well as his sides . . . till at last he said he had been struck with a notion that 'Miss Burney would begin her dramatic career by writing a piece called *Streatham*'.
>
> He paused, and laughed yet more cordially, and *then suddenly commanded a pomposity* to his countenance and his voice, and added, 'Yes! *Streatham – a Farce!*'[6]

Though Johnson's moments of mimicry or sheer buffoonery often surprised his friends, nothing puzzled them quite so much as his sense of farce. Boswell recounts Johnson's hilarity at the idea of his friend Bennet Langton making a will:

> I have known him at times exceedingly diverted at what seemed to others a very small sport. He now laughed immoderately, without any reason that we could perceive, at our friend's making his will; called him the *testator*, and added 'I daresay, he thinks he has done a mighty thing. He won't stay till he gets home to his seat in the country ... he'll call up the landlord of the first inn on the road; and, after a suitable preface upon mortality and the uncertainties of life, will tell him that he should not delay making his will; and here, Sir, will he say, is *my* will, which I have just made, with the assistance of one of the ablest lawyers in the kingdom. ...' Johnson could not stop his merriment, but continued it all the way till we got without the Temple-gate. He then burst into such a fit of laughter, that he appeared to be almost in a convulsion; and, in order to support himself, laid hold of one of the posts ... and sent forth peals so loud, that in the silence of the night his voice seemed to resound from Temple-bar to Fleet-ditch[7]

The joke did not amuse Langton's lawyer, who was one of the company. Most would agree with Boswell, that, at least in the way Johnson tried to explain the joke, it was 'very small sport', in proportion to the laughter it released. One is reminded, however, of *The Vanity of Human Wishes*, the Democritus passage, and its insistence that not only the 'robes of pleasure' but the 'veils of woe' 'aid[ed] the farce'. Human self-importance in any form was the legitimate target of this particularly anarchic form of laughter. When this includes 'a suitable preface upon mortality and the uncertainty of life', the ridicule reaches areas quite close to Johnson's own role as moral sage.

Among Johnson's favourite books, the only book that 'ever took him out of bed two hours sooner than he wished to rise' was Burton's *Anatomy of Melancholy*. The Preface of the *Anatomy* is called 'Democritus to the Reader'. The proximity of the melancholic to the hilarious is no very novel idea. In literature, many great writers are able to accommodate both in their work. The literature in which we least expect to find them combined, however, is work of a serious moral or theological character. This, however, is what Johnson aims for. Amid the 'mournful truth' of the bulk of the poem, other tones intermittently intrude. Sarcasm is one of them, whether at the expense of 'our supple tribes' (l. 95), or 'Ye nymphs of rosy lips and radiant eyes, / Whom Pleasure keeps too busy to be wise' (ll. 323–4). After the Wolsey portrait, we might expect a little conventional advice on ambition's golden mean. Johnson does not provide it:

> Speak thou, whose thoughts at humble peace repine,
> Shall Wolsey's wealth, with Wolsey's end be thine?
> Or liv'st thou now, with safer pride content,
> The wisest justice on the banks of Trent?
>
> (ll. 121–4)

Far from escaping censure, it is the humbler, the pettier pride which is most clearly despised. Some harsher tones survive from Juvenal's passage on the unsightliness of senility:

> From Marlb'rough's eyes the streams of dotage flow,
> And Swift expires a driv'ler and a show.
>
> (ll. 317–18)

Finally, there are those puzzling lines at the end of the 'scholar' passage, on the death of Laud:

> Mark'd out by dangerous parts he meets the shock,
> And fatal Learning leads him to the block:
> Around his tomb let Art and Genius weep,
> But hear his death, ye blockheads, hear and sleep.
>
> (ll. 171–4)

We meet many Johnsonian puns in this poem; but the last thing we expect here, at the climax of the passage most personal and intimate to Johnson, is the particularly schoolboyish – or schoolmasterly – pun of 'blockhead', with the 'block' on which Laud lost his head. It is as if, seeing the solemn funereal trappings, the weeping symbolic figures on his tomb, Johnson was momentarily convulsed by the sense of farce in 'the veil of woe'.

So, through the poem, Johnson intermittently holds in our mind the sense in which the vanity of human wishes (in which, according to Ecclesiastes, 'there is no new thing under the sun') may seem no more than a comedy, to 'feed with varied fools th'eternal jest' (l. 52). Both ideas are present in the poem. On the one hand, Man's own self-regard makes him grist to the comic mill. On the other, Man is trapped as *victim* of some divine 'eternal jest', since the human wish, vain though it is, is also intrinsic to the human condition.

Here, of course, Johnson's apparently conventional religious ending to the poem is of considerable interest. Once again, Johnson transforms his original. Juvenal concludes that if one *must* offer up entrails and sausages at the shrine, and ask for *something*, one might as well ask for a strong mind in a healthy body: one will need it; when all is said and done, stoical virtue is one's best protection. Johnson, too, sees self-discipline as a prayer and a wish worth making:

> Pour forth thy fervours for a healthful mind,
> Obedient passions, and a will resign'd.
>
> (ll. 359–61)

He adds to the short list love, patience and faith. Certainly, there is no survival here of Juvenal's sardonic recommendations. Yet, there is still a complication. Johnson sees that 'Hope and Fear' must find an 'object' (l.343). But the object he recommends is a state in which the choice of object is left to God: 'But leave to heav'n the measure and the choice' (l. 352). The solution is close to paradox. It defies the more orthodox interpretations that some critics would force on it. Arieh Sachs, quite correctly pointing out the poem's implied contrast between the narrow obsession and the 'extensive view', surely oversimplifies the poem in her conclusion that its function is to 'dispel these fixations upon particular notions and to restore our sanity by calling our attention to the general truths about the condition of man which are the truths of religion'.[8] D. V. Boyd comes much closer to the truth when he writes that 'Man is to hope, but not to hope for any *thing*. He is to implore God's benevolence, but resolutely refuse to imaginatively cast that benevolence in any specific terms. It is a state of absolute openness Johnson demands, a state akin, perhaps, to Heidegger's *besorgen*, but with a greater realization of the sheer discipline involved.'[9] One might add that this realisation seems to extend as far a sense of the impossible. In this, if Johnson is at least one step removed from the mass of mankind struggling, *without* a guide, in the 'clouded maze of fate', he rather resembles his own description of virtuous old age, 'Who set unclouded in the gulphs of fate'. The view is not appealing. Yet, what one remembers from the poem is not Johnson's impeccable orthodoxy, but his sense of at once the farce and the pity of his fellow man.

The Vanity of Human Wishes is so great a poem as seriously to challenge the view of him as, by nature, a writer of prose. It is a view still occasionally to be found, in unexpected places: for instance in the comments of the Yale editors of his poems, who feel that 'prose was more congenial to him than verse', and that 'the *Rambler* was to demonstrate that the sonority and balance of his great prose style made that eminently his forte'.[10] Yet Johnson's great poem transmits a unique excitement. One constantly has the simultaneous sense of words being used with the finest precision; and yet of the words developing an independent metaphoric life of their own. Every pun and every metaphor in the poem refers forwards or backwards to another pun, another metaphor. The coherence of the poem's style is closely tied up with the idea of echo and pattern, which is the poem's theme. It is a stylistic coherence which could only have been achieved by a surrender to the suggestive power of words. In this poem, so full of multiple meaning, Johnson turned lexicography from defence into attack. It is a source of lasting regret that, if he had other poems 'in his head', the neglect, in his own time, of his greatest poem caused him to keep them there.

6 *The Rambler*: 'those that aspire to the name of authors'

In *The Vanity of Human Wishes*, the man of learning was selected as one of the many obvious areas of vain or destructive wish. When Johnson came to write *The Rambler* – the literary work which is most centrally placed in his achievement, running parallel as it does to his greatest scholarly work, and forming his most sustained creative endeavour – the dream of literary greatness came almost inevitably to dominate. In the poem itself, Johnson had handled the wish for authorship more in terms of the obstructions which impede a legitimate wish than of the folly of the wish itself. In *The Rambler* too this thought tends to predominate. Johnson is far more tolerant of the phantoms of hope in an author than in perhaps any other area of existence. Not surprisingly, since the series coincides with the *Dictionary*, authorship is frequently treated defensively: exposing the low arts by which talent is dashed; and exhorting the author to brace himself, despite all opposition, for the task he must embrace. There is a strong drive away from the idea of mere fantasy, and towards the *enactment* of ambitions.

The second *Rambler* of the series here performs an interesting function. Explicitly dealing with hope, and the failure of the 'mind of man' to be 'satisfied with the objects immediately before it', it settles, after a preliminary discussion, on authorship as the principal area of hope in human life: 'perhaps no class of the human species requires more to be cautioned against this anticipation of happiness, than those that aspire to the name of authors'. Intriguingly, Johnson actually announces that his purpose in treating this subject is to fortify himself against the infection of this 'writer's malady'. He is writing about the near-hopelessness of authorial hope in order to stifle it in himself. His catalogue of the perils of authorship is accordingly long. Its principal interest is perhaps in the emphasis which develops, within this catalogue.

With fitting diffidence, Johnson begins with the thought that not every author is worthy of immortality, or even of notice:

> that, though the world must be granted to be yet in ignorance, he is not destined to dispel the cloud, nor to shine out as one of the luminaries of life. For this suspicion, every catalogue of a library will furnish sufficient reason; as he will find it crouded with names of men, who, though now forgotten, were once no less enterprising or confident than himself...

This thought, here so nobly expressed, is as long-standing in Johnson as his own earliest independent poem, *The Young Author*. A little earlier, the same diffidence had been expressed in the parallel of Don Quixote, who unexpectedly is used to illustrate the idea that 'there would be few enterprises of great labour or hazard undertaken, if we had not the power of magnifying the advantages which we persuade ourselves to expect from them'. However, as the essay reaches its last paragraph it becomes evident that the principal 'quixotry' in authorial hopes lies in expecting any attention from an ignorant and malicious world. In other words, the whole emphasis shifts away from self-doubt, towards an assault on the failings of those who obstruct the talented. The paragraph is worth giving in full, as it contains many ideas which are to be fully explored in the rest of the series:

> But though it should happen that an author is capable of excelling, yet his merit may pass without notice, huddled in the variety of things, and thrown into the general miscellany of life. He that endeavours after fame by writing, solicits the regard of a multitude fluctuating in pleasures or immersed in business, without time for intellectual amusements; he appeals to judges, prepossessed by passions, or corrupted by prejudices, which preclude their approbation of any new performance. Some are too indolent to read any thing, till its reputation is established; others too envious to promote that fame which gives them pain by its increase. What is new is opposed, because most are unwilling to be taught; and what is known is rejected, because it is not sufficiently considered, that men more frequently require

to be reminded than informed. The learned are afraid to declare their opinion early, lest they should put their reputation in hazard; the ignorant always imagine themselves giving some proof of delicacy, when they refuse to be pleased: and he that finds his way to reputation, through all these obstructions, must acknowledge that he is indebted to other causes besides his industry, his learning, or his wit.

Johnson is not exactly saying, at the end here, that success would have nothing to do with merit, but rather that merit also needs a little luck (and, by implication, that there are many just as talented, who end up *un*lucky). In fact, the series as a whole is notably generous in its impulses to fellow-authors, even to the untalented. Authorial pride comes across as a fitting and legitimate thing. It is however turned unremittingly against the mean artifices of neglect. At times, Johnson seems to launch himself into outright assault on a privileged and indifferent society. It is a side of Johnson not usually recognised. His respect of rank and wealth is well documented in his later life; yet the Chesterfield letter should sufficiently illustrate that if Johnson was injured, he would retaliate. One remembers the earlier incident when, feeling himself neglected by a genteel company, his reaction was aggressive; talking loudly to Reynolds about how much he could 'get' if he worked hard enough, as if the two of them were common workmen.[1] Johnson's charity in *The Rambler* goes out to his fellow-artisans. John Wain has ably demonstrated Johnson's deep sense of kinship with the outcast.[2] It is a sense which emerges artistically in the *Life of Savage* above all; with an uncritical warmth in Savage's cause, unique in *The Lives of the Poets*. The same sense of kinship with the struggling artistic outsider is almost equally to be found in *The Rambler*, when Johnson rises to his theme.

Judging by style, *The Rambler* seems anything but diffident. Johnson once force-fed Fanny Burney ('Dr Johnson made me eat cake at tea, for he held it till I took it'),[3] and *Rambler* readers are similarly force-fed with 'wisdom . . . not only convincing, but overpowering'.[4] This is perhaps not how Johnson himself regarded his prose style. In the final *Rambler*, he describes how 'I have laboured to refine our language to grammatical purity, and to clear it from colloquial barbarisms, licentious idioms, and irregular combinations'. Correspondingly, 'it has been my principal design to inculcate wisdom or piety'. There is a deliberate attempt to link moral purity with purity of style. Hence, stylistic impurity is expressed in more broadly cultural terms: 'barbarisms', 'licentious', 'irregular'. The link is one he comes later to make repeatedly, in *The Lives of the Poets*. Yet if Johnson believes his own style to be central and 'civilised', to others it appears highly idiosyncratic. As W. K. Wimsatt says, '*The Rambler* is, in the elaboration and complexity of its structures and in the weight of its vocabulary, the most concentrated, and in its length the most sustained example of the peculiarities which distinguish the prose of Johnson's maturity'.[5] It was a style which, as Boswell tells us, earned Johnson a host of 'ludicrous imitators'.[6] It can only be read in one way, at one pace, and with one tone. Yet, if tone arouses the suspicion of the writer's dogmatic certainty, structure and content tell another story:

> Self-condemned to write upon a stated day whether ready or not, Johnson found himself in a recurring compositional predicament which turned out to determine the *ad hoc* structure of most of the *Ramblers* as well as a great part of their substance. As we will see, many of them complicate their presumed topics surprisingly by setting out in one direction and then turning, oddly, in another. The anxiety-ridden compositional circumstances in which the *Ramblers* got written were inappropriate for the registration of any dogmatic certainties, or even for the achievement of a very seamless consistency. And in subject as in method they bear the mark of the way they were composed.[7]

The Rambler was written twice weekly for two years. Each essay tended to be delayed to the last possible minute to catch the press. The famous essay on procrastination was written as the printer's boy waited at the door. Inevitably, this meant that those concerns which were uppermost in Johnson's own preoccupations would tend to imprint themselves on the series. However ardently Johnson wished in these essays to contribute principally to 'the stability of truth' (the phrase is from the Shakespeare *Preface*), the end product turns out to be more volatile. However justly he is praised for his contributions to the stock of human perceptions, part of the fascination of *The Rambler* – not, of course, incompatible with 'truth' – is to detect in it the emergence of more personal concerns: the drive towards, to use another Johnson phrase, a mind 'defecated and pure'.[8] This too may be 'the achievement of Samuel Johnson' in *The Rambler*, an achievement to which he gives a personal and creative shape. Unexpectedly the series as a whole produces the sensation that we have entered an imaginative world. *The Rambler* lacks any single 'character' to compare in sustained realisation with, say, Sir Roger de Coverley. Its range of personae and its fictitious 'letters to the editor' have all been done before. Yet nevertheless it creates the two essential features which are usually defined as the basic essential features of another prose medium, the novel:[9] first, a sense of interrelationship between character and scene; second, a sense that that interrelationship is dynamic. While – evidently – *The Rambler* is neither novel nor even fiction, it exhibits something of the dynamism of self and scene of which novels are made.

In fact, this dynamic relationship is repeatedly *The Rambler*'s subject. First, as moralist, Johnson defines the individual moral flaw in terms of the corrupted social impulse. One gains the impression of personal integrity imperilled, and *only* imperilled, by the human context at large. Second, Johnson's own experiences as a struggling writer find their way into the series, and form themselves into a highly specialised version of the relationship of self and scene. This may be described as a preoccupation with the relationship, again a hostile one, between the talented and the wealthy.

A very high proportion of the essays of *The Rambler* can be related to one or other of these aspects of the 'self and scene' motif. The first aspect defines a theory of human conduct. The second gives specific malignant form to that theory, intensifying as the series proceeds.

As this implies, Johnson's view of human nature in these essays is one of essential solitariness. Enmity is a continual fact of life. However, the series gives some attention to the principal loving relationships open to man, and here too the stress is on human isolation in its own selfishness. Friendships are formed, Johnson concludes, on the basis of a community of faults. The thought goes back to *The Vanity of Human Wishes*, and the line 'For what but social guilt the friend endears?'

The essay (no. 28 in the series) develops the idea of a community of faults as the basis of attraction. Friends are selected in order to preserve our self-esteem: 'each palliates the other's failings, because they are his own'. Marriage is formed on still absurder impulses:

> some unite for life to those whom they have only seen by the light of tapers at a ball; when parents make articles for their children, without enquiring after their consent; when some marry for heirs to disappoint their brothers, and others throw themselves into the arms they do not love, because they found themselves rejected where they were more solicitous to please; when some marry because their servants cheat them, some because they squander their own money, some because their houses are pestered with company, some because they will live like other people, and some only because they are sick with themselves. (no. 45)

The sense of absurdity evidently grows as this sentence proceeds, with a greater and greater comic distance appearing between the logical connectives, 'because . . .' and the accelerating sequence of illogical whims of spite and pride. By such reductive accounts as these, the main benevolent human associations, of love and friendship, are speedily written off.

With benign relationships eliminated, Johnson is free to explore his general theme of relationships: the anxious and corrupting effect of the sense of self in relation to others. His impulse, of enquiry provides the driving force for the analytical essays. How do secrets come to be betrayed; what are the arts of self-delusions; why do men defend their known mistakes? The restlessness of the enquiry accounts for much of the instability of structure and the unpredictableness of direction which Fussell has noted. Yet, the answers he provides to the various questions turn out to be similar. The 'innocent' need for significance in the eyes of others is responsible for much guilt and frailty. So, with the betrayal of secrets:

> The vanity of being known to be trusted with a secret is generally one of the chief motives to disclose it; for however absurd it may be thought to boast an honour by an act which shews that it was conferred without merit, yet most men seem rather inclined to confess the want of virtue than of importance, and more willingly show their influence, though at the expense of their probity, than glide through life with no other

pleasure than the private consciousness of fidelity; which, while it is preserved, must be without praise, except from the single person who tries and knows it. (no. 13)

The need for importance is a standing temptation. Johnson shows that it is a need which can take particularly alluring forms. Love and friendship are among its disguises. 'Secrets are very frequently told in the first ardour of kindness, or of love, for the sake of proving, by so important a sacrifice, sincerity or tenderness.' Conscience itself in such cases assists with specious evasions. Johnson lists three typical excuses; and the way the sentence, with a faint sense of half-quotation, bundles them together, suggests that the habit of self-excuse is casual as well as multiple: 'He tells the private affairs of his patron, or his friend, only to those, from whom he would not conceal his own; he tells them to those, who have no temptation to betray the trust, or with a certain forfeiture of his friendship, if he discovers that they become public.' And so the secret is busily leaked to the world.

The effect of the passage is a double one. On the one hand, there is Johnson's reasoned contempt for the offence. He patiently points out consequences and fallacies. As for consequences, a secret passed on 'in the round of friendship' will inevitably reach 'them from whom it was the first intention chiefly to conceal it'. As to the fallacies of conscience by which the gossip persuades himself that the secret will go no further, 'he must upon reflection know [these] to be uncertain, because he finds them without effect upon himself'. Yet, at the same time, the rational balance of the passage, the clarity of paradox and antithesis by which the moral contradictions of the offence are spelled out, also produces an opposing effect. The balance of the passage creates a sense of a mechanism in human behaviour, beyond the reach of reason. 'Virtue' sits opposite to 'importance'. 'Influence' opposes 'probity'. The two are irreconcilable, since probity is 'private', 'without praise'. And since the passage attributes a stronger call to 'importance' than to 'virtue', it is not enlightenment which seems inevitable ('he *must* upon reflection know to be uncertain'), but rather betrayal. While the passage uses the tones of lofty scorn ('which shews that it was conferred without merit') and of sarcasm ('by so important a sacrifice') to crush the gossip, it is interesting that Johnson also confers on him the very sympathetic dread of 'glid[ing] through life' unremarked. 'Glide' is always an ambiguous term for Johnson. He attempts to use it as a term of praise for Dr Levet's life ('Unfelt, uncounted, glided by') and for virtuous old age in *The Vanity of Human Wishes* (which 'glides in modest innocence away'). Yet the same poems betray a dread of passivity to life; 'unfelt' in *Levet*, 'helpless' in *Vanity*. In the latter case, the stream of life which is the obvious metaphoric application of the word 'glide' (the *Dictionary* defines 'glide' as 'to flow gently and smoothly') becomes a hostile torrent: 'Must helpless man, in ignorance sedate, / Roll darkling down the torrent of his fate?' (ll. 345-6). The man who 'instead of enjoying the blessings of life, lets life glide away in preparations to enjoy them' featured in the second *Rambler*. For Johnson, the word 'glide' seems to have contained both an ideal of contentment, and a dread of obscure inertia. It is by no means clear which is uppermost in his description of those who prefer to experience a sense of importance in the eyes of others 'than glide through life with no other pleasure than the private consciousness of fidelity'.[10]

The essay impresses a sense of the corrupting effects of the need for self-consequence in relation to others. Similarly, no. 31, on the defence of known mistakes, traces the fault to the offender's conviction of his own perfection, compared with others: 'the conduct of those who so willingly admit the weakness of human nature ... seems to discern ... that most make it with a tacit reserve in favour of themselves'. By contrast, no. 28, on the arts of self-delusion, explains the comfort to be derived from a community of sin: 'each comforts himself that his faults are not without precedent, for the best and the wisest men have given way to the violence of sudden temptations'.

So far, Johnson's treatment of his theme is not without compassion and humour. Where his attitude hardens is where he perceives the need to be esteemed shading over into the fear of being excelled. It is here that the idea, which Professor Bate has identified as Johnson's master-theme, the idea of envy, enters the reckoning. It makes a first, rather unobtrusive appearance in no. 17. It is an essay with an orthodox moral message, 'The frequent contemplation of death necessary to moderate the passions.' On inspection, however, this orthodoxy is seen to turn on the general theme of the opinion of self in relation to others. Moral advice is tailored in a practical way to the individual's need for esteem. The difference is that the general theme shades over into the idea of envy:

> All envy is proportionate to desire; we are uneasy at the attainments of another, according as we think our own happiness would be advanced by the addition of that which he withholds from us; and, therefore, whatever depresses immoderate wishes, will, at the same time, set the heart free from the corrosion of envy. . . . Whoever reflects frequently upon the uncertainty of his own duration, will find out, that the state of others is not more permanent, and that what can confer nothing on himself very desirable, cannot so much improve the condition of a rival, as to make him much superior to those from whom he has carried the prize, a prize too mean to deserve a very obstinate opposition.

The distinctive development here of the theme of the need for esteem lies in the language of rivalry, superiority and prizes. It introduces a sense of life as a competition.

This idea is given a fairly full development in no. 49, on fame:

> This is the original of avarice, vanity, ambition, and generally of all those desires which arise from the comparison of our condition with that of others. He that thinks himself poor, because his neighbour is richer; he that, like Caesar, would rather be the first man of a village, than the second in the capital of the world, has apparently kindled in himself desires which he never received from nature, and acts upon principles established only by the authority of custom.

It is interesting that Johnson depicts the competitive urge as, in a sense, unnatural, yet acknowledges that it grows from an inevitable stretching out of energies to objectives; what he describes as feeling 'wants in consequence of our wishes'. It would be convenient to resolve this contradiction by some clear formula: for instance, that ambition, legitimate in itself, becomes vicious when it becomes emulous. No such formula exists. In fact, it is notable that Johnson spends very little time describing the legitimacy of competition and success. His stress rather lies with the unsuccessful, and the emotions which failure excites. A persistent target is a fraudulent pretence to despise success. So, no. 58 describes this kind of fraud:

> it will be, perhaps, seldom found that they value riches less, but

> that they dread labour or danger more than others; they are unable to rouse themselves to action, to strain in the race of competition, or to stand the shock of contest; but though they therefore, decline, the toil of climbing, they, nevertheless, wish themselves aloft, and would willingly enjoy what they dare not seize.

But Johnson's principal target is those whose hypocrisy is developed one stage further; who not only pretend to quarrel with the idea of success, but whose life's work is to slander the successful.

> Whoever rises above those who once pleased themselves with equality, will have many malevolent gazers at his eminence. To gain sooner than others that which all pursue with the same ardour, and to which all imagine themselves entitled, will be for ever a crime. When those who started with us in the race of life, leave us so far behind, that we have little hope to overtake them, we revenge our disappointment by remarks on the arts of supplantation by which they gained the advantage, or on the folly and arrogance by which they possess it. (no. 172)

Johnson detects the same malignancy operating even against the virtuous. The wicked 'envy an unblemished reputation, and what they envy they are busy to destroy: they are unwilling to suppose themselves meaner, and more corrupt than others, and therefore willingly pull down from their elevations those with whom they cannot rise to an equality' (no. 76).

Johnson's moral theme, then, concentrates not on the unfairness of 'the race of life', but on the malignancy of its failures. The motif of competition recurs time and again, in various arenas and locations. In one amusing 'letter to the editor' (no. 46), a young lady of fashion describes 'the mischief of rural faction': how 'malice and hatred descend here with an inheritance'. The country is the location for emulation in its rawest form. However, what concerns Johnson most keenly is the kind of competition and the kind of envy most closely related to his own situation; the situation of talent struggling in an indifferent or hostile world. As the series proceeds, we can piece together three recurring components in a pattern in which this most personal concern is enclosed. The first of these is the amount of attention the series gives to literary talent. The second is a hostile description of the society in which talent has to make its way, a society privileged but undeserving. The third component is the direct interaction of the first two, within the theme of envy: by an extraordinary twist, Johnson develops the argument that, though the struggling author is the needy suppliant of money and privilege, it is *they* who envy *him* his talent, and use all their energies to defeat him. This most vicious form of all envy draws the series to its peak of intensity.

From the beginning, the series gives prominence to the idea of literature and scholarship. Essays on apparently general themes often turn to concentrate on literary life. No. 25, on the relative merits of rashness and cowardice, concentrates almost immediately on the idea that it is better for the scholar and the student to be over-confident than too diffident. No. 27 on the miseries of dependence concentrates on the particular miseries of patronage and dedication. No. 19, on the importance of an early choice of life, illustrates its theme with the story of Polyphilus, the dilettante student. Numerous other essays are wholly dedicated to literature and writers. The largest and most obvious category is that of the critical essays. Bate counts thirty-one essays of literary criticism, and notes that 'perhaps another five could be added on general problems of writing'.[11] Clearly, part of the effect of the high proportion of such essays is to concentrate the series on literature and the writer. This concentration is maintained by a string of other essays; on the disproportion between an author's writings and his conversation (no. 14), on the unevenness of authors' writings (no. 21), or on the baffling effects of contradictory criticism on an author's judgement (no. 23). Needless to say, Johnson does not neglect the topic of success in the life of writing. The necessity for courage and hope, first touched on in no. 25, is a recurring one. There is a little group of such essays in nos 127, 129 and 137, bracing authorship against the threats it faces; threats to which Johnson himself gives a shape in no. 144, in his powerful description of the enmity talent provokes.

Set against his essays on authorship are his essays on 'society'. Significantly, as if to give this part of his composite structure a more documentary quality, this description is in great part conveyed by voices ostensibly not Johnson's own, in the fictitious 'letters to the editor'. They increase sharply in number in the second half of the series. Since they are frequently in the name of the victims of fashionable society, it is no surprise that the portrait which emerges is unflattering. Quite unlike *The Spectator*'s solidarity with 'society', these essays depict a class which is, at best, indifferent, vacuous and vain; and at worst vicious.

Rambler no. 194 is a 'letter' from the private tutor of a young nobleman, the sequel to an earlier letter, no. 132. It becomes an account, by the aggrieved and neglected tutor, of how patrician vacuity is studied and perfected by the young nobleman, brought to town.

> He became in a few days a perfect master of his hat, which with a careless nicety he could put off or on, without any need to adjust it with a second motion. This was not attained but by frequent consultations with his dancing-master, and constant practice before the glass, for he had some rustick habits to overcome; but, what will not time and industry perform? A fortnight more furnished him with all the airs and forms of familiar and respectful salutation, from the clap on the shoulder to the humble bow; he practices the stare of strangeness, and the smile of condescension, the solemnity of promise, and the graciousness of encouragement, as if he had been nursed at a levee; and pronounces, with no less propriety than his father, the monosyllables of coldness, and sonorous periods of respectful profession.
>
> He immediately lost the reserve and timidity which solitude and study are apt to impress upon the most courtly genius; was able to enter a crouded room with airy civility; to meet the glances of a hundred eyes without perturbation; and address those whom he never saw before with ease and confidence. In less than a month his mother declared her satisfaction at his proficiency by a triumphant observation, that she believed, 'nothing would make him blush'.

This splendid comic description is of an individual reduced to type; of behaviour stylised into 'airs and forms'; where no gesture is spontaneous, but rather a matter of 'practice' and, worse, 'profession'. The son becomes the copy of the father, and indeed of a whole class, in which one man is indistinguishable from another except by mannerism: 'one was detected by his gait, another by the swing of his arms, a third by the toss of his head, and another by his favourite phrase'. In an essay which insists that 'diffidence is found the inseparable associate of understanding', the young nobleman's acquisition of assurance must be seen as the extinction of intelligence, to match the mindlessness of his class.

This does not read like 'satire manqué',[12] Bate's phrase for what he believes to be Johnson's compassionate inability to commit himself to attack. Its commitment to ridicule is uninhibited. Other essays bring far weightier accusations than vacuity to bear against the privileged. It is evident that malice is Johnson's main allegation as early as no. 10, with its description of the gaming table: 'I saw their looks clouded at the beginning of every game with an uniform solicitude, now and then in its progress varied with a short triumph, at one time wrinkled with cunning, at another deadned with despondency, or by accident flushed with rage at the unskilful or unlucky play of a partner.' Greed and vindictiveness are thereafter constantly seen in action: in the antics of legacy hunters, and the cruelty with which the helpless and the unfortunate are treated. A recurring motif is the change of treatment occasioned by a change in financial fortunes. First touched on in no. 26, this receives extended treatment in the History of Melissa in no. 75. Melissa is little affected by her financial losses. To her former friends, however, she suddenly loses all claim to wit or beauty. She chronicles the insults she now has to suffer, and concludes, 'the rich and the powerful live in a perpetual masquerade, in which all about them wear borrowed characters; and we can only discover in what estimation we are held, when we can no longer give hopes or fears'. The theme is repeated in no. 153, while the tale of Victoria (130 and 133) tells an analogous tale of the disgrace of a victim of smallpox. Johnson is in effect enlarging on the story of Wolsey in *The Vanity of Human Wishes*, and describing the operation of a pack instinct. The pack turns on the fallen, and with an equal relentlessness protects its own exclusiveness, as Johnson shows, in the comic tale from a young trader who attempted to turn gentleman (nos 116 and 123). Always, the weak are exploited and victimised. No. 12 is a 'letter' describing the indignities of a poor relation, forced to depend on a rich cousin. Far more serious is the fate described in 'letters' from Misella (nos 170 and 171) of a prostitute, 'the drudge of extortion, and the sport of drunkenness'.

These, then, are the ingredients for Johnson's highly personal version of self and scene: the writer, and the privileged society. Gradually, through the series, they interact, as the writer strives to penetrate the obstacles he is faced with in this society. The very least handicap the man of talent suffers is the lack of those social graces in which the privileged are trained. This in itself is a strongly personal theme. One recalls that 'no praise was more welcome to Dr Johnson than that which said he had the notions and manners of a gentleman'.[13] Yet Johnson's uncouthness was legendary, and he re-enacts his own social awkwardness in no. 157, a 'letter' from a celebrated scholar invited to tea in polite society:

> There are not many situations more incessantly uneasy than that in which the man is placed who is watching an opportunity to speak, without courage to take it when it is offered, and who, tho' he resolves to give a specimen of his abilities, always finds some reason or other for delaying it to the next minute. I was ashamed of silence, yet could find nothing to say of elegance or importance equal to my wishes.

As to the former, the scholar has just succeeded in labouring his way to 'a very happy compliment' when, 'by too much attention to my own meditations, I suffered the saucer to drop from my hand. The cup was broken, the lapdog was scalded, a brocaded petticoat was stained, and the whole assembly was thrown into disorder.' The scholar slinks off in disgrace. The episode is a complete antithesis to the confidence of the fashionable young man of no. 132 that the world will listen attentively to the first thing that comes into his head. The scholar's humiliation gains, if anything, in comic force by our recollection of Johnson's own habit, in company, of emphasising a point by gesticulating wildly with a full cup of tea in his hand.[14]

However, as Johnson describes them, the scholar's misfortunes are certainly not confined to embarrassment. High among the perils of the writer is the envy which ability provokes. It will be recalled that *Rambler* no. 2 described how 'he that endeavours after fame by writing ... appeals to judges prepossessed by passions, or corrupted by prejudices'. It is a point which is given extended development later in the series. Increasingly, to succeed at all as a writer — by honest means, rather than by sycophancy and literary prostitution — comes to seem a near-impossibility.

The clear autobiographical element becomes increasingly clear as Johnson, from no. 40 onwards, begins to concentrate in particular on the *moral* writer's fate in an unresponsive world. The malignity of the moral writer's reception provokes some of the most forceful passages in the whole of *The Rambler*, as Johnson advises fellow moral-essayists not to blame themselves for their treatment by the world:

> He may suspect, but needs not hastily to condemn himself, for he can rarely be certain, that the softest language or most humble diffidence would have escaped resentment; since scarcely any degree of circumspection can prevent or obviate the rage with which the slothful, the impotent, and the unsuccessful, vent their discontent upon those that excel them. Modesty itself, if it is praised, will be envied; and there are minds so impatient of inferiority, that their gratitude is a species of revenge, and they return benefits, not because recompence is a pleasure, but because obligation is a pain. (no. 87)

The intensity of this passage is matched only by no. 144, on the various species of detractors of talent (including literary talent). We are prepared for this essay, perhaps, by the treatment the patron and the dedicator receive from Johnson in no. 136. Earlier treatments (no. 27, for instance) of the same species had been relatively indulgent. Now, Johnson does not spare his target. The dedicator is one who upon false principles of gratitude has 'ventured to extol wretches whom all but their dependents numbered among the reproaches of the species'. And in 144, after a relatively sportive treatment of the absurd character of the different kinds of detractor, Johnson's anger quickly concentrates again, when he considers the effects of their malice:

> Such the arts by which the envious, the idle, the peevish, and the thoughtless, obstruct that worth which they cannot equal, and by artifices thus easy, sordid, and detestable, is industry defeated, beauty blasted, and genius depressed.

The pounding rhythm of the prose is eloquent of the high feelings which neglect and envy provoke. He returns to his theme for the last time in no. 183: 'The genius, even when he endeavours only to *entertain or instruct* [my italics], yet suffers persecution from innumerable critics, whose acrimony is excited merely by the pain of seeing others pleased, and of hearing applauses which another enjoys.' Once again, the moral author is at the centre of the theme of envy; he is the particular victim of the vacuous and avid society he despises, and he is isolated and neglected by the very fact of possessing talent.

Isolation is in fact willingly embraced. Dedicated, whatever his fate, to the life of moral authorship, his is a position of injured isolation. Excluded by his inferiors, he gives full vent to his sense of injustice. The only examples which immediately spring to mind of 'satire manqué' and compassionate concern in the *Rambler* portraits are his fellow-victims of society; the youthful (e.g. no. 196), the impoverished, the defaced, the derided, and of course the talented. Around authorial figures sympathy naturally accumulates, even for their failings (no. 146, for instance, on the comic anticipation of an author, on publication-day). No. 145 is an overt plea that even the humblest hack writer 'deserves our kindness though not our reverence'. The rich and fashionable, by contrast, earn an increasingly fierce contempt. The two are poles apart. Early in the series, in no. 22, Johnson was still sufficiently an optimist to write a facile little allegory of wit and learning; in which wit, the prerogative of fashion, and the learning of the scholar, despite an initial quarrel, soon saw 'the necessity of union. They therefore joined their hands ... in perpetual concord', married, and produced 'a numerous progeny of Arts and Sciences'. It is the last instance of this kind of optimism. His subsequent treatment of wit is much harsher, and it is tempting to see no. 141 in particular as a kind of counter-piece and almost a revenge against poise and wit, in retaliation for the neighbouring account of the social agonies of the scholar. Johnson describes the social agonies, this time, of the 'wit':

> Think on the misery of him who is obliged to cultivate barrenness, and ransack vacuity; who is obliged to continue his talk when his meaning is spent, to raise merriment without images, to harrass his imagination in quest of thoughts which he cannot start, and his memory in pursuit of narratives which he cannot overtake; observe the effort with which he strains to conceal despondency by a smile, and the distress in which he sits while the eyes of the company are fixed upon him as their last refuge from silence and dejection.

There can be few more wounding accusations against the elegant easy wit than the accusation of 'effort'. So, Johnson condemns fashionable society to its own company; and accepts the isolation of his own society.

This is of some interest in connection with the ultimate tendency of Johnson's moral advice; which is to turn inwards on one's own moral resources. If society corrupts, then retreat from others will purify the self. The idea is first found in no. 7 which recommends that 'we weaken the temptations of the world, by retiring at certain seasons from it'. It is more forcefully restated in no. 28, on self-delusion, where Johnson recommends, as a means of disentangling ourselves from our own false motives, regular periods of contemplation: 'that we may, as Chillingworth expresses it, consider things as if there were no other beings in the world but God and ourselves; or to use a language yet more awful, "may commune with our own hearts, and be still" '. Johnson recounts, with a degree of envy, in no. 47 (on 'the proper means of regulating sorrow') that 'among soldiers and seamen, though there is much kindness, there is little grief'. Theirs is a life which imposes a certain necessary withdrawal from social concerns.

To such a state of tranquillity, the last *Ramblers* finally attain. The themes of envy and of injustice can be seen finally to exhaust themselves. If we look at a late moral essay such as no. 185, on revenge, the tone, compared with the last major essay on envy (183) seems suddenly much cooler and much less involved. The essay's emphasis is on the utilitarian and the reasonable. It stresses the *self*-torment of the revenger and its logic is overpowering: 'He that willingly suffers the corrosions of inveterate hatred, and gives up his days and nights to the gloom of malice, and perturbations of stratagem, cannot surely be said to consult his ease.' All the old lofty rationality of Johnson has here returned, and the last *Ramblers* of the series recover the best vein of sportiveness of some of the early numbers. Nos 204 and 205 are amusingly dedicated to the narrative of Emperor Seged of Ethiopia, who tried to banish misery from his entourage by force of edict. Johnson has much sport with the idea of such naivety, and clearly enjoys the crocodile which interrupts the fourth day's jollities. At this stage, having achieved a condition of some repose, in which even a literary dedicator is portrayed lightheartedly (no. 193), Johnson now finished writing *Ramblers*. He has, during the series, thought through his own condition as a writer in a society at best uncaring. He can now desist.

7 *The Idler*: the 'voluntary dream'

It is generally agreed that *The Idler* is altogether a lighter affair than *The Rambler*. The essays are shorter. There is a quite new sprinkling of topical material. There is an attempt to lighten the style. There is even, in the portrait of 'the ponderous dictator of sentences' (31) or of Sober (36), a parody of Johnson's *Rambler* persona. Even where the *Rambler* tone detectably creeps back, there is a far lower level of moral exhortation than in the earlier periodical.

However, in one sense, *The Idler* is more daring than its predecessor. It handles material of a deep and radical nature; material of which Johnson had a lifelong fear.

The point of entry to such topics is the title-theme of idleness itself. It is a theme of the utmost personal importance to Johnson, obsessed as he was with idleness as sin. Needless to say, the development of this and its related topics is at the expense of others. The first issue of the magazine, establishing the 'Idler' persona, claims that 'scarcely any name can be imagined from which less envy or competition is to be dreaded'. This in itself gives an indication of how completely *The Rambler*'s master-theme of envy now disappears. There are perhaps just two sur-vivals of the powerful theme of neglected merit: the naturalist–author of no. 55, and Gelaleddin the scholar in no. 75. There are only two survivors (nos 29 and 42) of stories of the miseries of dependants. Again, there are just a couple of stories on the subject of marital miseries (nos 28 and 54).

Idleness, on the other hand engrosses the series. There is little of the *Rambler*'s tendency to stress the brevity of life, and the proper use of time as a sacred duty. Rather, the general topic of idleness is used as an invitation to study the seductive distractions of the mind; or the comparative force exerted by mind over sensation. There are eight key essays on such topics in the series. The first is no. 18. In it, the 'correspondent' undertakes to look into a kind of error which, since it is pleasurable in its effects, is rarely examined ('The mind is seldom quickened to very vigorous operations but by pain. . . . We do not . . . willingly decline a pleasing effect to investigate its cause'). This error is, that 'Pleasure is . . . seldom such as it appears to others, nor often such as we represent it to ourselves.' Johnson proceeds to advance, with utter plausibility, the theory that happiness is a kind of conspiracy of appearances. Starting with the mixed motives of, for instance, concert-goers, among whom more go to be seen, than to hear, Johnson finds his real theme with the idea that each individual's pleasure on such occasions is the result of what might be described as mutual self-deception:

> To every place of entertainment we go with expectation, and desire of being pleased; we meet others who are brought by the same motives; no one will be the first to own the disappointment; one face reflects the smile of another, till each believes the rest delighted, and endeavours to catch and transmit the circulating rapture. In time, all are deceived by the cheat to which all contribute. The fiction of happiness is propagated by every tongue, and confirmed by every look, till at last all profess the joy which they do not feel, consent to yield to the general delusion; and when the voluntary dream is at an end, lament that bliss is of so short a duration.

This exquisite paragraph is unmatched by anything *The Rambler* has to offer. The only trace of a judgement passed is in the splendid comic final clause. The rest is an analysis that strikes the strongest chord of recognition. From the earlier periodicals, the closest Johnson approaches to this kind of analysis is in *The Adventurer* no. 120, some five years earlier; which pronounces that 'The world, in its best state, is nothing more than a larger assembly of beings, combining to counterfeit happiness which they do not feel.' This, however, turns out to be only a matter of keeping up the appearance of wealth. The *Idler* essay is a considerable development. Its only omission is of any explanation of the apparent contradiction, that all are eager to catch the universal rapture, and 'are deceived' by it, yet 'do not feel' the joy they profess. It is an omission which, in due course, Johnson proceeds to correct. No. 50 is the immediate sequel to one of *The Idler*'s many portraits. This portrait is of 'Will Marvel' the raconteur, who embellishes the ordinary occurrences of his life into heroic adventures. Its sequel proceeds to excuse Will Marvel, on the grounds that his is merely an extreme manifestation of a universal tendency. Johnson describes how every man enhances what he experiences, either for the benefit of others, or of himself:

> It is certain that without some artificial augmentations, many of the pleasures of life, and almost all its embellishments, would fall to the ground. If no man was to express more delight than he felt, those who felt most would raise little envy. If travellers were to describe the most laboured performances of art with the same coldness as they survey them, all expectations of happiness from change of place would cease. The pictures of Raphael would hang without spectators, and the gardens of Versailles might be inhabited by hermits. All the pleasure that is received ends in an opportunity of splendid falsehood, in the power of gaining notice by the display of beauties which the eye was weary of beholding, and a history of happy moments, of which, in reality, the most happy was the last.
>
> The ambition of superior sensibility and superior eloquence disposes the lovers of arts to receive rapture at one time, and communicate it at another; and each labours first to impose upon himself, and then to propagate the imposture.

The last paragraph is the significant one, which solves the contradiction between the idea of 'rapture' and 'coldness'. Pleasure is not experienced spontaneously, but is an act of will, albeit an unconscious one. The mind is willed into a receptive and gullible state, so that it may deceive itself as to the quality of the sensory experience transmitted to it. As the reiterated words of 'labour' indicate, much effort is expended, both by the eye itself, and by the struggle to be enraptured. The mind is relieved when it is all over. The 'most happy' moment is 'the last'.

No. 24 is a similar essay. Taking its subject as mental torpor, it somewhat tormentingly fluctuates between direct philosophical discussion, with specific allusions to Locke and Malebranche, and frivolous caricatures of those who live without thought: 'of the sportsman in a rainy month, of the annuitant between the days of quarterly payment, of the politician when the mails are detained by contrary winds'. Its fourth paragraph, however, is entirely serious:

> It is reasonable to believe that thought, like everything else, has its causes and effects; that it must proceed from something known, done or suffered; and must produce some action or event. Yet how great is the number of those in whose minds no source of thought has ever been opened, in whose life no consequence of thought is ever discovered; who have learned nothing upon which they can reflect; who have neither seen nor felt any thing which could leave its traces on the memory; who neither foresee nor desire any change of their condition, and have therefore neither fear, hope, nor design, and yet are supposed to be thinking beings.

At first sight, this seems less depressing in its implications than the essays already discussed. The scathing tone at least implies the *availability* of sensation and reflection. These things are available by acts of will, and the essay concludes by urging that such efforts must be made. Another passage of the essay, however, is less sanguine:

> The waking hours are not denied to have been passed in thought, yet he that shall endeavour to recollect on one day the ideas of the former, will only turn the eye of reflection upon vacancy; he will find, that the greater part is irrevocably vanished, and wonder how the moments could come and go, and leave so little behind them.

The observation is offered as a universal one. The experience was a personal one. It was something he came to record in his *Diaries*, a few years later: 'my time has been unprofitably spent, and seems as a dream that has left nothing behind. My memory grows confused, and I know not how the days pass over me.'[1] Johnson's awareness of the power of fantasy, present since *London*, combines, in this *Idler* essay, with one of his most potent metaphors, of a void. The 'eye of reflection', seeking some solid recollection of yesterday's experiences, finds only 'vacancy'. The passage leaves us with the unspoken question, whether the 'thought' of yesterday was not, even at the time, more illusory than real. It is intriguing that the essay's concluding exhortations to arouse the mind from torpor, still uses the language of illusion: 'the passage of life will be tedious and irksome to him who does not *beguile* it by diversified ideas'. The phrase, 'the passage of life', containing once again the metaphor of travel, also contains the ambiguous suggestion, reminiscent of his comments in the *Diaries*, of life passing over the traveller, rather than the other way about.

Three essays later, Johnson grapples with another aspect of 'idleness', and the relationship between mind and matter; the power of habit. He begins by looking at the commonplace moral advice, to know oneself and to reform. He argues that few have the moral energy to do so, preferring an inert 'plunge into the current of life'; but that even those who make the attempt at resolution are defeated by the force of habit. Once again, Johnson is dealing here with a strongly personal theme. No reader of his *Diaries* can miss the frequency with which he forms resolutions of better conduct, at the spiritual climacterics of each year. Each year, too, Johnson records in agony how the last resolutions have been broken. In recognising, in *Idler* 27, the power of habit, Johnson is, moreover, delivering a blow against one of his most cherished spiritual doctrines; of the freedom of the moral will:

> There is nothing which we estimate so fallaciously as the force of our own resolutions, nor any fallacy which we so unwillingly and tardily detect. He that has resolved a thousand times, and a thousand times deserted his own purpose, yet suffers no abatement of his confidence, but still believes himself his own master, and able, by innate vigour of soul, to press forward to his end, through all the obstructions that inconveniences or delights can put in his way.

There is no more telling concession in Johnson than that a man merely 'believes' himself to be his own master. The breach of resolutions is not, he insists, a matter of hypocrisy. 'There is very little hypocrisy in the world.' 'We resolve to do right, we hope to keep our resolutions, we declare them to confirm our own hope ... but at last habit prevails.' Not surprisingly, Johnson retreats from this extreme honesty by the end of the essay. Those who are in the power of evil habits 'must' conquer them. Those who are not yet subject to their influence 'may, by timely caution, preserve their freedom'. Yet, these saving clauses, and the use of cautious words such as 'most' and 'commonly' elsewhere, have to fight against at least one downright denial of free-will. Speaking of resolutions, Johnson says that, when forming a good intention, 'the whole soul yields itself to the predominance of truth, and readily determines to do what, when the time of action comes, will be at last omitted'.

This is a very considerable reversal of what Johnson has to say in his *Sermons*. Sermon 5, an important discussion of the problem of evil in the world, and of its compatibility with religious belief, offers the hypothetical prospect of a far happier state of man. If man were simply to improve, he might, 'by the general practice of the duties of religion', 'secure him[self] from misery'. Johnson sternly warns, 'Let no man charge this prospect of things, with being a train of airy phantoms; a visionary scene.... To effect all this, no miracle is required; men need only unite their endeavours, and exert those abilities, which God has conferred upon them, in conformity to the laws of religion.' The same Sermon upholds the very concept of free will. Without it, 'Men would be no longer rational, or would be rational to no purpose.' Yet, the ease with which he believes it can be exerted ('men need *only* unite their endeavours') is fundamentally at odds with the conclusions of *Idler* no. 27. In the Sermon, the vision of human improvement is real, not 'airy' or 'visionary'. This ties in with what one normally assumes to be Johnson's strong insistence on the real. One recalls his hatred of Berkeley's philosophy, his common-sense insistence that 'sensation is sensation'. Yet, time and again, the *Idler* essays seem to depict life itself as a kind of dream.

The idea is most fully developed in no. 32. This essay begins on the topic of sleep. Johnson notes with satisfaction the blow to human arrogance that the failure to explain so simple a thing as sleep represents. To sleep, perchance to dream. The rest of the essay turns to the subject of dreams; the dreams both of night and day. In *The Rambler*, Johnson had dealt with dreams in terms of a 'formidable and obstinate disease of the intellect' (no. 89). In *The Idler*, his handling of the subject is both more sensitive and more sympathetic. The relevant passage merits extended quotation:

> There is reason to suspect that the distinctions of mankind have more shew than value, when it is found that all agree to be weary alike of pleasures and of cares, that the powerful and the weak, the celebrated and obscure, join in one common wish, and implore from nature's hand the nectar of oblivion.
>
> Such is our desire of abstraction from ourselves, that very few are satisfied with the quantity of stupefaction which the needs of the body force upon the mind. Alexander himself added intemperance to sleep, and solaced with the fumes of wine the sovereignty of the world. And almost every man has some art, by which he steals his thoughts away from his present state.
>
> It is not much of life that is spent in close attention to any important duty. Many hours of every day are suffered to fly away without any traces left upon the intellects. We suffer phantoms to rise up before us, and amuse ourselves with the dance of airy images, which after a time we dismiss for ever, and know not how we have been busied.
>
> Many know no happier moments than those that they pass in solitude, abandoned to their own imaginations, which sometimes puts sceptres in their hands or mitres on their heads, shifts the scene of pleasure with endless variety, bids all the forms of beauty sparkle before them, and gluts them with every change of visionary luxury.
>
> It is easy in these semi-slumbers to collect all the possibilities of happiness, to alter the course of the sun, to bring back the past, and anticipate the future, to unite all the beauties of all seasons, and all the blessings of all climates, to receive and bestow felicity, and forget that misery is the lot of man. All this is a voluntary dream, a temporary recession from the realities of life to airy fictions; and habitual subjection of reason to fancy.
>
> Others are afraid to be alone, and amuse themselves by a perpetual succession of companions, but the difference is not great, in solitude we have our dreams to ourselves, and in company we agree to dream in concert. The end sought in both is forgetfulness of ourselves.

In this wonderful, mournful essay, Johnson drives deeper and deeper into his theme. Only with the 'sceptres' passage does the impetus slow down for elaboration. The essay is of course less radical than others in the series. It maintains its clear distinction between on the one hand a plain if painful reality and on the other a state of fantasy into which the mind voluntarily retreats. All the same, this is a far stronger acknowledgement of the power of fancy than the more orthodox Johnson would usually permit, being remarkably free from moralising. In fact, when 'misery is the lot of man', and it is acknowledged that 'Many have no happier hours' than their hours of fantasy, the passage conveys no strong sense that Johnson is prepared to condemn the dreamer. Elsewhere, he is far more severe. The fantasy which is here described as 'forgetfulness of ourselves' is represented in the *Sermons* – Sermon 3 is a good example – as forgetfulness of God. Arieh Sachs, working mostly from the *Sermons*, has stressed the side of Johnson which saw the power of fantasy in terms of spiritual danger, to be repressed. Yet here, in an *Idler* essay which is once again unmistakably self-inclusive, particularly in its final paragraph, Johnson extends an uncharacteristic absolution for his own failings and those of other men.

So far, then, Johnson has described a state (no. 24) in which existence almost loses its reality. Even when it seems more real, man may lose his ability to connect with it and influence it, because of the power exercised by mechanical habit (no. 27). He describes (no. 18) the necessity of 'enhancing' experience, so that its impact seems more real. He describes the mind's continual retreat from reality, since reality is painful (no. 32). All this has vital bearing on the topic of idleness, which entirely loses its sinful status when reality and decision are either illusory or unbearable. Johnson's last contribution to the analysis of mind and matter is his treatment of memory in essays 44 and 72.

In no. 44, he describes, in effect, the darkening of life. Acknowledging the existence of a period of life when all is new, and much delightful, he goes on to describe how this openness to experience diminishes with age, and how 'Then it is that the magazines of memory are opened.' Unfortunately, memory is invariably an afflictive power. Its 'agency is incessant'. Without it, 'there could be no other intellectual operation'. These are the opening assumptions of the essay. Yet, when, later in the essay, he comes to handle memory as an aspect of middle age, the 'treasures of remembrance' are seen to be 'blasted'. Memory is not a pure repository of truths, but rather is coloured by the pain of living experienced by each individual:

The pleasure of recollecting speculative notions would not be much less than that of gaining them, if they could be kept pure and unmingled with the passages of life; but such is the necessary concatenation of our thoughts, that good and evil are linked together, and no pleasure recurs but associated with pain. Every revived idea reminds us of a time when something was enjoyed that is now lost, when some hope was yet not blasted, when some purpose had not yet languished into sluggishness or indifference.

The essay concludes with Themistocles' preference that, rather than learn an art of memory, he could be taught the art of forgetfulness. In a way which is strongly reminiscent of *Idler* 32, and the search for 'forgetfulness of ourselves', this essay decides that 'all shrink from recollection, and all wish for an art of forgetfulness'.

No. 72 pursues the same argument. It begins with the idea of the evanescence of human experience. As in *Idler* 24, Johnson argues how little real impact experience makes on the mind. He puts forward the idea that, if ways could be found of discarding what is useless, the mind would be more free to imprint forcibly what is significant. The rest of the essay, however, records the difficulty of such an idea. The 'memory' which he goes on to describe is one which is abandoned to its own embittered associations, its time being 'uselessly or painfully passed in the revocation of events, which have left neither good nor evil behind them, in grief for misfortunes either repaired or irreparable, in resentment of injuries known only to ourselves, of which death has put the authors beyond our power'. This essay turns out, somewhat unexpectedly, to be the most positive of the key essays of the series. 'Reason will, by a resolute contest, prevail over imagination.' Johnson urges constant employment, since only those 'to whom the present offers nothing will often be looking backward on the past'. He still acknowledges that 'The incursions of troublesome thoughts are often violent and importunate; and it is not easy to a mind accustomed to their inroads to expel them immediately by putting better images into motion.' In the end, the essays on memory take their place alongside the essay on fantasy and daydreams, in describing the mind's retreats from reality. The only difference is that, for Johnson, the memory seems far less pleasurable, handling, as it does, material which has once belonged to reality.

Throughout the key essays, Johnson is directly handling the controversial material of Enlightenment philosophy. He makes continual reference to the philosophers. The whole issue of idleness is jokingly cast in the mode of philosophy in the first essay of the series: 'Some philosophers have called [man] a reasonable animal. . . . Perhaps man may be more properly distinguished as an idle animal.' Johnson touches on the existence of matter, on the nature of mind, on the processes of mind including perception and memory, and on the topics of habit and identity. Finally, in the last and most significant of the key essays, no. 89, he turns to metaphysics. All the other essays have in a sense been preparing for this one. Continually underlying his examinations of daydreams, or memory, or the enhancement of experience is the assumption that 'misery is the lot of man'. The mind's flight from reality is a flight from pain. Even the failure to engage with reality is a failure to engage with pain; though torpor is itself a miserable condition. *Idler* no. 89 proceeds to ask the ultimate question, the question 'why': 'why the only thinking being of this globe is doomed to think merely to be wretched, and to pass his time from youth to age in fearing or in suffering calamities'.

The first explanation offered is of course the orthodox one of the fall of man. 'Misery and sin were produced together.' This is mentioned, however, only to be dismissed. The Garden of Eden is a 'state so remote from all that we have ever seen, that . . . our speculations upon it must be general and confused'. As a 'reason' for pain, therefore, the Fall is set aside. Johnson adopts instead a pragmatic theory that evil at least produces some good: 'Almost all the moral good which is left among us, is the apparent effect of physical evil.' He goes on to explain how none of the three traditional aspects of goodness (soberness, righteousness and godliness) would be practised, but for the enforcements of pain.

To find such a passage in Johnson is nothing short of astonishing. The ferocity with which he could attack any attempt glibly to explain away the presence of evil is adequately illustrated by his review, two years earlier, of Soame Jenyns's *Free Enquiry into the Nature and Origin of Evil*. Jenyns's argument is brutally summarised as follows, in Johnson's review: 'The religion of man produces evils, because the morality of man is imperfect; his morality is imperfect, that he may be justly a subject of punishment: he is made subject to punishment, because the pain of part is necessary to the happiness of the whole: pain is necessary to happiness no mortal can tell why or how.'[2] What clearly infuriates Johnson above all else is the blitheness with which Jenyns can try to explain away evils and tribulations of which he has no real conception. Of this, Johnson is clearly not guilty himself. Yet *Idler* 89 would appear to be venturing, as Jenyns had done, to attach a useful function to misery, a function nothing if not pragmatic.

The evil of disease enforces on the cautious a sober life. The evils of anarchy enforce a righteous one, since 'the pain of suffering wrong was greater than the pleasure of doing it'; and more positively, 'we are in danger of the same distresses, and may sometime implore the same assistance'. Finally, the evil of discontentment enforces a godly life. This is the most interesting part of the theory:

> Godliness, or piety, is elevation of the mind towards the supreme being, and extension of the thoughts to another life. The other life is future, and the supreme being is invisible. None would have recourse to an invisible power, but that all other subjects had eluded their hopes. None would fix their attention upon the future, but that they are discontented with the present. If the senses were feasted with perpetual pleasure, they would always keep the mind in subjection. Reason has no authority over us, but by its power to warn us against evil.

There are really two alternative explanations here, for the mind's potential resistance to the concept of a god. The one offered at the end of the paragraph is that the mind would, if permitted, be content with present gratifications. Only dissatisfaction in this life encourages the mind to look for gratification elsewhere. The other explanation is only half stated, but can be detected in the sentences, 'The other life is future, and the supreme being is invisible. None would have recourse to an invisible power, but that all other subjects had eluded their hopes.' These sentences seem to say more than that an afterlife is difficult to imagine. They imply that, to the human imagination, an afterlife is an unpalatable concept. But for the misery of the present existence, it would not be believed.

This essay has been accorded varying status in Johnson's thought, according to the persuasions of the interpreter. In Stuart Gerry Brown's article in *Marxist Quarterly*,[3] it is of major significance. In Arieh Sachs's[4] exposition of Johnson's Christian orthodoxy, it is not once mentioned.

Johnson's philosophical affiliations in this essay are perhaps somewhat unexpected. His theory of 'godliness' finds him citing the idea of a social compact which, he says, 'one of the heathen sages [Plato] has shewn with great acuteness'. But what is not of course acknowledged is that the theory had been pursued far more recently by Hobbes, whom Johnson professed to abominate.[5] As to the invisible power and the supreme being as aspects of human wishes, Johnson's closest companion here is Hume, whose comments on 'belief' include the theory that its 'effect ... is to raise up a simple idea to an equality with our impressions, and bestow on it a like influence on the passions. This effect it can only have by making an idea approach an impression in force and vivacity.'[6] Hume was another for whom Johnson professed loathing – with a violence which shocked Boswell[7] – but there is a suggestive comment here from Johnson's contemporary, Richard Porson:

> A very old gentleman, who had known Johnson intimately, assured me that the bent of his mind was decidedly towards scepticism: that he was literally afraid to examine his own thoughts on religious matters; and that thence arose his hatred of Hume and other writers.[8]

In fact, even in the *Sermons*, where one might expect to find Johnson at his most orthodox, echoes of Hume are to be found. Sermon 9 is a good example:

> All sin that is committed by Christians, is committed either through an absolute forgetfulness of God, for the time in which the inordinate passion ... prevails; or because, if the ideas of God and religion were present to our minds, they were not strong enough to overcome and suppress the desires excited by some object. So that either the love or fear of temporal good or evil, were more powerful than the love or fear of God.
>
> All ideas influence our conduct with more or less force, as they are more or less strongly impressed upon the mind; and they are impressed more strongly, as they are frequently recollected or renewed. For every idea, whether of love, grief, fear, or any other passion, loses its force by time. . . . But by dwelling upon, and indulging any idea, we may increase its efficacy and

force... and raise it to an ascendant over our passions.

The terminology of Hume is all here, but perversely and confusedly used. 'Idea' seems at one time cognate with 'passions' ('For every idea, whether of love, grief, fear, or any other passion'): at another time it seems to be superior to the passions ('By dwelling upon... any idea, we may... raise it to an ascendant over our passions'). The answer is of course that Johnson grants to the passions the status of an 'idea' when they are directed towards a worthy end. The 'love or fear of God' amounts to 'the *ideas* of God and religion'. The 'love or fear of temporal good or evil' remains, however, at the level of the 'desires', and should be extirpated. Likewise, *Rambler* no. 203 distinguishes between irrational hopes of mortal happiness, and a rational hope of heaven: 'that hope only is rational, of which we are certain that it cannot deceive us'. In all these examples, Johnson was using some of his own most basic terminology. 'Hope and fear, desire and hate' had been heavily used, from *The Vanity of Human Wishes* on. It was a terminology he applied equally to mundane desires and the ideas of religion. There was always the possibility in such a terminology that he might one day leave off the safety-catch of a separation of rational and irrational hopes. When that happened, God would emerge as the emanation of human wishes. This is what happened in *Idler* 89. There is only one other example in Johnson, and that is a private one: the note in his *Annals*, 'Faith in some proportion to Fear'.[9] *Idler* 89 strongly resembles Hume's theory of belief raising up an idea to an equality with our impressions. The only substantial difference is that, rather than the idea influencing the passions, as in Hume, Johnson's passions seem to create the idea. God becomes the ultimate human wish, on which the disappointment of all else 'forces him to fix'. Religion takes its place among the other Johnsonian mechanisms of the mind.

Idler no. 89, and its conclusion that the 'vanity' of life '*forces* him to fix his hopes upon another state', is the culminating point of the personal doubts explored in the key essays of the series. It contains in particularly concentrated form all the major images which Johnson uses in connection with his fears. Chains, rivers, gulphs, mists (familiar from *The Vanity of Human Wishes*) and bubbles are all present. Worldly concerns, he concludes, 'chain down the mind... to the present scene; nor is it remembered how soon this mist of trifles must be scattered, and the bubbles that float upon the rivulet of life be lost for ever in the gulph of eternity'. Contrary to the impression of Porson's 'very old Gentleman', Johnson could and did confront his fears. It is moving to see the great Christian moralist do so. The only surprise is that his doubts are explored in so comparatively light-weight a context.

There are, as in *The Rambler*, many small-portraits among the 'letters to the editor'. The difference is that, as the correspondents' names might indicate, the portraits – of Sukey Savecharges, Zachary Treacle, Betty Broom and the rest – tend to the frivolous. Nearly a third of the total number of *Idlers* are nevertheless composed of these portraits, and it is worthwhile enquiring whether they serve, here, any useful function.

The answer would seem to be that, while the key essays explore the topics of dreamlike unreality in life, the portraits provide the examples. The sequence is packed with hapless dilettantes, all craving to establish some real imprint on life. The most chronic case is Dick Linger of no. 21, a living illustration of the 'enhancement of life' theory in its negative aspect; who vainly tries to 'Kindle in myself an artificial impatience for intelligence of events'. Others, more successful than Linger, in that they at least succeed in stirring themselves to activity, nevertheless enjoy only the illusions of a willed existence. Jack Whirler of no. 19 is the embodiment of purposeless activity. Tom Restless (no. 48) is an intellectual parrot, who, at the end of each day 'lies down full of ideas, and rises in the morning empty as before'. Dick Minim (60 and 61) is a far more extended exercise in the same kind of mind. Minim is a 'critick' by rote, responding to stock theories and stock phrases. His remarkably successful career is a life of habit, and the essays are full of such lives, from needlewomen (13) to debaters (78 and 83), from projectors (17) to collectors (56). The 'fantasy-life' is another recurring pattern. The scribbler-tradesman of no. 47 is echoed in the tradesman's son who has delusions of gentility in no. 95; while the story of Dick Shifter, in no. 71, is a study of a gentleman's pathetic pastoral longings. No. 92 has been praised[10] for its portraits' accurate anticipation of various modern psychological concepts, including the paranoia of Tom Double and Ned Smuggle. In truth, however, the whole sequence of portraits is a gallery of distortions: the mind's distortions and codifications of reality. As Professor Bate points out,[11] *The Idler*'s portraits are far more sympathetic in tone than those of Johnson's earlier periodicals. But then, the key essays seemed to argue that distortion and codification were the inescapable lot of the human mind, placed in such a tormenting relationship with reality: the 'only thinking being of this globe . . . doomed to think merely to be wretched'.

8 *Rasselas*: the 'phantoms of hope'

Rasselas is, of all Johnson's prose works, the one which arouses the highest expectations. It is a short work. It is Johnson's closest approach to the familiar literary form of the novel. It comes at the end of a highly productive decade, so arousing the hope that it will in some way set the seal on that decade. Finally, it was written under the pressures of time, and – apparently – of emotional distress; factors which were frequently, if not invariably, productive of the best in Johnson.

The emotional distress in this case was caused by the death of Johnson's mother in Lichfield. Boswell makes a direct connection between the death of Sarah Johnson and the writing of *Rasselas*, and his account is much quoted: 'soon after [the death] he wrote his *Rasselas, Prince of Abyssinia;*... the late Mr Strahan the printer told me, that Johnson wrote it, that with the profits he might defray the expence of his mother's funeral, and pay some little debts which she had left. He told Sir Joshua Reynolds that he composed it in the evenings of one week, sent it to the press in portions as it was written, and had never since read it over.'[1]

Boswell's account creates a most interesting picture of duty, haste and distress. The true story however is still more fascinating. Where Boswell's account is erroneous is in his supposition that the book was written after Sarah's death. In fact, it was written as she was dying.

We have a series of letters from Johnson to his ninety-year-old mother, and to Lucy Porter, his stepdaughter, who took care of her. In the first, dating from 13 January 1759, Johnson has clearly only just heard of his mother's illness, and the account, he says, 'pierces my heart'. He recommends a herbal remedy, 'a strong infusion of the bark', but, even in this first letter, is clearly thinking of the illness as terminal. He urges her to ask Lucy to recite her 'from time to time the Passion of our Saviour, and sometimes the sentences in the Communion Service, beginning *"Come unto me, all ye that travail and are heavy laden, and I will give you rest"* '. The same somewhat contradictory combination of themes is again taken up in the next letter to his mother, three days later: a letter which, unfortunately, cannot be read with an entirely straight face:

> DEAR HONOURED MOTHER,
> Your weakness afflicts me beyond what I am willing to communicate to you. I do not think you unfit for death, but I know not how to bear the thought of losing you. Endeavour to do all you can for yourself. Eat as much as you can.
> I pray often for you; do you pray for me. I have nothing to add to my last letter.
> I am, dear, dear mother
> Your dutiful son,
> SAM. JOHNSON.

Two days later, and another letter:

> DEAR HONOURED MOTHER,
> I fear you are too ill for long letters; therefore I will only tell you, that you have from me all the regard that can possibly subsist in the heart. I pray God to bless you for evermore, for Jesus Christ's sake. Amen.
> Let Miss write to me every post, however short.
> I am, dear mother,
> Your dutiful son,
> SAM. JOHNSON.

Finally, two days later, on 20 January, his last letter to his mother:

> DEAR HONOURED MOTHER,
> Neither your condition nor your character make it fit for me to say much. You have been the best mother, and I believe the best woman in the world. I thank you for your indulgence to me, and beg forgiveness of all that I have done ill, and all that I have omitted to do well. God grant you his Holy Spirit, and receive you to

everlasting happiness, for Jesus Christ's sake. Amen.
Lord Jesus receive your spirit. Amen.
    I am, dear, dear mother,
        Your dutiful son,
        SAM. JOHNSON.

This sounds pretty final, and indeed his mother was dead by the time the letter arrived; possibly she was dead even as he wrote. His next letter is to Miss Porter, three days later – the day of the funeral – and Johnson expresses his grief as follows: 'You will conceive my sorrow for the loss of my mother, of the best mother. If she were to live again, surely I should behave better to her. . . . I shall send a bill of twenty pounds in a few days, which I thought to have brought to my mother; but God suffered it not.'

'Which I thought to have brought to my mother; but God suffered it not.' One of the most striking things about this correspondence is that Johnson's tender farewells to his mother are all by post. On the other side of the paper are letters to Miss Porter, in which he promises that he is all but on his way to Lichfield ('I will, if it be possible, come down to you. God grant I may yet [find] my dear mother breathing and sensible. Do not tell her, lest I disappoint her. If I miss to write next post, I am on the road'). In fact, he continued to hang on in London until she was dead. Of course, he had good excuses, and biographers have often put them forward on his behalf. It is also possible to put these excuses into perspective: 'It is, I think, incontestable that Johnson avoided an actual interview with his mother. He was short of money, yes; loaded with work, yes; the roads were bad and travel uncertain, yes; but he did get himself as far as Oxford in 1754, and spent week after week there doing very little, and Lichfield could have been reached easily enough from there if he had really wanted to reach it.'[2] Johnson actually revisited Oxford later in 1759. His grief was certainly great, when his mother died. The event left him 'as little able to sustain the shock as he would have been had this loss befallen him in his nonage'.[3] It is possible, however, that the depth of his feelings derived as much from a sense of guilt as of devotion.

Certainly, the most intriguing letter of all from Johnson's correspondence in this period is the letter to his printer concerning *Rasselas*: 'When I was with you last night I told you of a story which I was preparing for the press. The title will be "The Choice of Life" or "The History of — Prince of Abyssinia".' He goes on to bargain with Strahan about the price: 'The bargain I made with Mr Johnson was seventy five pounds (or guineas) a volume, and twenty five pounds for the second edition. I will sell this either at that price or at sixty the first edition, of which he shall himself fix the number, and the property then to revert to me, or for forty pounds, and share the profit, that is retain half the copy. I shall have occasion for thirty pounds on Monday night, when I shall deliver the book which I must entreat you upon such delivery to procure me.'[4] As it happens, he was in the end beaten down to a hundred for the first edition, and twenty-five for the second. For all the businesslike tone of the letter to Strahan, Johnson had no business head. As Baretti says, 'any other man with the degree of reputation he then possessed would have got £400 for that work, but Johnson never understood the art of making the most of his productions'. What is striking about the letter, though, is not the businesslike tone (there is after all, no total contradiction between grieving and making money), but the date of the letter.

The letter is dated 20 January, the same day on which he wrote so conclusive a valedictory letter to his mother. It is clear that Boswell is entirely wrong in supposing that *Rasselas* was written 'soon after' his mother's death. It is possible that Bate too is wrong in saying that the 'result and not the intention'[5] is what we must bear in mind, in thinking of Johnson writing *Rasselas* to 'defray the expenses of his mother's funeral'. Johnson wrote *Rasselas* instead of going to see his mother while she still survived. It was written in anticipation of her funeral.

There is no doubting Johnson's generosity, and no question but that the 'thirty pounds' advance he demanded from Strahan was destined for his mother; and indeed most of that sum did eventually make its way to Lichfield. We might add that, for years, Johnson had supported his mother, and borne the mortgage on the Lichfield property. After her death, with a typical gesture, he offered the house to Lucy Porter for as long as she needed it. What one doubts is not Johnson's financial generosity, and his intention to convey to his mother some of the money he made from *Rasselas*, but only the genuineness of his intention 'to have *brought* [it] to my mother'. The finality of his letters of farewell argues decisively against accepting his word on this score.

One other point is of interest. On the day of his mother's funeral – which, of course, he did not attend – he composed a prayer in which he asked that a new 'purity of mind' be granted 'unto me that am now about to return to the common comforts and business of the world'. Hill compared this with the forty days that had elapsed before Johnson, in his prayers on the death of his wife, seven years earlier, permitted himself to 'return to the duties of my present state'.[6]

Great though Johnson's need of money seems to have been at this time – in March, he gave up the struggle to maintain his house in Gough Square, and moved to rooms in Staple Inn – his return to 'the common ... business of the world' was not a return to full employment. There was *The Idler*; but that demanded no more than two or three pages a week. There was a contribution to the controversy over the design of Blackfriars Bridge; but that was not until December. There was the edition of Shakespeare, but it is quite clear that that project was by now completely stationary. There was an Introduction, written for the publisher John Newberry, to a collection of voyages and travels, called *The World Displayed*; but he owed Newberry money (a sum roughly equivalent to a year's rent of the house at Gough Square), and this assignment may have been forced on him, to clear his debt. *The Idler* was enough to keep him alive. The impression of him at this time is otherwise one of lassitude rather than of industry. Murphy, writing of Johnson in the beginning of 1759, and of the move to Staple Inn, described him as living 'in poverty, total idleness, and the pride of literature. ... Mr Fitzherbert used to say that he paid a morning visit to Johnson, intending from his chambers to send a letter into the city; but to his great surprise, he found an author by profession without pen, ink, or paper.'[7] In his prayer for Easter Day of this year (15 April) Johnson prays for 'Grace to break the chain of evil custom. Enable me to break off idleness and sloth ... to be diligent in my calling, that I may support myself and relieve others.'[8]

It is clear, then, that Johnson's haste to return to the world after the death of his mother was not dictated by the pressure of his commitments. On the day of his mother's death, he wrote an amusing *Idler* (no. 40) mocking advertisers. The next he had to provide was for 27 February. It took the form of a 'letter to the editor' from a fictitious correspondent who had just seen the death of a mother. It strikes all the proper notes of mournful piety. Yet its laudable conclusion that 'these are the calamities by which Providence gradually disengages us from the love of life', is somewhat contradicted by Johnson's own return to the common comforts and business of the world, four days earlier.

Hawkins conjectures a direct link between the loss of Johnson's mother, and what he takes to be the tone of *Rasselas*: 'it was composed at a time when no spring like that in the mind of Rasselas urged his narrator; when the heavy band of affliction almost bore him down, and the dread of future want haunted him: . . . he poured out his sorrow in gloomy reflection, and being destitute of comfort himself, described the world as nearly without it'.[9] This seems on the face of it a fair assumption. *Rasselas* is commonly taken to be a depressing book. Even Boswell will not deny that 'the "morbid melancholy" in Johnson's constitution may not, perhaps, have made life appear to him more insipid and unhappy than it generally is'.[10] Certainly, Johnson's mood at this time seems both gloomy and apprehensive. However, Hawkins's interpretation of *Rasselas* still represents a misreading both of the tone of the work itself, and of the direct connection of this with the death of Johnson's mother.

In fact, the true relationship between *Rasselas* and Sarah's death may more properly be seen as inverse. As he saw the approach of his mother's extinction, he chose to write a story, not about the leaving of life, but about the entering of it. More interestingly still, Rasselas's flight from the Happy Valley may be seen as a kind of escape from the womb.

The plot is an Eastern romance. It opens in a place called the Happy Valley in which the heirs to the kingdom of Abyssinia are confined from birth, until they should be called to the succession. Since the titular hero of the book is only the fourth in line to the throne, Rasselas's confinement is likely to be lifelong. The royal prisoners are provided with a variety of amusing companions, and competition to gain entry to the Valley is keen. However, as Rasselas grows to maturity, he begins to long only for escape. Eventually, he achieves this, together with his sister Nekayah, her maid Pekuah, and the poet–philosopher Imlac. Imlac of course has seen the outside world before. The others have not, and the remainder of the story shows their introduction to the world, and their eventual formation of a 'choice of life'.

The source of the story is in folklore, but the specific idea of the confinement of heirs to the throne he took from Father Lobo's *Voyage to Abyssinia*, which he had translated twenty-four years earlier. What is interesting is the changes Johnson made to the nature of the place of confinement. In the *Voyage to Abyssinia*, that place had been a bare mountain top. Here, Johnson preferred to follow instead a secondary source, a seventeenth-century travel book, *Purchas: His Pilgrimage* which describes the place as being 'many fruitful and pleasant valleys'.

Accordingly, in the one passage of full and evocative geographical description which the book contains, the Happy Valley is depicted as follows:

> The place which the wisdom or policy of antiquity had destined for the residence of the Abyssinian princes, was a spacious valley in the kingdom of Amhara, surrounded on every side by mountains, of which the summits overhang the middle part. The only passage by which it could be entered, was a cavern that passed under a rock, of which it has long been disputed whether it was the work of nature or of human industry. The outlet of the cavern was concealed by a thick wood, and the mouth which opened into the valley was closed with gates of iron, forged by the artificers of ancient days, so massy that no man could without the help of engines open or shut them.
>
> From the mountains on every side, rivulets descended, that filled all the valley with verdure and fertility, and formed a lake in the middle, inhabited by fish of every species, and frequented by every fowl whom nature has taught to dip the wing in water. This lake discharged its superfluities by a stream, which entered a dark cleft of the mountain on the northern side, and fell with dreadful noise from precipice to precipice till it was heard no more.
>
> The sides of the mountains were covered with trees; every blast shook spices from the rocks, and every month dropped fruits upon the ground. All animals that bite the grass, or browse the shrub, whether wild or tame, wandered in this extensive circuit, secured from beasts of prey by the mountains which confined them. . . . All the diversities of the world were brought together; the blessings of nature were collected, and its evils extracted and excluded.
>
> The valley, wide and fruitful, supplied its inhabitants with the necessaries of life, and all delights and superfluities were added at the annual visit which the emperor paid his children, when the iron gate was opened to the sound of music, and, during eight days, every one that resided in the valley was required to

propose whatever might contribute to make seclusion pleasant, to fill up the vacancies of attention, and lessen the tediousness of time. Every desire was immediately granted. All the artificers of pleasure were called to gladden the festivity; the musicians exerted all the power of harmony, and the dancers showed their activity before the princes, in the hope that they should pass their lives in this blissful captivity, to which those only were admitted whose performance was thought to add novelty to luxury.

Such was the appearance of security and delight which this retirement afforded, that they to whom it was new always desired that it might be perpetual; and as those on whom the iron gate had once closed were never suffered to return, the effect of longer experience could not be known. Thus every year produced new schemes of delight, and new competitors for imprisonment.

As his mother lay dying, Johnson produced in this passage a description of a valley which is extraordinarily womb-like. There is almost complete enclosure by the overhanging mountains (Johnson never tries to explain how sunlight entered!). The valley is full of moisture, and in and around this moisture is a kind of universal breeding-ground, for every conceivable species except predators. There is one exit for drainage, through a single narrow cleft. There is another separate entry, used for paternal access; gated, and with a 'mouth' concealed on the outside by a thick wood. *Rasselas* predates the first occasion (1774) on which the word 'confinement' was used in relation to childbirth, but the confinement of Rasselas and the others in the Happy Valley seems like an imprisonment in the womb. Interestingly, it also carries one of the properties of death, since those who enter it can never return. *Idler* 41, the one in which Johnson almost directly wrote of the loss of his mother, carries an intriguing image for bereavement: 'the life which made my own life pleasant is at an end, and the gates of death are shut upon my prospects'. It might be anticipated that the image would normally be applied to the dead person, rather than the bereaved one; so that it would be the dead person on whom the gates of death would close, cutting off the prospect of life. The change is an arresting one, drawing attention to the bereaved person's sense of hopelessness. In *Rasselas*, the same image is used, but in the obvious way. The gates close on those to whom the world is denied, and it is a kind of death. There is a notable absence of 'prospects': instead there are the uterine labyrinths of the palace, in which 'to every room there was an open and a secret passage'. When Rasselas escapes, it is an escape into prospects; an escape into life.

Johnson had always taken a strong interest in the condition of youth as a kind of blank sheet, capable of taking impressions from others. Possibly his most extended pronouncement on the responsibility this placed on others is in *Rambler* no. 4. The essay is on the contemporary novel, or, as it is called here, 'the comedy of romance', which, unlike older forms of romance, concerns itself with recognisable contemporary scenes, 'when an adventurer is levelled with the rest of the world, and acts in such scenes of universal drama, as may be the lot of any other man'. On such a hero, the young readers fix their eyes 'with closer attention, and hope by observing his behaviour and success to regulate their own practices'. Accordingly, Johnson urges the modern novelist that 'the highest degree of reverence should be paid to youth, and that nothing indecent should be suffered to approach their ears and eyes. . . . The purpose of these writings is surely not only to show mankind, but to provide that they may be seen hereafter with less hazard; to initiate youth by mock encounters in the art of necessary defence, and to increase prudence without impairing virtue.' As a recipe for literary composition, this is somewhat repugnant. Johnson believes that he is quoting the precepts of Juvenal (*reverentia*), but Satire XIV urges only that fathers should not commit their moral outrages before their children's faces. This seems fair enough, but, for Johnson, the threshold of evil influence seems much lower. It is perhaps surprising that an author who in his Shakespeare criticism insisted that an audience had a sense of the fictitious nature of the play, should here have so strong a sense of an audience's potential involvement in the fiction; or, in the terminology of the pornography law, of the power of literature to deprave and corrupt. The theory is relentlessly applied. Johnson castigates the Fieldings and Smolletts of his age who 'so mingle good and bad qualities in their principal personages, that they are both equally conspicuous'. In such cases, 'we lose the abhorrence of their faults . . . or, perhaps, regard them with some kindness for being united with so much merit'. The novel attracts a young and impressionable readership. Its only defensible way of proceeding is diligently to separate good from bad; and, if 'vice is necessary to be shewn, [it] should always disgust'.

Johnson's own early work is occasionally directly formed on these principles. His poem, *To a Young Lady on her Birthday*, spends no more than half-a-dozen lines on birthday greetings and compliments before getting down to the serious theme:

> My fair, be mindful of the mighty trust,
> Alas! 'tis hard for beauty to be just.
> Those sovereign charms with strictest care employ,
> Nor give the generous pain, the worthless joy.
> With his own form acquaint the forward fool,
> Shewn in the faithful glass of ridicule;
> Teach mimick censure her own faults to find,
> No more let coquets to themselves be blind,
> So shall Belinda's charms improve mankind.

In *Rasselas*, the chosen mentor for youth is, more realistically, not beauty but age; the middle-aged poet–philosopher Imlac. Under his guidance, moral survival becomes a much less hazardous business than it had been for the youthful royal principals of *Irene* similarly assailed by alien culture. In his own 'romance', Johnson creates at once a fable of release, and a scheme of enlightenment. It is quite clear from the strongly evocative nature of the former, that one part of Johnson the writer strongly identifies with the euphoria of release from minority. On the other hand, since Imlac is equally clearly a Johnsonian alias, the *surrogate* parental voice which the novel contains is also Johnson's own. In fact, the impression that Johnson is imaginatively involved both as novice and as guide is enhanced by the marked similarity of cadence between Imlac's speech and that of any of his charges. As Professor Bate remarks, the similarity develops into something closer than cadence: 'by the later part of the story, they themselves have progressed to the point at which they think and talk about experience in the way that Imlac would'.[11] Given the coalescence of pupil and teacher, *Rasselas* becomes something far more lively and heterodox than, on the evidence of *Rambler* no. 4, one might ever imagine Johnson capable of producing. It becomes a myth not only of quest and discovery, but of independence and self-creation.

To take the idea of quest first, the search for a choice of life naturally generates a kinetic plot, and an episodic one; as episodic as the mode of composition he adopted, sending it 'to the press in portions as it was written'. The four escapees become travellers through foreign countries, and through other modes of life. Those they meet tend to be stationary when encountered; waiting as it were for the travellers to inspect the choice of life they have made. However, often, they recount a history of the same kind of pilgrimage or quest, before the choice was made, and in three conspicuous cases, the chosen life is discarded in favour of a new quest, under the stimulus of the encounter with Rasselas and his companions. The first such case is Imlac himself, whose life-story recounted in Chapters VIII–XII is entirely one of quest. Eventually, when 'wearied', he had made a choice of life, to be employed in the Happy Valley. Almost at once, he had repented his choice. He now seizes the chance to exchange choice for a renewal of quest, which Rasselas's own restlessness now offers. At the end of the book, when the time comes for the others to make a choice of life, it is clear that for Imlac quest is itself a sufficient choice of life. Another example is provided by the hermit of Chapter XXI. He became a hermit when baulked in an earlier choice of a military career, 'being disgusted at the preferment of a younger officer'. However, the story of his retirement from life is one of growing dissatisfaction:

> When the pleasure of novelty went away, I employed my hours in examining the plants which grow in the valley, and the minerals which I collected from the rocks. But that inquiry is now grown tasteless and irksome. I have been for some time unsettled and distracted: my mind is disturbed with a thousand perplexities of doubt and vanities of imagination, which hourly prevail upon me, because I have no opportunities of relaxation or diversion. I am sometimes ashamed to think that I could not secure myself from vice, but by retiring from the exercise of virtue, and begin to suspect that I was rather impelled by resentment, than led by devotion, into solitude. My fancy riots in scenes of folly, and I lament that I have lost so much and gained so little. . . . I have been long comparing the evils with the advantages of society, and resolve to return into the world tomorrow.

The last figure who 'returns to the world' is the astronomer, of the latter parts of the book, whom the travellers meet, cure of his delusions, and adopt as a companion. At the end of the book, he makes his choice of life along with the others, and his choice is the same as Imlac's. In line with Professor Bate's observation on the growing wisdom of the younger members of the group, it is not Imlac but Nekayah who sums up the theme of quest in the book's antepenultimate chapter:

> 'Such', said Nekayah, 'is the state of life, that none are happy but by the anticipation of change: the change itself is nothing; when we have made it, the next wish is to change again. The world is not yet exhausted; let me see something tomorrow which I never saw before.'

In the case of the hermit, the search for change is simplified into an oscillation between the world and the retreat. As he gazes on the city 'with rapture', it is predicted of him that he 'would, in a few years, go back to his retreat, and perhaps, if shame did not restrain or death intercept him, return once more from his retreat into the world'.

The other part of the fable is of independence and self-creation. It is a theme which has a negative as well as a positive aspect. Solitariness is repeatedly the theme, implied or explicit, of many sections of the narrative. Hostility and loneliness are again and again encountered. It is as much an imperative of this theme as of the narrative itself that the four escapees from the Happy Valley spend considerable portions of the narrative in isolation from each other. Pekuah is kidnapped, and the effect on Nekayah of the loss of her favourite is closely observed. For a longish stretch of the book, the figure of Imlac simply disappears. In his absence, Rasselas and Nekayah, rather than clinging together, embark on independent quests. It is Nekayah who comes up with the idea of a divided quest (Chapter XXIII): 'you shall try what is to be found in the splendour of courts, and I will range the shades of humbler life. Perhaps command and authority may be the supreme blessings, as they afford most opportunities of doing good; or, perhaps, what this world can give may be found in the modest habitations of middle fortune, too low for great designs, and too high for penury and distress.' They meet again only to compare notes, and announce the failure of both areas of enquiry. It might be added that, for much of the time, it is a matter of the solitary observers observing other solitaries.

However, even when the scene is a crowded urban one, the narrative insists on the solitariness of the lives observed. Imlac tells of his early experience with the merchants of a caravan:

> My companions, for some reason or other, conjecturing that I was rich, and, by my inquiries and admiration, finding that I was ignorant, considered me as a novice whom they had a right to cheat, and who was to learn at the usual expense the art of fraud. They exposed me to the theft of servants and the exaction of officers, and saw me plundered upon false pretences, without any advantage to themselves, but that of rejoicing in the superiority of their own knowledge. (Chapter IX)

It is the first of several occasions in the book on which hostility of this kind is experienced. It is largely the absence of any such belief in one's own superiority, or the absence of any such desire to inflict defeat, which separates those on the quest from at least the inferior minds they encounter. Imlac promptly gives another example of the same impulse in the learned men he had encountered: 'some were unwilling to teach another what they had with difficulty learned themselves; and some showed that the end of their studies was to gain the dignity of instructing'. Similar examples later in the book include the scholarly debating society of Chapter XXII, in which 'every one was desirous to dictate to the rest, and every one was pleased to hear the genius or knowledge of another depreciated'. Then (Chapter XXV) there are the ladies of noble families encountered by Nekayah, whose 'pleasures, poor as they were, could not be preserved pure, but were embittered by petty competitions and worthless emulation. They were always jealous of the beauty of another.' In much the same way, Pekuah announces, the women of the harem behaved, whom she observed during her kidnap: the Arab who owned them was not 'much obliged by that regard, of which he could never know the sincerity, and which he might often perceive to be exerted, not so much to delight him as to pain a rival' (Chapter XXXIX). At the bottom of the social scale there are the peasants of Chapter XIX, of whom 'it was evident that their hearts were cankered with discontent, that they considered themselves as condemned to labour for the luxury of the rich, and looked up with stupid malevolence toward those that were placed above them'.

With this sort of competitive malice as the ruling impulse of all the lesser figures in the book, it is no surprise that the whole tendency of the narrative is away from, rather than towards relationships. The encounters between those on the quest, and those who display modes of life for their benefit tend to be less meetings than, at best, collisions. Each episode tends to be brief, demonstrative and comic. In the case of the stoic philosopher, Johnson adopts the eighteenth-century cliché of the stoic bereaved; in which, as usual, despite his stoical preachings, the stoic behaves with extravagant grief (Chapter XVIII). In other episodes, the incidents described may not amount to cliché, but they are designed to provide just enough evidence to provide the voice of the narrator with a dismissive punch-line. In Chapter XXII, Rasselas finds, among the scholarly debaters, one man whose views have some appeal. He preaches a life according to nature. On enquiry, of course, his views turn out to be cant:

> 'When I find young men so humble and docile', said the philosopher, 'I can deny them no information which my studies have enabled me to afford. – To live according to nature, is to act always with due regard to the fitness arising from the relations and qualities of causes and effects; to concur with the great and unchangeable scheme of universal felicity; to co-operate with the general disposition and tendency of the present system of things.'
>
> The prince soon found that this was one of the sages whom he should understand less as he heard him longer. He therefore bowed and was silent; and the philosopher, supposing him satisfied, and the rest vanquished, rose up, and departed with the air of a man that had co-operated with the present system.

The parody is so broad, and the comic despatch so rapid, that there is hardly the slightest glimpse in Rasselas of any substantial impulse of gullible attraction. The evidence is shown only for instant demolition. Similarly, in the next chapter, Rasselas explores the attractions of political power: but, again, his willingness to believe in the advantages of this aspect of life is given only such scope as is necessary for emphatic deflation. At first, Rasselas believes the man of power to be happy, but worries that the subjection of the many should be necessary to the happiness of the one:

These thoughts were often in his mind, and he found no solution of the difficulty. But as presents and civilities gained him more familiarity, he found that almost every man who stood high in employment hated all the rest, and was hated by them, and that their lives were a continual succession of plots and detections, stratagems and escapes, faction and treachery. Many of those who surrounded the Bassa, were sent only to watch and report his conduct; every tongue was muttering censure, and every eye was searching for a fault.

At last, the letters of revocation arrived, the Bassa was carried in chains to Constantinople, and his name was mentioned no more.

'What are we now to think of the prerogatives of power?' said Rasselas to his sister; 'is it without any efficacy to good? or, is the subordinate degree only dangerous, and the supreme safe and glorious? Is the Sultan the only happy man in his dominions? or, is the Sultan himself subject to the torments of suspicion, and the dread of enemies?'

In a short time the second Bassa was deposed; the Sultan who had advanced him was murdered by the Janizaries, and his successor had other views and different favourites.

There is no attempt here to make credible the 'evidence', in terms of Rasselas's encounters with the powerful. Quite clearly, the events described extend over too long a period for credible narration. Instead, Johnson keeps his terminology of time purposely vague: 'often', 'continual', 'at last', 'no more', 'in a short time'. By doing so, he is not only able to condense time, but to obscure the whole issue of Rasselas's part in all this. Here and elsewhere, Rasselas seems particularly remote from the events he is supposed to witness. However, the narrative is not contained in what he sees, and his observations do not govern the book's perspective. Rather, the knowing narrator disposes a series of encounters between fallible modes of life and naive observer. The book becomes for at least half of its length a series of moments of enlightenment, and the sole interaction between scene and observer in which Johnson is interested is the transition from gullible belief to clarity. After each brief episode, the innocence of the observing eye is fully re-established for the next encounter. This is no great feat, when the moment of enlightenment is so lightly registered anyway. The most forceful of such moments amounts to no more than this: 'the prince ... went away convinced of the emptiness of rhetorical sound, and the inefficacy of polished ... sentences'. More typical is the group's reaction to the hermit's confession: 'they heard his resolution with surprise, but after a short pause, offered to conduct him to Cairo'. Even a sharp rebuff – for instance the derisive reception given to Rasselas's counsel of sobriety by the young revellers (Chapter XVII) – is rapidly digested, and forgotten: 'he recovered his tranquillity, and pursued his search'.

There is hardly any more substantial sense of relationship at first between the major characters. Early on, Nekayah discovers the escape-tunnel being dug by Rasselas and Imlac, and begs to join the venture. Rasselas agrees, since he 'loved Nekayah above his other sisters'. His affection hardly seems to amount to rapture, though. His first reaction is one of vexation 'that he had lost an opportunity of showing his confidence by a voluntary communication'. Later, the affection between Nekayah and her favourite, Pekuah, is made the subject of the same kind of analytical scrutiny. The episode here is the one in which Pekuah is kidnapped. The grief of Nekayah is remotely and impersonally observed. The first phase is of self-reproach; if Nekayah had ordered Pekuah to enter the pyramids with the rest of the party, none of this would have happened. Reasoned out of this phase by Imlac, she enters a second, which consists of an obsession with the memory of Pekuah, in which, increasingly, despite attempts to divert her, 'her mind, though forced into short excursions, always returned to the image of her friend'. It is the final phase, however, which most interests Johnson, and which is recounted at greatest length. It concerns the gradual effacement of Pekuah's memory:

> Nekayah, seeing that nothing was omitted for the recovery of her favourite ... began imperceptibly to return to common cares and common pleasures. She rejoiced without her own consent at the suspension of her sorrows, and sometimes caught herself with indignation in the act of turning away her mind from the remembrance of her, whom yet she resolved never to forget.
>
> She then appointed a certain hour of the day for meditation on the merits and fondness of Pekuah, and for some weeks retired constantly at the time fixed, and returned with her eyes swollen and her countenance clouded. By degrees she grew less

scrupulous, and suffered any important and pressing avocation to delay the tribute of daily tears. She then yielded to less occasions; sometimes forgot what indeed she was afraid to remember, and at last wholly released herself from the duty of periodical affliction.

Her real love of Pekuah was yet not diminished. . . . 'Yet what', said she, 'is to be expected from our pursuit of happiness, when we find the state of life to be such, that happiness itself is the cause of misery. . . . I shall henceforth fear to yield my heart to excellence however bright, or to fondness however tender, lest I should lose again what I have lost in Pekuah.' (Chapter XXXVI)

The process we watch is identical to the experience of bereavement. It is intriguing, reading a book written on the occasion of a close bereavement, to see the process so dispassionately and even comically noted. Notably, Nekayah is observed as she began 'imperceptibly to return to common cares and common pleasures', and this comes close to Johnson's own formula, of 'return to the common comforts and business of the world'. If Nekayah's period of mourning is far longer than Johnson's own, her persistence earns her something close to ridicule, as the mechanisms of grief turn mourning into an exercise in perversity; with its mechanically graded phases, its self-regard and even, finally, its self-protection. The affection is conceded to be 'real', but the emotional displays and daily tears are made to seem fraudulent. It is not the gradual effacement of Pekuah's memory which is mocked, but the artificial attempt to preserve it fresh. The episode provides strong reinforcement to the impression the book elsewhere makes; that the essential human condition is solitary, and even the most intimate contact remote.

Of special interest then, is the discussion between Rasselas and Nekayah on marriage and the family; which, given the fact that sexual and romantic love never features in the book, is the only evidence we have on this important topic. The discussion is long, and centrally placed (Chapters XXV–XXIX). It takes place between Rasselas and his sister, following their resolution to divide the work of observation, of public life and private, between them. But when they meet to report their findings, it is almost exclusively the conduct of private life which engrosses the conversation.

The first topic is not matrimony but parenthood, and the relationship between parents and children is depicted as one of faction:

> Parents and children seldom act in concert: each child endeavours to appropriate the esteem or fondness of the parents, and the parents, with yet less temptation, betray each other to their children; thus, some place their confidence in the father, and some in the mother, and by degrees the house is filled with artifices and feuds. (Chapter XXVI)

Worse, there is active and direct hostility between parent and child: 'kindness seldom continues beyond the years of infancy: in a short time the children become rivals to their parents; benefits are allayed by reproaches, and gratitude debased by envy'. Ultimately, the relationship of parent and child is totally embittered to one of anger and contempt: 'age looks with anger on the temerity of youth, and youth looks with contempt on the scrupulosity of age. Thus parents and children, for the greatest part, live on to love less and less.' The theme is returned to in Chapter XXIX, in the context of the topic of youthful marriage: 'from those early marriages proceeds likewise the rivalry of parents and children. The son is eager to enjoy the world before the father is willing to forsake it, and there is hardly room at once for two generations. The daughter begins to bloom before the mother can be content to fade, and neither can forbear to wish for the absence of the other.' The theme is familiar enough from *The Rambler* (nos 55, 148, etc.), but here is given far greater prominence, occurring as it does in one of the two major discussions of the book. Similarly, the discussion on matrimony itself gives a new prominence to thoughts familiar from *The Rambler*:

> Such is the common process of marriage. A youth and maiden, meeting by chance or brought together by artifice, exchange glances, reciprocate civilities, go home, and dream of one another. Having little to divert attention, or diversify thought, they find themselves uneasy when they are apart, and therefore conclude that they shall be happy together. They marry, and discover what nothing but voluntary blindness before had concealed: they wear out life in altercations, and charge nature with cruelty.

This pitiless sardonic simplification of courtship to, not lust, but the delusions of vacancy, is entirely of a piece with Johnson's treatment of Nekayah's mourning; except that, in this case the emotion is not conceded to be 'real' at all. In any case, the mechanisms of falling in love are so far condensed by Johnson that amusement is here less notable than contempt. Unfortunately, late marriage, though not comically treated in this Chapter (XXIX), seems equally doomed:

> it is dangerous for a man and woman to suspend their fate upon each other, at a time when opinions are fixed, and habits established; when friendships have been contracted on both sides; when life has been planned into method, and the mind has long enjoyed the contemplation of its own prospects.

The only shred of comfort which this discussion on marriage and parenthood offers is that the single state is in its own way just as bad, consisting as it does of living 'without feeling or exciting sympathy' (Chapter XXVI).

Rasselas, then, gives very full scope to the idea of solitariness, the ubiquitous presence in human relationships of either envy or contempt, and the fallaciousness of hopes of human love. This is the negative side of the theme of self-determination: that the price to be paid is being alone.

There is, however, a positive side. The relationship between parent and child might be embittered, but then the book at least offers the prospect of youth breaking free of the parental tyranny, and making its own choices. Rasselas and his sister are of course not only escapees from the Valley, but rebels against the parental and hereditary will. Their father is a remote figure who visits them once a year, but by their escape they in effect renounce their parentage and entirely cancel the relationship. Their father, and indeed the rest of their family, is mentioned again in the book only once, where Rasselas reproaches himself that, in his daydreams of inheriting power in Abyssinia, he had contemplated so lightly the necessary destruction of his father and elder brothers.

It is notable that the mentor-figure of Imlac himself provides a parallel instance of renunciation of the parental tie. His life-history, in Chapter VIII, begins with the story of Imlac's mutiny against his father's intention to make him follow his own profession, of commerce. Here, Imlac's account precisely anticipates the account of the fate of the parent–child tie of Chapter XXVI. Two maxims in particular are illustrated in advance: that 'the old man pays regard to riches, and the youth reverences virtue', and that increasingly the attitude of youth towards age is one of 'contempt'. In the case of Imlac, he soon began to diverge from his father's ideas:

> when I had once found the delight of knowledge, and felt the pleasure of intelligence and the pride of invention, I began silently to despise riches, and determined to disappoint the purpose of my father, whose grossness of conception raised my pity.

Eventually Imlac, like Johnson himself, came to despise his very teachers, and an independent choice of life became inevitable. As soon as Imlac's father entrusted his son with a stock of capital, which he was supposed to use for his apprenticeship in commerce, Imlac decamped. He was never to see his father again, and did not revisit his native country until twenty years had elapsed. One notes the exact correspondence here with Johnson's own case, whose own last visit to Lichfield had been precisely twenty years earlier.

Another example of similar personal renunciations is the moral hero of the last phase of *Rasselas*, the astronomer, who twice speaks, albeit with regret, of his deliberate isolation from human relationships of any kind: 'I have neither mother to be delighted with the reputation of her son, nor wife to partake the honours of her husband. I have outlived my friends and my rivals.' Here (Chapter XLV), for all his regret, is another figure who renounces family relationships in favour of independence; and whose relationships are solely those of friendship and rivalry. Only when friends and rivals are dead does he regret the absence of other ties.

Here, then, is a clear and reiterated pattern, of initiatives necessarily formed at the expense of the parental will, and fulfilled at the expense of sacrificing the filial tie. Within the quest itself, it is noticeable that the pseudo-parent, Imlac, becomes the subject of small stirrings of rebellion in Rasselas and Nekayah. It comes just before the important central section on marriage and parenthood. In fact, the resolve which Rasselas and his sister form, to explore public and private life respectively, and consult only with each other, originates in their impatience with the pseudo-parental circumspection and pessimism of Imlac:

Rasselas returned home full of reflections, doubtful how to direct his future steps.... He communicated to Imlac his observations and his doubts, but was answered by him with new doubts, and remarks that gave him no comfort. He therefore discoursed more frequently and freely with his sister, who had yet the same hope with himself, and always assisted him to give some reason why, though he had been hitherto frustrated, he might succeed at last.

'We have hitherto', said she, 'known but little of the world: we have never yet been either great or mean. In our own country, though we had royalty, we had no power; and in this, we have not yet seen the private recesses of domestic peace. Imlac favours not our search, lest we should in time find him mistaken. We will divide the task between us.' (Chapter XXIII)

Possibly, they are doing Imlac an injustice. Later on in the book, after their encounter with an old man, they attempt to reason away the latter's depressive view of his own old age, which left 'his audience not much elated with the hope of long life' (Chapter XLV). 'Imlac, who had no desire to see them depressed, smiled at the comforts which they could so readily procure to themselves, and remembered, that at the same age he was equally confident of unmingled prosperity, and equally fertile of consolatory expedients. He forbore to force on them unwelcome knowledge, which time itself would too soon impress.'

Imlac, then, demonstrates himself to be the perfect parent, with a charitable recall of his own youthful errors. However, the impulse to break free even from Imlac provides Rasselas and Nekayah with their most important learning experience. In the debate on marriage and parenthood, and on statecraft, we have the best example of how, 'by the later part of the story, they themselves have progressed to the point at which they think and talk about experience in the way that Imlac would'.

The first feature of this new-found capacity is of course the confidence with which each dissects human affairs; the confidence born of careful observation, and rational inference. Each in turn therefore pronounces resonant general truths about the section of life they have seen. Since the truths pronounced are always pessimistic, this places the speaker in the customary position of Imlac; and in the same relative position to the hearer, of sweeping aside optimistic incredulity. Where Imlac's life-story had provoked

Rasselas's resistance ('I am not yet willing', said the prince, 'to suppose that happiness is so parsimoniously distributed to mortals', Chapter XII), it is now Nekayah who leaves him groping for comfort ('the prince having considered his sister's observations, told her, that she had surveyed life with prejudice, and supposed misery where she did not find it', Chapter XXVII). Promptly their roles are exchanged, and it is the prince who presses his reasoned pessimism against his sister's resistance, on the subject of statecraft.

But possibly the more important symptom of a quite new maturity is the way the discussion begins to open out, once each has stated a view of public or private life. There are moments in the dialogue when brother and sister become contentious intellectual equals, trying out ideas on each other. The first notable development of this kind is where Nekayah, returning to the subject of marriage, concludes that she sometimes is 'disposed to think with the severer casuists of most nations, that marriage is rather permitted than approved, and that none, but by the instigation of a passion too much indulged, entangle themselves with indissoluble compacts'. Rasselas pounces on an apparent inconsistency: ' "You seem to forget", replied Rasselas, "that you have, even now, represented celibacy as less happy than marriage. Both conditions may be bad, but they cannot both be worst." ' In Nekayah's reply, she gets on to interesting ground, relating to the general matter of judgement and perception:

> 'I did not expect', answered the princess, 'to hear that imputed to falsehood which is the consequence only of frailty. To the mind, as to the eye, it is difficult to compare with exactness objects vast in their extent, and various in their parts. Where we see or conceive the whole at once, we readily note the discriminations, and decide the preference; but of two systems, of which neither can be surveyed by any human being in its full compass of magnitude and multiplicity of complication, where is the wonder, that, judging of the whole by parts, I am alternately affected by one and the other, as either presses on my memory or fancy?'

In arguing that perception is rarely reasonable, but usually determined by the fluctuations of memory or fancy, the princess, though she does not press the point, is well on the way to recognising that one half of the motive for the quest is seriously suspect. The quest is of course for a choice of life. It is begun, with the evident belief that it is humanly possible to observe, form reasonable perceptions, and make a rational choice based on those perceptions. And if the implication of the princess's argument is that no such reasonable perception is possible, the last part of the chapter (XXIX) sees her commenting on choice itself. Rasselas presses her on the issue of whether there is no middle way between marrying too early and marrying too late. Instinctively, Nekayah again broadens the issue:

> 'Every hour', answered the princess, 'confirms my prejudice in favour of the position so often uttered by the mouth of Imlac, – That nature sets her gifts on the right hand and on the left. Those conditions which flatter hope and attract desire, are so constituted, that, as we approach one, we recede from another. There are goods so opposed that we cannot seize both, but, by too much prudence, may pass between them at too great a distance to reach either. This is often the fate of long consideration: he does nothing who endeavours to do more than is allowed to humanity. Flatter not yourself with contrarieties of pleasure. Of the blessings set before you, make your choice, and be content. No man can taste the fruits of autumn while he is delighting his scent with the flowers of the spring: no man can, at the same time, fill his cup from the source and from the mouth of the Nile.'

In this emphatic passage, Nekayah, with the very voice of Imlac, dismisses the whole concept of careful choice. The only concept of choice endorsed here is arbitrary. In this very lengthy stretch of the narrative, we watch Rasselas and Nekayah develop minds of their own. Abjuring temporarily the influence of Imlac, they gain a way of thinking identical to his; but though the thinking may be the same, it is self-made. Admittedly, only a little later, they relapse into comparative ignorance; belittling the study of the past (Chapter XXX), or callously mocking the derangement of the astronomer (Chapter XLIII). At the end of the book, the decisions made by Rasselas and Nekayah, and for that matter by Pekuah, are the decisions of youth. They are nevertheless informed decisions, independently reached.

It is in the various choices of life, of course, that the book's final meanings receive form. In many ways, it seems that, in these choices of life, the positive sense of quest and self-fulfilment implied in the fable is negated. It is perhaps a logical development of the 'marriage debate' that this should be so, when the marriage debate itself concludes in the thought that there is no basis for rational choice. It is a thought which only confirms Imlac's comment to Rasselas at the outset of the journey: ' "very few", said the poet, "live by choice. Every man is placed in his present condition by causes which acted without his foresight, and with which he did not always willingly co-operate." ' If Rasselas and particularly Pekuah, in their debate, have increasingly turned away from the idea of careful perception and rational choice, their own choices of life can only be interpreted in terms of fantasy and wish-fulfilment. Given that it seems to them that a choice must be made, these are the motives which dictate their choice.

If we look at the choices made by Rasselas, Nekayah and Pekuah, we find the following:

> Pekuah was never so much charmed with any place as the convent of St Anthony, where the Arabs restored her to the princess, and wished only to fill it with pious maidens, and to be made prioress of the order; she was weary of expectation and disgust, and would gladly be fixed in some unvariable state.
> The princess thought, that of all sublunary things knowledge was the best: she desired first to learn all sciences, and then proposed to found a college of learned women, in which she would preside, that, by conversing with the old, and educating the young, she might divide her time between the acquisition and communication of wisdom, and raise up for the next age models of prudence, and patterns of piety.
> The prince desired a little kingdom, in which he might administer justice in his own person, and see all the parts of government with his own eyes; but he could never fix the limits of his dominion, and was always adding to the number of his subjects.

It is interesting to compare this with a passage in Chapter XLIV, in which each confesses a persistent and alluring daydream:

> 'I will no more', said the favourite, 'imagine myself the queen of Abyssinia. I have often spent the hours which the princess

gave to my own disposal, in adjusting ceremonies and regulating the court; I have repressed the pride of the powerful and granted the petitions of the poor; I have built new palaces in more happy situations, planted groves upon the tops of mountains, and have exulted in the beneficence of royalty, till, when the princess entered, I had almost forgotten to bow down before her.'

'And I', said the princess, 'will not allow myself any more to play the shepherdess in my waking dreams. I have often soothed my thoughts with the quiet and innocence of pastoral employments, till I have in my chamber heard the winds whistle and the sheep bleat; sometimes freed the lamb entangled in the thicket, and sometimes with my crook encountered the wolf. I have a dress like that of the village maids, which I put on to help my imagination, and a pipe on which I play softly, and suppose myself followed by my flocks.'

'I will confess', said the prince, 'an indulgence of fantastic delight more dangerous than yours. I have frequently endeavoured to image the possibility of a perfect government, by which all wrong should be restrained, all vice reformed, and all the subjects preserved in tranquillity and innocence. This thought produced innumerable schemes of reformation, and dictated many useful regulations and salutary edicts. This has been the sport and sometimes the labour, of my solitude; and I start when I think with how little anguish I once supposed the death of my father and my brothers.'

In the case of the prince, the final choice of life is identical with the daydream he has renounced. It was a daydream which he knew to be pure fantasy. Quite apart from his own observation of governments threatened or overthrown, he had concluded, during the 'marriage debate', that no system of government will ever be perfect; that vice will sometimes go undetected and virtue unrewarded; and that no ruler 'will be able to persist for ever in the fixed and inexorable justice of distribution'. Yet, knowing the meretriciousness of fantasy, he still permits himself a choice of life which is purely fanciful. It is difficult to see which kingdom he might have laid his hands on; and his continual multiplication of his prospective subjects stretches wider and wider the distance from any real and feasible system of personal rule.

In the case of the princess, her daydream, too, had been sustained against the evidence of her own observation, this time her own observation of the 'envious savages' (Chapter XIX) of whom pastoral life was in reality composed. At least her final choice of life is different. However, it seems equally fanciful. First, Nekayah has never shown the least aptitude or previous inclination for a life of science, during the book. Second, her choice seems to be founded, if not on her own previous daydreams, at least on the dreams of others. At one stage (Chapter XL) the prince had been drawn in this direction: 'the prince began to love learning, and one day declared to Imlac, that he intended to devote himself to science'. The princess might equally have remembered her encounters with the hermit or the astronomer; the latter with his observatory, and the former in his cave with book, pens and paper, and 'mechanical instruments of various kinds' (Chapter XXI). More likely, however, she was recalling Pekuah's success as 'a prodigy of genius' (Chapter XLVI), when she paraded for the benefit of the astronomer the astronomical knowledge she had gained during her captivity. In any case, the motive is much the same as Rasselas's: to form an institution 'in which she would preside'.

As to Pekuah, hers seems the least culpable of the three wishes. Her desire for religious retreat is in keeping with the pious tone of the latter stages of the book. Chapters XLVII and XLVIII debate precisely this topic of retreat, and come down firmly in favour of convents and monasteries, and of the lives they enjoin, of charitable labour, 'incited by an adequate and reasonable motive'. Even Pekuah, however, is placed within the context of fantasy by her wish 'to be made prioress of the order'.

It is not, surely, that Johnson is trying to imply that the three choosers have learned nothing from their observation of life. Rasselas has at least learned better, thanks to the example of the solitaries he has met, than to vow to 'pass all the rest of his days in literary solitude', as he had earlier intended (Chapter XL). Above all, the last page of the book insists that all of them 'knew well' that 'of these wishes ... none could be obtained'. Yet, shielded by experience from making the most disastrous errors of choice, and from naive expectations of success in any choice, their youth still dictates that a choice be made. No criticism is implied of this. It is merely a fact of life that choices of life must be made.

What the book then offers is the comforting prospect that, in age, finally, there might be some release from the absurd but necessary treadmill of choice and of labour to fulfil it. Imlac and the astronomer had both, equally, once been the victims of the same malady. Now, in age, both are finally released.

In fact, Imlac has long since enjoyed such a release. The 'performance' which ensured his admittance to the Happy Valley seems to have been his last act as a poet. Still capable of feeling the 'enthusiastic fit' when describing his calling to Rasselas (Chapter XI), Imlac is nevertheless a writer who writes nothing, who feels no urge to write anything, and who only *gains* by his inertia. Likewise, it is only when the astronomer is persuaded to renounce his chosen calling that he can be reclaimed to sanity.

In effect, with both these figures, the resources of mind which, earlier in their lives were turned outwards, into career achievements, are now turned inwards, into the endeavour to achieve a sufficiency of self. This is not the same as solitude. Solitude was the cause of the astronomer's insanity. It consists, rather, of a kind of passive drifting in the 'stream of life', absorbing experience from the world, and converting that experience into a sustaining store of ideas. In the Happy Valley, Imlac argued that he is at least 'less unhappy than the rest, because I have a mind replete with images, which I can vary and combine at pleasure. I can amuse my solitude by the renovation of the knowledge which begins to fade from my memory, and by recollection of the incidents of my past life.' In the previous chapter (XI) he had urged that 'knowledge is certainly one of the means of pleasure, as is confessed by the natural desire which each mind feels of increasing its ideas. ... I am therefore inclined to conclude, that if nothing counteracts the natural consequence of learning, we grow more happy as our minds take a wider range.' Possessing an essentially curious mind, Imlac has collected a great store of information which on the face of it is useless; for instance 'learning from the sailors the art of navigation, which I have never practised' (Chapter IX). Yet, in effect, the possession of such a hoard of experience equips Imlac with a profound sense of identity. The mind has then only to practise its own sufficiency. It is a process which Imlac refers to (Chapter XLV) as 'recreat[ing]' oneself. Interestingly, it is only when the astronomer is released from his choice of life, and from the needless self-reproach it entails — of 'time squandered' (Chapter XLV); or of 'the attainment of sciences ... but remotely useful to mankind' (Chapter XLVI) — that he can achieve a state comparable with Imlac's. It is an essentially passive condition in which both are 'contented to be driven along the stream of life, without directing their course to any particular port'.

Interestingly, it is a condition which, unlike the final states of mind of the book's younger principals, is completely free from fantasy and imagination.

In the case of the astronomer, far more than in the final choices of life by Rasselas, Nekayah and Pekuah, the sense of awesome duty to a career is directly coupled with the idea of insanity. However, in the chapter in which Imlac discusses with the others the astronomer's mental condition, he reaches the conclusion that '*all* power of fancy over reason is a degree of insanity' (Chapter XLIV, my italics). By the word 'fancy' a great deal is covered. There is in this book no distinction made between fancy and imagination. The words seem, indeed, interchangeable. When for instance the young choosers confess their favourite daydreams, in this same chapter, their fantasies take the terminology of 'imagination'. Pekuah will no longer 'imagine myself the queen of Abyssinia'. Nekayah will no longer wear her pastoral costume 'to help my imagination'. The prince renounces his endeavour 'to image the possibility of a perfect government'. There is not even a separate category of fancy given to active creativity. When this is discussed at all, it too is discussed in terms which imply its delusiveness. The most relevant passage here is in Chapter XXXII, in Imlac's discourse on the creation of the Egyptian pyramids:

> no reason has ever been given adequate to the cost and labour of the work. The narrowness of the chambers proves that it could afford no retreat from enemies, and treasure might have been reposited at far less expense with equal security. It seems to have been erected only in compliance with that hunger of imagination which preys incessantly upon life, and must be always appeased by some employment. Those who have already all that they can enjoy, must enlarge their desires. He that has built for use, till use is supplied, must begin to build for vanity, and extend his plan to the utmost power of human performance, that he may not be soon reduced to form another wish.

It is notable that this passage in fact accords no separate status to active creativity as a primary urge. It is, rather, the incongruous by-product of a far more basic mechanism: the mind's search for something to do. It is this – and *not* active creativity – to which the phrase 'hunger of the imagination' applies in this passage.

Professor Bate reminds us of Mrs Thrale's comment that the vacuity of life had at some time 'so struck upon the Mind of Dr Johnson that it became by repeated Impression his favourite hypothesis; and the general Tenor of his reasonings commonly ended in that. the Things therefore which other Philosophers attribute to various and contradictory Causes, appeared to him uniform enough – all was done to fill up the Time, on his Principle.'[12] Professor Bate seems to associate the formation of this master-theory with the approximate period in which *Rasselas* was written. Its impact on the book's fable is clear enough. It produces an episodic plot, and the guiding impulse, shared by the old and the young alike, to 'see something tomorrow which I never saw before' (Chapter XLVII). Yet, as the passage on the pyramids shows, the mechanism of *doing* something to 'fill up the time' is seen as a cruel and ridiculous gesture of appeasement. *Rasselas* seems to reach the surprising conclusion that true happiness consists of the ability to defy the mechanisms of the vacuity of life. In fact, happiness consists of the capacity to do nothing. Imlac already possesses the capacity. The astronomer achieves it, when at last he manages to 'abstract my mind from hopes and cares, which, though reason knows them to be vain, still try to keep their old possession of the heart' (Chapter XLV).

In a sense, of course, Imlac's contented inertia as a writer is a fantasy of Johnson's own. The 'vacuity of life' theory is perhaps best seen as a robust corrective to an oppressive work-conscience. This was the period which saw the acutest conflict in Johnson between his sense of the duty of work, and his own resistance to the demands he made of himself. *Rasselas* in a sense glorifies that resistance. Paradoxically, though itself a created fable, it preaches against both the duty to create, and against the hunger of the imagination itself.

Suspicion of the imaginative power is not exactly new in Johnson. *Rambler* no. 96 contains an allegory on the subject of fiction. In it, Truth and Falsehood, sent down to earth simultaneously by Jupiter, quarrel, part company and form hostile factions against each other. Truth wins few followers, and begs Jupiter to release her from the world. Instead, Jupiter clothes Truth in the garments of fiction: whereupon 'she now went out to conquer with more success; for when she demanded entrance of the passions, they often mistook her for Falsehood, and delivered up their charge; but when she once had possession, she was soon disrobed by Reason, and shone out in her original form, with native effulgence and resistless dignity'. Fiction here is a desperate last resort for Truth. Since the passions will believe only Falsehood, Truth is compelled to adopt fiction. It is adopted as a kind of trick, and discarded at the earliest opportunity. By the time of writing *Rasselas*, however, Johnson's distaste for fiction seems to have become far more forceful. Fantasy is the same thing as insanity, and the creative imagination is more or less the same thing. It is perhaps no accident that *Rasselas* is succeeded by an almost complete silence in terms of creative work, and by the depressing conviction that 'no man but a blockhead ever wrote but for money'. Unfortunately for Johnson, he seems to have gained, himself, very little contentment in the mere possession of a 'mind replete with images'.

9 *A Journey to the Western Islands*: 'imagination' and 'idea'

In his pleasurably anecdotal account of Johnson in the Highlands and Islands (*The Journal of a Tour to the Hebrides*), Boswell occasionally comments on one singularity in particular of his celebrated travelling companion: 'Last night Mr Johnson gave us an account of the whole process of tanning, and of the nature of milk and the various operations upon it, as making whey, etc. His variety of knowledge is quite amazing, and it gives one much satisfaction to find such a genius bestowing his attention to the useful arts. . . . A strange thought struck me: to try if he knew anything of an art, which is no doubt very useful in life, but which certainly lies far out of the way of a philosopher and poet – I mean the trade of a butcher.' Johnson duly showed 'that he knew something even of butchery'.[1] On another occasion he explained all the 'operation of coining, and, at night, all the operation of brewing spirits. . . . Mr MacQueen said when he heard the first he thought he had been bred in the Mint. When he heard the second, that he had been bred a brewer.'[2] A few days earlier, Johnson's range had been further extended: 'Lady Raasay showed him the operation of *wawking* cloth, that is, thickening it as is done by a mill. Here it is performed by women who kneel upon the ground, .. and ... rub it with both their hands, . . . singing an Erse song all the time. He was asking questions in the time of it, and amidst their loud and wild howl his voice was heard even in the room above.'[3] At Fort George, he 'talked of the proportions of charcoal and saltpetre in making gunpowder, of granulating it, and of giving it a gloss. He made a very good figure upon these topics. He said afterwards that he had talked *ostentatiously*.'[4]

These small incidents are instructive. Most obviously, they illustrate one of Johnson's major concerns in his record of what he saw of Highland life, his preoccupation with utility and improvement in common life. More generally, however, they are symptoms of his inexhaustible intellectual curiosity. It was a habit of enquiry which frequently fixed on topics of method, or mensuration or of experiment. What Boswell, in the *Life of Johnson*, mentions as a trifling hobby – 'He sometimes employed himself in chymistry, sometimes in watering and pruning a vine, sometimes in small experiments, at which those who may smile should recollect that there are moments which admit of being soothed only by trifles'[5] – actually amounted to a whole cast of mind. Johnson's own *Diaries* frequently record the passion for experimentation and scientific enquiry, albeit in small matters. Having accidentally shaved a fingernail, he measures the mark, and proceeds to discover 'the growth of nails'.[6] He deliberately shaves the hair from an arm, again to measure the processes of growth; and having done this in winter, repeats the experiment in summer.[7] As to the vine referred to by Boswell, it too came in for scientific study: 'I cut from the vine 41 leaves which weighed five oz. and half and eight scruples. I lay them upon my bookcase to try what weight they will lose by drying.'[8] On his visit to France, Johnson fully combines both interests, the scientific and the interest in the practical processes of life, in his long and detailed description of the manufacture of mirrors.[9]

It is just such a combination which we find again, informing his *Journey to the Western Islands*. Finding in his travels 'quite a different system of life',[10] he energetically discovers and records, analyses and assesses it. If in many instances, his Scottish contemporaries were predictably offended by anything less than effusiveness, others saw the fairness of the observations, and the basic standards of utility on which they are founded. Boswell quotes several testimonials on this score, including the following:

> I have often admired the accuracy, the precision, and the justness of what he advances respecting both the country and the people. The Doctor has everywhere delivered his sentiments with freedom, and in many instances with a seeming regard for the benefit of the inhabitants, and the ornament of the country. ... He ... felt for the distresses of the Highlanders, and explodes with great propriety the bad management of the grounds, and the neglect of timber in the Hebrides.[11]

When, therefore, Johnson lost his stout walking stick, near the end of the journey, the loss bore upon two of the obsessional interests of the tour. First, trees, on the dearth of which Johnson is continually commenting, as a central symbol of the waste of a rich inheritance and a neglect of the future. So, on the loss of his stick, Boswell 'could not persuade him out of a suspicion that it had been stolen. "No, no, my friend", said he, "it is not to be expected that any man in Mull who has got it will part with it. Consider, Sir, the value of such a *piece of timber* here!" ' Second, measurement, of which his stick was, additionally, an implement, 'for one nail was driven into it at the length of a foot; another at that of a yard'.[12] A little later, therefore, Johnson found himself comparatively ill-provided, when, in order to measure the dimensions of a cave, he had only a walking-pole of unknown size, 'of which I guessed the length by standing against it'. Conceding that the margin of error was probably quite small, he still complains that 'more nicety however is better, and no man should travel unprovided with instruments for taking heights and distances'. He goes on to discuss the importance of recording measurements as soon as possible, before the memory begins to jumble exactness into confusion.[13] No matter how emotionally exciting the experience may be, for instance on Iona, Johnson rarely neglects the habits of a scientific mind. He attempts an equal precision in matters of computation. From time to time, he tries to assess the population of an island, and plunges into calculations involving the number of men alleged to have been called for military service, the proportion of the population this is likely to represent, the area of an island, the degree of error likely in such reported measurements, and whether the density of population arrived at agrees with observation.[14]

Frequently, even in matters of pure computation, he finds himself having to contend with what he rapidly discovers to be highly unreliable native witnesses. Even in matters of easily verifiable physical fact, he finds it impossible to trust what he is told. He hears of 'a cavern by the sea-side, remarkable for the powerful reverberation of sounds',[15] but finds it to be devoid of echo. At Iona, he is shown the ruins of a Bishop's House, whose 'chimney' proves to be 'only a nich, without perforation'.[16] On matters which cannot be immediately verified, the unreliability of testimony is far more vexing; whether they belong to the present or to the past. Johnson is unable to discover whether 'brogues' are easy or difficult to make. By one witness, he is told that these 'artless shoes stitched with thongs' are 'the work of an hour . . . a domestic art which every man practised for himself'. By another, he is informed that 'a brogue-maker was a trade, and that a pair would cost half-a-crown'. He is given 'both accounts in the same house within two days'.[17] Regarding more ancient local history, he finds the question of bards and senachies equally vexed. One man tells him that the bard was the poet, and the senachie was the historian; that each great family had one of each; and that they had existed within living memory. Another tells him that bard and senachie was one and the same thing ('This variation discouraged me!'). A third informs him that though the two offices were distinct, neither had existed 'for some centuries'.[18]

On this occasion Johnson goes on to deplore the oral tradition in general, as providing every incentive to inaccuracy. More broadly, the whole matter of unreliable testimony becomes one of the identifying features of the culture Johnson is studying. It comes to indicate for him a quality of fecklessness in Scottish life. It becomes, rather like the topic of trees, an indication of an improvident national character. Discussing bards and senachies, Johnson calls the Scots a 'nation wholly illiterate'. Earlier, however, he had conceded that 'from the middle of the sixteenth century, almost to the middle of the seventeenth, the politer studies were very diligently pursued. The Latin poetry of *Deliciae Poetarum Scotorum* would have done honour to any nation; at least till the publication of May's *Supplement*, the English had very little to oppose.' He puts this forward, in order to argue that it is peculiar to the Scots to have 'attained the liberal, without the manual arts'.[19] Yet the liberal tradition has in its turn perished. Boswell records a conversation in which Johnson argues vehemently the deficiency of learning in Scottish clergy, and their lack of any significant contribution to pious scholarship.[20] The Reformation, indeed, was responsible for much in this direction, according to Johnson; and the complaint of a neglected and decayed liberal tradition is closely allied with his distress at the destruction of Scotland's ancient cathedrals and universities. Boswell records, in his own account, how Johnson was 'affected with a strong indignation, while he beheld the ruins of religious magnificence' at St Andrews; adding that he seemed 'quite wrapt up in the contemplation of the scenes which were now presented to him'.[21]

Johnson himself speaks of its ruins filling 'the mind with mournful images and ineffectual wishes'.[22] With less overt emotion, he records other ruined places of worship in Aberbrothick, Aberdeen, Elgin, Raasay, Mull and Ulva; but on Inch Kenneth he again confesses that 'it was not without some mournful emotion that we contemplated the ruins of religious structures and the monuments of the dead'.[23] On Iona, indignation again surfaces. Confronted with the ruins of the chapel of the nunnery 'now used by the inhabitants as a kind of general cow-house', he records that now 'the inhabitants are remarkably gross, and remarkably neglected: I know not if they are visited by any minister. The island, which was once the metropolis of learning and piety, has now no school for education, nor temple for worship, only two inhabitants that can speak English, and not one that can write or read.'[24]

Yet, the Highlander as the *victim* of neglect is not exactly his theme. The Reformation, far from being something inflicted on a nation, is a predictable part of a national culture, being related to that part of the national character which is slackest and most idle. This might seem an odd account of puritanical frenzy, but this is Johnson's version of events, from the earliest part of his narrative:

> The change of religion in Scotland, eager and vehement as it was, raised an epidemical enthusiasm, compounded of sullen scrupulousness and warlike ferocity, which, in a people whom idleness resigned to their own thoughts, and who, conversing only with each other, suffered no dilution of their zeal from the gradual influx of new opinions, was long transmitted in its full strength from the old to the young, but by trade and intercourse with England, is now visibly abating, and giving way too fast to that laxity of practice and indifference of opinion, in which men, not sufficiently instructed to find the middle point, too easily shelter themselves from rigour and constraint.[25]

It is with considerable irony that, later in the narrative, provoked by the sight of a ruined chapel on Raasay, he comments on the laziness of Catholicism: 'over the sleepy laziness of men that erected churches, we may indulge our superiority with a new triumph, by comparing it with the fervid activity of those who suffer them to fall'.[26]

Johnson relates the Highlander's lack of veracity to this kind of vacancy of mind, 'where there was neither shame from ignorance, nor pride in knowledge; neither curiosity to inquire, nor vanity to communicate'.[27] Or again, 'they have inquired and considered little, and do not always feel their own ignorance. They are not much accustomed to be interrogated by others; and seem never to have thought upon interrogating themselves.'[28] Or again, the typical 'fearlessness of assertion was either the sport of negligence, or the refuge of ignorance'.[29] Of course, if this cast of mind is responsible for the ruin of the culture of the past, it is equally responsible for the lack of progress. Again, there is a constant stream of complaint from Johnson on this topic. What begins as a joke on Boswell's account – 'Dr Johnson laughed to hear that Cromwell's soldiers taught the Aberdeen people to make shoes and stockings, and brought in cabbages'[30] – becomes a fully fledged theme in Johnson; a theme of wonder, 'that that which was so necessary and so easy was so long delayed'.[31] Again and again there are similar refrains: that sash windows at Bamff were without weights or pulleys (when there were windows at all); that at Raasay, the inhabitants made do without a regular landing place, where one would have been easy to build; that on Skye the oats are separated from the husk by parching, which destroys valuable fodder; that a crupper will be improvised from straw in a place (Ostig) where hemp will grow 'and therefore ropes may be had'. As Johnson comments, 'they supply their wants with very insufficient shifts, and endure many inconveniences, which a little attention would easily relieve'.[32]

It is the same mental idleness which is at the root of the superstitions and frauds which Johnson groups together for discussion: in particular, the alleged gift of 'second sight', and the existence of the poems of 'Ossian'. Towards the first, at least, Johnson professes an open mind, but both fail his strict requirements of evidence and probability. It is hard to see how they could have done otherwise. Both phenomena are orally transmitted. In the same section of the *Journey*, Johnson discusses the Erse language and the oral tradition. It was unlikely that either would appeal to the great upholder and recorder of a literary tradition. Erse is pronounced to be 'the rude speech of a barbarous people who had few thoughts to express, and were content, as they conceived grossly, to be grossly understood'. Never having become a written language, it 'could therefore receive little improvement'. As to the oral tradition, it is productive of fiction, and the constant prey of oblivion. A bard was 'a barbarian among barbarians', and Johnson regards it as an impossibility that such a man should ever achieve a composition of significance or length. He makes a direct connection between illiteracy and mental primitiveness in his rhetorical question, 'what principles of ratiocination, what comprehension of knowledge, and what delicacy of elocution has ... any man attain[ed] who cannot read',[33] and finally, both 'second sight' and the poems of Ossian are dismissed as the products, respectively, of incomprehension and invention. They are believed, only because people want to believe them. In the case of second sight, the main incentive to belief is 'the indistinct cry of national persuasion, which may be perhaps resolved at last into prejudice and tradition'. In the case of Ossian, 'a Scotchman must be a very sturdy moralist, who does not love Scotland better than truth: he will always love it better than inquiry: and if falsehood flatters his vanity, will not be very diligent to detect it'.[34]

The joke is almost affectionate. Nevertheless, the concern which is violated by this credulous patriotism is probably the most central one in Johnson. Mrs Thrale tells us that his 'Incredulity amount[ed] almost to Disease'.[35] She had good reason to know, since she constantly suffered correction at Johnson's hands, when her own sprightly gift of exaggeration collided with Johnson's passion for truth. Boswell recounts an episode when Johnson urged that Mrs Thrale should adopt towards her children the same role he adopted with her: ' "Accustom your children", said he, "constantly to this; if a thing happened at one window, and they, when relating it, say that it happened at another, do not let it pass, but instantly check them; you do not know where deviation from truth will end." ... Our lively hostess, whose fancy was impatient of the rein, fidgeted at this, and ventured to say, "Nay, this is too much. If Dr Johnson should forbid me to drink tea, I would comply, as I should feel the restraint only twice a day; but little variations in narrative must happen a thousand times a day, if one is not perpetually watching." JOHNSON: "Well, Madam, and you *ought* to be perpetually watching. It is more from carelessness about truth than from intentional lying, that there is so much falsehood in the world." '[36]

In the light of this constant preoccupation, Johnson's *Journey to the Western Islands of Scotland* can be seen as a kind of search for truth, pursued in the face of resistance from an incredulous and ignorant native population, unreliable in their information and feckless in their character. Indeed, these characteristics might be seen both as an obstruction to the search for truth and also its subject; since Johnson is attempting to describe not only the physical characteristics of an undeveloped region, but the mental characteristics in a people which determine and preserve its primitiveness.

Unquestionably, Johnson does think like a scientist, or at the very least, as a social scientist; his interest being, as he stresses, in 'the manners of a people'.[37] His *Journey* has indeed been explicitly compared with the work of modern sociology, analysing not 'this or that isolated novelty, but . . . a social and cultural totality operating on principles very different from what Johnson had previously known'.[38]

The scientific remoteness from the subject which this implies tends to be borne out in Johnson's extremely insistent use of the simple third-person-plural pronoun, in discussing the Scots: 'Their strength is proportionate to their size, but they are accustomed to run upon rough ground, and therefore can with great agility skip over the bog, or clamber the mountain.'[39]

Yet, an imaginative response, however modified and even transformed, is not only detectable but evident in the work. It provides, indeed, the impulse to visit Scotland in the first place. Boswell recounts a conversation, early in their acquaintance, in which Johnson described how 'his father had put Martin's account of those islands into his hands when he was very young, and that he was highly pleased with it'. On the basis of Martin's description, he had formed, as Boswell says, 'a wish that then appeared to me a very romantic fancy' to visit the Highlands and Islands. It was clearly on the basis of Martin's account that Johnson had formed 'his notion of the dignity of a Scotch landlord' and of the patriarchal authority of the Highland chiefs, of which his impression was extremely exalted.[40] With such strong imaginative preconceptions Johnson was fired to visit Scotland, and Boswell describes moments of high Johnsonian glee, when Johnson was able to imagine himself in the light of a Highland chief, 'quite feudal'.[41]

Indeed, Johnson permitted himself, in the early part of his narrative, a degree of imaginative enthusiasm even towards the Scottish landscape. Such was very far from his usual response. He greatly discomfited an Ayrshire gentleman, on his return, who had dared to ask him how he liked the Highlands. Boswell remarks that 'the question seemed to irritate him, for he answered, . . . "Who *can* like the Highlands? I like the inhabitants very well." The gentleman asked no more questions.'[42] Johnson was no lover of uncultivated prospects. Yet, at Anoch, on entering the Highlands, a certain excitement is confessed in Johnson's account. 'Regions mountainous and wild, thinly inhabited, and little cultivated, make a great part of the earth, and he that has never seen them, must live unacquainted with much of the face of nature, and with one of the great scenes of human existence.' It is consequently of man's helplessness in scenes of natural wildness of which Johnson thinks; and thinks, in terms of imaginative excitement: 'the imaginations excited by the view of an unknown and untravelled wilderness are not such as arise in the artificial solitude of parks and gardens, a flattering notion of self-sufficiency, a placid indulgence of voluntary delusions, a secure expansion of the fancy, or a cool concentration of the mental powers. The phantoms which haunt a desert are want, and misery, and danger; the evils of dereliction rush upon the thoughts; man is made unwillingly acquainted with his own weakness, and meditation shews him only how little he can sustain, and how little he can perform.'[43] He adds that it was here that he first conceived the thought of writing the *Journey*; so that, just as the idea of the visit was stimulated by an imaginative response to Martin's account, so the idea of writing his own account of the region had its genesis in an imaginative response to the location. This response is not, incidentally, the first of its kind in the book. There are two earlier examples, one at Slanes Castle and the second at the Fall of Fiers. On both occasions, Johnson seems actively to wish to excite his own responses; and finding, in both cases, that the season is too tame for him to see what he might have seen, sets his imagination to work, to heighten the scene. At Slanes Castle, built on a perpendicular rock, 'the eye wanders over the sea that separates Scotland from Norway, and when the winds beat with violence must enjoy all the terrifick grandeur of the tempestuous ocean. I would not for my amusement wish for a storm; but as storms, whether wished or not, will sometimes happen, I may say, without violation of humanity, that I should willingly look out upon them from Slanes Castle.'[44] At the Fall of Fiers, his imagination works with more detail: 'But we visited the place at an unseasonable time, and ... were left to exercise our thoughts, by endeavouring to conceive the effect of a thousand streams poured from the mountains into one channel, struggling for expansion in a narrow passage, exasperated by rocks rising in their way, and at last discharging all their violence of waters by a sudden fall through the horrid chasm.'[45] These passages coexist alongside others, in which come the expected disclaimers: in the passage on mountainous regions, the eye's first reaction is to be 'astonished and repelled by this wide extent of hopeless sterility'.[46] Shortly after the description of Slanes Castle, Johnson visits by boat the cliff basin known as the Buller of Buchan. For a while, he speaks of his 'recoil of ... mind' at the thoughts of 'unknown profundity of water', and evil spirits. Briskly, however, he resumes his equilibrium: 'But terror without danger is only one of the sports of fancy, a voluntary agitation of the mind that is permitted no longer than it pleases. We were soon at leisure to examine the place with minute inspection.'[47] At this stage of the *Journey*, however, the imaginative response seems to be able to hold its own.

The question is, whether it continues to hold its own when it becomes apparent that Martin's impression of Highland life has been long superseded. As Mary Lascelles points out, in the Introduction to her Yale edition of the *Journey*, he found, not an original and isolated system of life, but 'a people in the throes of change, threatened with hasty innovation, and surrounded with evidence of the havoc which former innovation had wrought'.[48] She points out various occasions in which Johnson registers his sense of this change by significant changes of tense. In an instance similar to the ones she lists, Johnson comments, 'Such are the effects of habitation among mountains, and such were the qualities of the Highlanders, while their rocks secluded them from the rest of mankind.' The sentence comes in a separate chapter, entitled 'The Highlands', coming after the last outpost of civilised life, Fort Augustus, is left behind. It is a chapter in which Johnson lists the characteristics of highland peoples, isolated from the general progress of a community. The chapter ends, 'They are now losing their distinction, and hastening to mingle with the general community.'[49] In Mary Lascelles view, 'What Johnson found ... was to prove more engrossing than what he sought.'[50]

It is not clear, however, that the engrossment was of the same kind as his stimulation by Martin. George Savage is something of a rarity among interpreters of the *Journey* in his insistence on seeing a mythic and imaginative ingredient in Johnson's handling of the theme of change: seeing in particular certain Homeric allusions as evoking an 'ancient tale of homeless man desperately beating through the avatars of barbarism to regain the continuity of family, to reunite with the mainland of civilised humanity, to reaffirm identity, with which Johnson illumines his theme'.[51] Such a reading seems in fact a falsification of the text's emotional tone, and equally an over-simplification of its theme. It is by no means as clear as this suggests that Johnson's commitment to the ideal of progress and uniformity is as unequivocal as this. For every critic who suggests as much,[52] there is another to deny it, and to maintain that towards 'the rise of middle-class progressive culture ... Johnson maintains an ambivalent attitude'.[53]

Indeed, what happens, is that Johnson sets both attitudes off against each other. More interestingly, the method he employs to do so is to create an imaginative image of each cultural ideal, as if in opposition, and to subject both images to scrutiny and adjustment. These images are firstly of the old Highland life, or at least what remained of it in the earlier part of the century; and second, of the ideal of progress in the wilderness. Of the old Highland life, Johnson writes as follows:

> It affords a generous and manly pleasure to conceive a little nation gathering its fruits and tending its herds with fearless confidence, though it lies open on every side to invasion, where, in contempt of walls and trenches, every man sleeps securely with his sword beside him; where all on the first approach of hostility come together at the call to battle, as at a summons to a festal show; and committing their cattle to the care of those whom age or nature has disabled, engage the enemy with that competition for hazard and for glory, which operate in men that fight under the eye of those, whose dislike or kindness they have always considered as the greatest evil or the greatest good.
>
> This was, in the beginning of the present century, the state of the Highlands. Every man was a soldier, who partook of national confidence, and interested himself in national honour. To lose this spirit, is to lose what no small advantage will compensate.
>
> It may likewise deserve to inquire, whether a great nation ought to be totally commercial? whether amidst the uncertainty of human affairs, too much attention to one mode of happiness may not endanger others?[54]

The last thought seems a peculiarly modern one, in its concern to respect and protect alternative ways of life which are threatened by the dominant commercial one. The previous two paragraphs indicate that Johnson's attitude towards this minority culture was capable of extending beyond tolerance to enthusiasm. Yet, immediately, Johnson subjects the pleasing vision to scrutiny. Already, a little earlier in the passage, he has asked himself whether, after Culloden, it was right to disarm the clans; and has set against the state's undoubted right of 'taking away the weapon that is lifted against it' the obligation of the state – apparently neglected – to protect those it has disarmed.[55] He goes on to argue, however, that the threat of an invader is a rarity, whereas domestic quarrels had been a frequent occurrence. By depriving the clans of the power to hurt each other, the state had quietened 'a very troublesome and pernicious animal'.[56] But once again, the argument expands, as Johnson goes on to consider whether the chiefs of clans, deprived of their ancient martial dignity, should not receive an alternative and compensating dignity; the dignity of money. He goes on to set power against money as the two driving desires of man, ending, however, with a simile which does little honour to the latter: 'Youth therefore flies at power, and age grovels after riches.'[57] The vicious circle is completed by Johnson's observation that, rather than bringing dignity, money brings an obliteration of rank, when, with the laird letting land to the highest bidder, the tenant 'treats with the laird upon equal terms, and considers him not as a chief, but as a trafficker in land'. In the meantime, the original tenant is evicted, and emigrates.[58] After a long discussion of the persistently occurring topic of emigration, Johnson concludes that 'To hinder insurrection, by driving away the people, and to govern peaceably, by having no subjects, is an expedient that argues no great profundity of politicks.'[59] He therefore returns to the original cause of the whole process of change, the disarming of the Highlands, and concedes, 'If the restitution of their arms will reconcile them to their country, let them have again those weapons, which will not be more mischievous at home than in the Colonies.'[60] In effect, Johnson has by the end completely doubled back on his earlier arguments. The idea of the proud, tough little nation is set back somewhat by the idea of its being a troublesome and pernicious animal to the state at large. However, if by disarming it, it turns itself into still more troublesome and pernicious animal in America, it would be better to restore its arms after all. It is not, however, to the vision of a brave little country that Johnson returns. While he lists as a disadvantage of the commercial renting of land that 'the clan is broken',[61] and speaks of pensions to the chiefs to keep them quiet, and damp down their greed,[62] the emphasis is by the end of the passage on the general peace and prosperity of Britain, rather than on the need to preserve or protect the clan system. What seems to Johnson a far more significant argument than the break-up of the clan system is the ruin of the countryside itself. While higher rents may bring some land-improvement, large-scale emigration will ensure that Scotland will 'remain a desert'; and 'where there was formerly an insurrection, there is now a wilderness'.[63] When Johnson goes on to discuss the migration of Scots alongside those of the Goths, the picture of the brave little nation sinks without trace. Very briefly, Johnson later revives an image of a fierce and noble patriarchal society, when describing the laird of Col with his clansmen running to touch him; or, later, the McLean who said of his chief, 'I would cut my bones for him'.[64] However, we still have to remember the earlier pronouncement that this 'insular subordination' produced a happiness which was 'a muddy mixture of pride and ignorance'.[65] Later, Johnson speaks of a more legitimate pride: that which consists of contributing to a larger progressive community: 'that security, that dignity, that happiness ... which a prosperous community throws back upon individuals'.[66] The narrative seems prepared to entertain flattering imaginative images of clan life, but they hardly seem to survive examination.

There is an alternative kind of image in the *Journey*, of which a handful of examples occur. These are the images of progress; or, more precisely, of spots of cultivation created in the wilderness. While much praise is given to young Col, a Johnsonian paragon, who is improving his land, building a road, and who above all plans to plant trees; the passages in which his praises are sung contain no imaginative images as such. These tend rather to occur when Johnson encounters small communities of refined *people* in the Islands, an occurrence which always seems to take him by surprise. The first time he encounters a lady in the Highlands, the surprise is openly confessed: 'we were surprised by the entrance of a young woman, not inelegant either in mien or dress, who asked us whether we would have tea'.⁶⁷ At Coriatachan, he remarks on being 'treated with very liberal hospitality, among a more numerous and elegant company than it could have been supposed easy to collect'.⁶⁸ At Raasay, however, the occurrence finally touches the imaginative impulse:

> Our reception exceeded our expectations. We found nothing but civility, elegance, and plenty. After the usual refreshments, and the usual conversation, the evening came upon us. The carpet was then rolled off the floor; the musician was called, and the whole company was invited to dance, nor did ever fairies trip with greater alacrity. The general air of festivity, which predominated in this place, so far remote from all those regions which the mind has been used to contemplate as the mansions of pleasure, struck the imagination with a delightful surprise, analogous to that which is felt at an unexpected emersion from darkness into light.⁶⁹

There is a similar passage, on returning to Coriatachan:

> The fictions of the Gothick romances were not so remote from credibility as they are now thought. In the full prevalence of the feudal institution, when violence desolated the world, and every baron lived in a fortress, forests and castles were regularly succeeded by each other, and the adventurer might very suddenly pass from the gloom of the woods, or the ruggedness of moors, to seats of plenty, gaiety, and magnificence. Whatever is imaged in the wildest tale, if giants, dragons, and enchantment be excepted, would be felt by him, who, wandering in the mountains without a guide, or upon the sea without a pilot, should be carried amidst his terror and uncertainty, to the hospitality and elegance of Raasay or Dunvegan.⁷⁰

In this second passage, the compliment seems at first to be a little back-handed, in its analogy with the experiences available to barbarians several centuries before. However, it turns out that the analogy is a deliberately synthetic one. It *might* be possible to approximate to the terrors stimulated formerly by violence, by imagining being lost in the surrounding wilderness. Certainly, where the ancient baron could offer 'plenty, gaiety and magnificence', the modern assembly offers instead something far more advanced: hospitality and *elegance*. The term is used in the Raasay passage itself: 'nothing but civility, elegance, and plenty'. The air of festivity might be common to both eras. Refinement is uniquely modern. To find it in the middle of a desert is like encountering light after darkness, and is an imaginative experience analogous to romance.

However, romance or not, it is still a Johnsonian ideal to see civilised life reclaiming the Highlands to the general community. It is at Dunvegan that Johnson confesses to have 'tasted lotus',[71] in the company of Lady MacLeod 'who had lived many years in England, and was newly come hither with her son and four daughters, who knew all the arts of southern elegance, and all the modes of English economy'.[72] As to McLeod of Raasay, while Johnson remarked to Boswell, 'This is truly the patriarchal life. This is what we came to find',[73] his own narrative mentions only the tutor employed to educate the sons, and the family's general cultivation: 'More gentleness of manners, or a more pleasing appearance of domestick society, is not found in the most polished countries.'[74] He again concludes his compliments with another passage which acknowledges the imagination stimulated by progress in a wild place:

> Raasay has little that can detain a traveller, except the Laird and his family; but their power wants no auxilliaries. Such a seat of hospitality, amidst the winds and waters, fills the imagination with a delightful contrariety of images. Without is the rough ocean and the rocky land, the beating billows and the howling storm: within is plenty and elegance, beauty and gaiety, the song and the dance. In Raasay, if I could have found an Ulysses, I had fancied a Phaeacia.[75]

The last compliment is neatly turned, since the Phaeacians excelled in refinement, rather than virility; and Johnson certainly did not have in mind the rather suspect quality of that refinement when he made the compliment.

These, then, are the images of progress which counterpoise the images of feudalism. In much the same way, these images too come under inquiry. On Col, Johnson sees a primitive system turning itself into a modern one. 'Cultivation is likely to be improved by the skill and encouragement of the present heir, and the inhabitants of those obscure vallies will partake of the general progress of life.'[76] The cultivation of land will lead to a more cultivated people. At the moment, such a thing is still in prospect. Johnson finds himself confessing a degree of social deprivation: 'Without intelligence man is not social, he is only gregarious; and little intelligence will there be, where all are constrained to daily labour, and every mind must wait upon the hand.'[77] Without plenty, there can be no leisured society; and on Col, that plenty is still to be created. To this extent, even Johnson's paragon of progress falls short of the imaginative ideal of other passages; and Johnson goes on to speak for the first time of the difficulties of improving an intractable landscape. Earlier, his optimism had been almost airy: 'To drop a seed into the ground can cost nothing, and the trouble is not great of protecting the young plant, till it is out of danger; though it must be allowed to have some difficulty in places like these, where they have neither wood for pallisades, nor thorns for hedges.'[78] Now, he returns to the subject, with a much greater sense of realism:

> To drop seeds into the ground, and attend their growth, requires little labour and no skill. . . . But there is a frightful interval between the seed and timber. He that calculates the growth of trees, has the unwelcome remembrance of the shortness of life driven hard upon him. He knows that he is doing what will never benefit himself; and when he rejoices to see the stem rise, is disposed to repine that another shall cut it down.
>
> Plantation is naturally the employment of a mind unburdened with care, and vacant to futurity, saturated with present good, and at leisure to derive gratification from the prospect of posterity. He that pines with hunger, is in little care how others shall be fed. The poor man is seldom studious to make his grandson rich. It may be soon discovered, why in a place, which hardly supplies the cravings of necessity, there has been little attention to the delights of fancy, and why distant convenience is unregarded, where the thoughts are turned with incessant solicitude upon every possibility of immediate advantage.
>
> Neither is it quite as easy to raise large woods, as may be conceived. . . . Ground sown with trees must be kept useless for a long time, inclosed at an expence from which many will be discouraged by the remoteness of the profit, and watched with

> Sir James MacDonald, in parts of the wastes of his territory, set or sowed trees, to the number, as I have been told, of several millions, expecting, doubtless, that they would grow up into future navies and cities; but for want of enclosure, and of that care which is always necessary, and will hardly ever be taken, all his cost and labour have been lost, and the ground is likely to continue an useless heath.[79]

Where the need is greatest for change, the obstructions to change seem most formidable. Earlier, Johnson seems not to notice the incongruity of the idea that there might be some difficulty in finding wood to stake new trees, because there aren't any trees. In this later passage, the same kind of impasse is diligently explored. It is with the thought in mind, from a couple of pages earlier, of the need to give the mind some relief from the toil of the hand, that he here speaks of the need of a mind vacant to futurity, to think of planting trees. When every item of Highland life dictates a subsistence economy, where, as he says elsewhere in this chapter, the 'consequence of a bad season is not scarcity but emptiness',[80] it is precisely that necessary freedom of the mind to imagine for the future which is least likely to emerge. It is against the obstacles to imaginative progress that Johnson's own imaginative excitement collides. At the beginning of the narrative, he had announced that 'we are well or ill at ease, as the main stream of life glides on smoothly, or is ruffled by small obstacles and frequent interruption. The true state of every nation is the state of common life... in the streets, and the villages, in the shops and farms; and from them collectively considered must the measure of general prosperity be taken. As they approach to delicacy a nation is refined, as their conveniencies are multiplied a nation... must be denominated wealthy.'[81] Yet, on Mull, Johnson's impatience at the Scots' apparent inattention to 'conveniencies', their feckless failure to remove 'small obstacles' and approach delicacy, falls away in the face of his realisation that the true obstacles are not 'petty': 'But where the climate is unkind, and the ground penurious, so that the most fruitful years will produce only enough to maintain themselves; where life unimproved, and unadorned, fades into something little more than naked existence, and every one is busy for himself, without any arts by which the pleasures of others may be increased; if to the daily burden of distress any additional weight be added, nothing remains but to despair and die.'[82] True, at the end of the book, he returns once again to his theme of improvement; but this time it is in the sober context of a comparison with the feat of teaching deaf mutes to be literate and numerate.

So, both imaginative visions, of the primitive and of the refined, are evoked only to be overwhelmed by fact and analysis. In effect, it is Johnson's final assessment that the truth lies or rather falls somewhere between the two. Already, the clan system is broken and the old primitive ways have passed. Yet, the progressive benefits of a money economy are still a mere prospect. The old has been destroyed, but there is as yet nothing to replace it. Johnson's early optimism about the advent of a money economy ('they are now acquainted with money, and the possibility of gain will by degrees make them industrious'[83]) gives way in the end to a joke concerning the patriotic desire of all Scotsmen to represent their country as richer than it was: 'Money and wealth have by the use of commercial language been so long confounded, that they are commonly supposed to be the same; and this prejudice has spread so widely in Scotland, that I know not whether I found man or woman, whom I interrogated concerning payments of money, that could surmount the illiberal desire of deceiving me, by representing everything as dearer than it is.'[84]

This assessment is Johnson's final 'idea' of the Highlands and Islands. The term is his own, and seems to rank, in this text, altogether higher than the imagination. In effect, the perfected 'idea' supersedes the imperfect imagination.

The term is first used at Anoch, in Johnson's opening dissertation on mountainous regions. In this passage, Johnson defends the need for personal experience of phenomena, in order to complete the 'idea' of them. While we may often be compelled to content ourselves with others' accounts, 'these ideas are always incomplete, and that at least, till we have compared them with realities, we do not know them to be just. As we see more, we become possessed of more certainties, and consequently gain more principles of reasoning, and found a wider basis of analogy.'[85]

In the *Life of Johnson*, Boswell records Johnson's rather testy

'A Journey to the Western Islands'

vigilance against the misuse of words, hardly surprising in a lexicographer: 'He was particularly indignant against the almost universal use of the word *idea* in the sense of *notion* or *opinion*, when it is clear that *idea* can only signify something of which an image can be formed in the mind. We may have an *idea* or *image* of a mountain, a tree, a building; but we cannot surely have an *idea* or *image* of an *argument* or *proposition*.'[86] The distinction here is not only between the visible and the abstract; but between the certain and the tendentious. The actual experience of a phenomenon helps to establish its certainty. It becomes clearer, then, what he means, on Inch Kenneth; when he discusses the need to record information accurately and early; knowing as he does, how, otherwise, 'the succession of objects will be broken, how separate parts will be confused, and how particular features and discriminations will be compressed and conglobated into one gross and general idea'.[87] In fact, the word 'idea' is incompatible with indistinctness, but is the product of the particular and the precise. It is interesting that this was not the first time Johnson had used the word in connection with travel. *Idler* 97 lists the various failings of most travel-literature, being usually 'such general accounts as leave no distinct idea behind them, or such minute enumerations as few can read with either profit or delight'.[88] Neither extreme is productive. The general account needs particular observation, to convert it into an idea. The minute observation needs to be linked to an instructive theme. It is clear that this is what Johnson achieves in the *Journey*. As he writes, his theme is adjusted as new facts and evidence are drawn into range, until the idea is completed. Probably the best known comment by Johnson on his voyage is that 'I got an acquisition of more ideas by it than by any thing I remember.'[89]

He also told Boswell, 'Our ramble in the islands hangs upon my imagination.'[90] It would be surprising if it had not. Boswell's parallel account is full of marvellous imaginative sallies. In recording one of them, Boswell demonstrates how ill he himself understands the word, 'idea':

> There is a beautiful little island in the Loch of Dunvegan, called Isay. MacLeod said he would give it to Mr Johnson, on condition of his residing on it three months in the year, nay, one month. Mr Johnson was highly pleased with the fancy. I have seen him please himself with little things, even with mere ideas,

as this was. He talked a great deal of this island – how he would build a house, how he would fortify it, how he would have cannon, how he would plant, – how he would sally out, and *take* the Isle of Muck; and then he laughed with a glee that was astonishing, and could hardly leave off.[91]

However, Johnson's imaginative stimulation was either entirely 'off the record': or was present only to be adjusted, or demolished or superseded by ideas. At Fort George, he betrays his 'official' attitude to the imagination in this book; where he refuses to give a description of the fort, since 'I cannot delineate it scientifically, and a loose and popular description is of use only when the imagination is to be amused.'[92] He is prepared of course to defend, in theory, the significance of, say, 'local emotion' stirred by the imagination of the past. The famous passage on Iona abhors the man 'whose patriotism would not gain force upon the plain of Marathon, or whose piety would not grow warmer among the ruins of Iona'.[93] Yet, amusingly, in practice, Johnson permits himself – at least on paper – to experience no such thing. At the end of the Iona visit, he alludes to 'those illustrious ruins, by which Mr Boswell was much affected'; though he does add, 'nor would I willingly be thought to have looked upon them without some emotion'.[94] Yet Boswell's account of the visit to Iona insists that Johnson was 'no less affected by it than I was'.[95] If he is right, then it seems that Johnson's determination to write scientifically is one which relegates the imagination to such a subordinate position, that it can hardly be admitted. Interestingly, at Slanes Castle, or at Anoch, or at the Fall of Fiers, the imagination is recruited only to help to perfect the idea of a wild landscape, which the benignness of the season denied to the eye itself. For the rest, if Johnson's terminology of the 'idea' is reminiscent of Hume, his treatment of the imagination is reminiscent of Locke's relegation of 'wit' to the role of amusement. If *Rasselas* discovers a fear of fancy, as being close to insanity, the *Journey*, his first major literary composition since *Rasselas*, enacts the discipline of the imagination, and its replacement by the idea.

10 The Literary Criticism: 'propriety of thought'

In his early poem, *The Young Author*, Johnson mockingly sets out the fate of the hopeful scribbler, yearning for immortality. Warned in vain that 'These dreams were Settle's once and Ogilby's', he launches his first pamphlet, into what turns out to be a scathing, derisive reception. He flees back to obscurity, 'Glad to be hid, and proud to be forgot.' When Johnson accepted the commission for the *Lives of the English Poets*, he set himself a task which involved, many times over, the scrutiny of authorial hopes and their fate, over the previous hundred years. The very nature of the subject entailed the continual confrontation of briefly-held hopes with the perspective of a century. If the *Lives of the Poets* includes neither Settle nor Ogilby, it contains its Blackmores and Philips as well as its Dryden and Pope; and though the careers he considers were often far more locally successful than the 'young Author's', time still has the last say on hopes of immortality. Even with relatively major figures, the pattern into which their lives are shaped by Johnson often seems to be an ironic one, of blasted hope.

The first of the sequence, Cowley, fits the 'young Author's' pattern in more than one respect. Johnson depicts Cowley's career, as a Royalist civil servant, as having little or no connection with his productions as a poets. However, when the narration reaches the Restoration period, Johnson begins to connect the two, and the connection is in terms of disappointment:

> At the Restoration, after all the diligence of his long service, and with consciousness not only of the merit of fidelity, but of the dignity of great abilities, he naturally expected ample preferments; and, that he might not be forgotten by his own fault, wrote a Song of Triumph. But this was a time of such

general hope that great numbers were inevitably disappointed, and Cowley found his reward very tediously delayed. He had been promised by both Charles the first and second the Mastership of the Savoy, but he 'lost it', says Wood, 'by certain persons, enemies to the Muses'.

The neglect of the court was not his only mortification: having, by such alteration as he thought proper, fitted his old Comedy of *The Guardian* for the stage, he produced it to the publick under the title of *The Cutter of Coleman-street*. It was treated on the stage with great severity, and was afterwards censured as a satire on the king's party.

With the apparent failure of all his hopes of immortality, and certainly of immediate reward and celebrity, Cowley's reaction much resembles that of the 'young Author':

His vehement desire of retirement now came again upon him. 'Not finding', says the morose Wood, 'That preferment conferred upon him which he expected, while others for their money carried away most places, he retired discontented into Surrey.'

However, here too, hopes met disappointment. Johnson publishes Cowley's letter to Sprat, complaining of a cold and a fall, of truculent tenants and encroaching cattle. Immediately after the letter comes the comment, 'He did not long enjoy the pleasure or suffer the uneasiness of solitude for he died at the Porch-house in Chertsey in 1667, in the 49th year of his age.'[1] In fact, since Johnson gives dates, it is evident that two years elapsed between letter and death, but the brevity of Johnson's dismissal of Cowley's hopes of pastoral peace create the impression of death pressing hard and mockingly on the heels of his first anxious days of retirement.

It is a technique which Johnson uses many times in the sequence. The best example is probably in the Life of the 'other' Philips: John. In this case, Johnson is handling the life of a diffident man, who caught the public attention almost despite himself, and who had to be induced to publish more work, though his public were ready to acclaim new successes. Finally, he began to believe in his own abilities. It is at precisely this point in the brief narrative of his life that irony is introduced, in Johnson's neat juxtaposition of the title of his last projected work with his imminent death:

> He then grew probably more confident of his own abilities, and began to meditate a poem on *The Last Day*, a subject on which no mind can hope to equal expectation.
> This work he did not live to finish; his diseases, a slow consumption and an asthma, put a stop to his studies, and on Feb. 15, 1708, at the beginning of his thirty-third year, put an end to his life.[2]

Johnson repeats the same kind of grim irony at the expense of Denham; who was rewarded, unlike Cowley, at the Restoration; who promptly lost his reason during a disastrous second marriage; who 'regained his full force of mind ... for he wrote afterwards his excellent poem upon the death of Cowley, whom he was not long to survive; for on the 19th of March, 1668, he was buried by his side'.[3] There is Otway, a writer whose 'principal power was in moving the passions'. The was a gift which he 'drew originally, by consulting nature in his own breast', and his passions duly play their part in his death. In great destitution, 'he went out, as is reported, almost naked, in the *rage of hunger*, and, finding a gentleman in a neighbouring coffee-house, asked him for a shilling. The gentleman gave him a guinea, and Otway going away bought a roll, and was choaked with the first mouthful.'[4] Rather similar is the life of Gay, whose up-and-down literary career exactly matched his character; 'a man easily incited to hope, and deeply depressed when his hopes were disappointed'; and whose death matches his life, since he 'languished, though with many intervals of ease and cheerfulness, till a violent fit at last seized him, and hurried him to the grave, as Arbuthnot reported, with more precipitance than he had ever known'.[5]

Then there is the career of Fenton, whose writings are frequently associated, by Johnson, with collaboration and borrowing. He wrote part of Pope's translation of the *Odyssey*. In 1723 he had a play performed, which had been brutally rejected by Cibber (who advised him 'to engage himself in some employment of honest labour, by which he might obtain that support which he could never hope from his poetry'). The play was successful with another company, but Johnson points out that Fenton completed it from hints supplied by Southern. Finally, Fenton issued a new edition of Waller; whose useful notes, however, were 'too much extended by long quotations from Clarendon'. It is with these collaborations and plagiarisms in mind that Johnson, with an almost straight face, relates his death:

> He died in 1730 at Easthampstead in Berkshire, the seat of the lady Trumbal; and Pope, who had been always his friend, honoured him with an epitaph, of which he borrowed the two first lines from Crashaw.[6]

However, the most extended exercise of charnel irony is devoted to a great author. This is Johnson's account of the funeral of Dryden; an account which he believes to be apocryphal, but which he retails, just the same. Having described at great length all Dryden's 'schemes and labours' for contemporary dignity and lasting fame, Johnson is in effect making a kind of comment on Dryden's immortal longings, in his detailed story of how the funeral was intercepted, with 'the Abbey lighted, the ground opened, the choir attending, an anthem ready set, and [the bishop] waiting for some time without any corpse to bury'; as, meanwhile, the rakish Lord Jefferies, promising a far more regal burial, ordered the corpse to be sent to an undertaker's in Cheapside to await embalmment – only subsequently to declare that 'those who observed the orders of a drunken frolick deserved no better; that he remembered nothing at all of it; and that [the undertaker] might do what he pleased with the corpse'.[7]

It is in this context, of lives and hopes which frequently turn out to be ironic, that Johnson contributes his own assessments of the work of his fifty-two subjects. His tone is notably cool, and frequently acid. He is particularly scathing about Charles Montague, Earl of Halifax, a minor poet, whose patronage secured a rapturous reception for his poems:

> Many a blandishment was practised upon Halifax which he would never have known, had he had no other attractions than those of his poetry, of which a short time has withered the beauties. It would now be esteemed no honour, by a contributor to the monthly bundles of verses, to be told that, in strains either familiar or solemn, he sings like Montague.[8]

However, if it is (predictably) a patron who is most roughly handled, virtually no writer, however great, emerges entirely unscathed.

What is interesting is to discover what kinds of writing were most likely to win his approval. What emerges is an attitude to the writers' imagination which is at least as distrustful and negative as his attitude towards their hopes. It is notable that his view of the imagination, in the years after his great creative decade (in the *Preface to Shakespeare* as well as *The Lives of the Poets*) becomes far more constrained than before.

His earlier pronouncements are to be found in the twenty or so literary-critical numbers of *The Rambler*. Many of these are admittedly fairly technical in nature – on the genre of pastoral, on Milton's versification, on contemporary Spenserianisms, on neoclassical critical rules. They occasionally contain, however, accounts of the imaginative faculty which look uninhibitedly enthusiastic, compared with later ones. Tackling the subject of generic definitions in literature, he spells out the main difficulty as being the imaginative power itself; by nature

> a licentious and vagrant faculty, unsusceptible of limitations, and impatient of restraint [which] has always endeavoured to baffle the logician, to perplex the confines of distinction, and burst the enclosures of regularity. There is therefore scarely any species of writing, of which we can tell what is its essence, and what are its constituents; every new genius produces some innovation, which, when invented and approved, subverts the rules which the practice of foregoing authors had established.[9]

If the faculty is 'licentious', it is nevertheless only by genius that literary forms are advanced. 'Regularity' tries in vain to impose order and reason after the event. It is in a *Rambler* essay, not in Johnson's later critical work that we find the famous pronouncement, 'No man ever yet became great by imitation.'[10] Conversely, a reader could be forgiven for believing that the equally famous comment on the 'blanket of the dark' speech in *Macbeth* comes from the notes of the Shakespeare edition, or from the *Preface*. Actually, it comes from *Rambler* no. 168. The essay does indeed contain a strong ingredient of the nit-picking criticism which often characterises the *Shakespeare*. Johnson objects that 'We do not immediately conceive that any crime of importance is to be committed with a *knife* ... an instrument used by butchers and cooks in the meanest employments'; and declares that 'I can scarcely check my risibility when the expression ['Nor Heaven peep through the blanket of the dark, / To cry, hold, hold'] forces itself upon my mind; for who, without some relaxation of his gravity, can hear of the avengers of guilt "peeping through a blanket"?' Yet this same essay also comments on the same passage of *Macbeth* in the following terms: 'In this passage is exerted all the force of poetry, that force which calls new powers into being, which embodies sentiment, and animates matter.'[11] In Johnson's later criticism there is no section equal to this, in its enthusiastic acknowledgement of the sheer creativity of the imagination. After 1760, he tends to define poetic excellence in quite different terms.

In the *Lives of the Poets*, it is Dryden who comes closest to Johnson's ideal as a writer. Just as Dryden himself had celebrated Congreve's achievement in taming the rugged national genius, so Johnson celebrates Dryden's contribution as a refiner of English poetry: 'he found it brick and left it marble'.[12] As an earlier passage shows, his talent consisted of the perfect balance of three essential elements. His success here was enough to cancel out the effect of his negligence as a writer, and again Johnson implies the theme of progress: 'He had more musick than Waller, more vigour than Denham, and more nature than Cowley.'[13] All these three are key terms in Johnsonian criticism. Each is essential in a poet. Each is displayed in individual ascendancy by a great English writer, in other sections of the *Lives of the Poets*. Leopold Damrosch, adopting an earlier observation of Jean Hagstrum, notes that Johnson associates Pope with the musical or beautiful, Milton with the vigorous or the sublime, and Shakespeare with the natural or 'pathetick'.[14] However, it is Dryden alone who achieves the necessary poise and balance between the three distinct qualities. It is a balance which equips him best for the kind of poetry which Johnson most admires, the poetry of pronouncement.

By comparison, each of the other three great geniuses suffered from an imbalance of gifts. In the case of Pope, the deficient component is evidently vigour, as emerges in the comparison between Pope and Dryden. Dryden's range of knowledge is wider. He also has the power to enliven that knowledge:

> Of genius, that power which constitutes a poet; that quality without which judgement is cold and knowledge is inert; that energy which collects, combines, amplifies and animates – the superiority must, with some hesitation, be allowed to Dryden.[15]

Johnson does indeed add that Pope must not therefore be thought of as possessing only little vigour. Apart from Dryden, 'every other writer since Milton must give place to Pope' in terms of energy. Nevertheless, the preference is made. Quite probably what guides it is Johnson's conviction that Dryden had the stronger mind. Certainly, when Pope tries to follow Dryden, and reason in rhyme, the resulting *Essay on Man* amounts only to 'penury of knowledge and vulgarity of sentiment . . . happily disguised'.[16] Certainly, in the comparison between Dryden and Pope, 'genius' is defined in predominantly intellectual terms. It becomes the talent of organising materials; collecting, combining, amplifying, animating. Animation sounds promising, but clearly what is involved there is something not very different from the other terms; the lively disposition of materials already assembled. This version of the imaginative process – of collecting material, and then working on it – is developed as the comparison proceeds. Dryden, says Johnson, is hastier than Pope. He collects all the material he can in one quick swoop: 'what his mind could supply at call, or gather in one excursion, was all that he sought, and all that he gave'. In fact, here, the operations of disposition seem to be performed simultaneously with the act of gathering. Pope, on the other hand, with his 'dilatory caution', was a far more conscious workman. His habit of care 'enabled him to condense his sentiments, to multiply his images, and to accumulate all that study might produce, or chance might supply'. Pope's very care is in a sense debilitating. Yet, even the quality of vigour is defined in terms of organisation, however instantaneous.

As to Shakespeare, he has 'nature' in great abundance. Johnson repeatedly praises this, and defends him in the *Preface* from the kind of criticism which gives precedence to critical rules over nature. On these grounds, he defends his characterisation, his mingling of tragedy and comedy, his violation of the unities. However, Johnson's contentment with Shakespeare's naturalism is at least equalled by his irritation at Shakespeare's failings. The first of these and the most serious objection is the lack of a serious and sustained didactic purpose. On the face of it, this moral criterion seems to be quite unconnected with Johnson's three normal criteria of music, vigour and nature. It seems to constitute a separate fourth quality, usually unstated, but called on in special cases either of blame (Shakespeare or Fielding) or praise (Milton). In fact, the moral criterion in Johnson is actually closely connected with the first of his normal criteria, of music (or more broadly, of beauty). As will shortly be seen, technical correctness is often closely associated in Johnson's mind with moral correctness; refinement of writing with refinement of morals or manners. Certainly, in the Shakespeare *Preface*, Shakespeare's neglect of an overt moral purpose is seen as simply one aspect of a general technical negligence, which also includes the loose formation of his plots, his errors of anachronism, his hasty conclusions, his failures of propriety and above all his indulgence of verbal quibbling. Collectively, these lapses appear to Johnson as Shakespeare's 'deformities', and if he was deficient in beauty it was because he failed to attempt to satisfy even 'his own ideas of perfection'.[17] When it comes to a particular example of Shakespeare's neglect of a moral, it can again be shown that the moral argument is expressed in aesthetic terms. *Hamlet* is praised for variety, but finally condemned on moral grounds:

> The poet is accused of having shewn little regard to poetical justice, and may be charged with equal neglect of poetical probability. The apparition left the regions of the dead to little purpose; the revenge which he demands is not obtained but by the death of him that was required to take it; and the gratification which would arise from the destruction of an usurper and a murderer, is abated by the untimely death of Ophelia, the young, the beautiful, the harmless, and the pious.[18]

Of course, every observation here is true. It is simply a matter of whether these facts are the source of blame or praise. Johnson's distaste for Shakespeare's moral scheme is expressed in terms of violations of 'poetical justice' and 'poetical probability'. In other words, Johnson appeals to senses of justice and probability peculiar to art; and, incidentally, quite at odds (especially 'probability') with those found in the 'nature' which Shakespeare everywhere imitates. Shakespeare violates the expectations of art, its evolved codes and patterns. His preference for nature is therefore a kind of violation of the sense of form. The same kind of argument is used in the criticism on *King Lear*, with reference to the death of Cordelia. Acknowledging that, in life, virtue does often perish, Johnson still argues that, 'if other excellencies are equal, the audience will ... always rise better pleased from the final triumph of persecuted virtue'.[19] The doctrine of pleasure makes clear how closely akin Johnson's moral criterion is to his criterion of beauty. The argument which we might expect to be consistently framed in terms of *docere* is suddenly translated into the terms of *diligere*.

In the case of Milton, the deficiency is of 'nature', and also, to a certain extent, of beauty. In vigour, he has certainly no failings. In *Paradise Lost*, 'the thoughts which are occasionally called forth in the progress, are such as could only be produced by an imagination in the highest degree fervid and active, to which materials were supplied by incessant study and unlimited curiosity. The heat of Milton's mind might be said to sublimate his learning, to throw off into his work the spirit of science, unmingled with its grosser parts.'[20] This very enthusiastic account of the Miltonic imagination is of a quality far more active than that ascribed to Dryden. More than a mere disposition of materials supplied by learning, the imaginative process transforms the material it works with. Johnson begins his account of *Paradise Lost* tamely enough. Poetry is 'the art of uniting pleasure with truth, by calling imagination to the help of reason'.[21] Imagination supplies the pleasing vehicle, but the principal use of poetry is not artistic but moral. Epic poetry simply provides a vehicle of suitable magnitude to convey pre-existing truths. However, as the section develops, Johnson finds himself celebrating imagination as a capacity to 'form new modes of existence'.[22] Milton's delight was to 'sport in the wide regions of possibility; reality was a scene too narrow for his mind'. At this point in the *Life of Milton*, Johnson approaches quite close to the conception of the imagination power which he had permitted himself in the *Rambler* essay on *Macbeth*, as the quality of creativity. Unfortunately, he feels unable to give to this kind of imagination his unqualified approval. The key sentence is the one which declares that 'reality was a scene too narrow for his mind'. Ultimately, whatever the sublimity of Milton's imagination, and his capacity to satisfy that of his reader ('he never fails to fill the imagination'),[23] Milton's departures from nature must ultimately be viewed as a failing. *Paradise Lost* introduces us to Heaven and Hell and to the parents of mankind; but since 'human passions did not enter the world before the Fall, there is in the *Paradise Lost* little opportunity for the pathetick ... the passions are moved only on one occasion; sublimity is the general and prevailing quality in this poem. ... The want of human interest is always felt. *Paradise Lost* is one of the books which the reader admires and lays down, and forgets to take up again. None ever wished it longer than it is.'[24] Here very clearly expressed is a distinction between the sublime and the pathetic, in which the pathetic is associated with 'nature', and found wanting in Milton. Vigour and the sublime are abundantly present. Nature and the pathetic are deficient, and the failure is crippling, since the reader needs to experience a sense of common mind with his author. When Johnson subsequently goes on to consider the quality of music or beauty in Milton, towards the end of the *Life*, the same kinds of criteria operate. Milton 'formed his style by a perverse and pedantick principle. He was desirous to use English words with a foreign idiom. This in all his prose is discovered and condemned; for there judgement operates freely, neither softened by the beauty, nor awed by the dignity of his thoughts; but such is the power of his poetry that his call is obeyed without resistance, the reader feels himself in captivity to a higher and a nobler mind, and criticism sinks in admiration.' Johnson goes on to use Butler's phrase of a *'Babylonish Dialect*, in itself harsh and barbarous, but made by exalted genius and extensive learning the vehicle of so much instruction and so much pleasure that, like other lovers, we find grace in its deformity.'[25] Milton compels our admiration of his verse, by the sheer force of his personality. However, coolly considered, it is not beauty but deformity that we see. That it is so, is largely the result again of his remoteness from the common stock. True, his remoteness is 'exalted'. It is nevertheless 'perverse and pedantick'.

One is particularly struck by the phrase, 'harsh and *barbarous*'. Johnson frequently speaks of the 'beauties' of *Paradise Lost*, but of only *Paradise Regained* does he use the word 'elegant'.[26] Again, behind Johnson's treatment of the Miltonic sublime, and the consequent absence of the pathetic, lies a preference for softer and more refined artistic experiences; for 'natural curiosity or sympathy'.[27] However, to find Milton described as a barbarian is still something of a surprise.

As Warren Fleischauer has pointed out, the word 'harsh 'in Johnson usually means something other than 'dissonant'.[28] Usually, it implies remoteness from normal meaning. In this sense, it is frequently found in the detailed comments on Shakespeare's plays:

> We have with a leaven'd and prepared choice . . .
> No emendation is necessary. Leaven'd choice is one of Shake-

speare's harsh metaphors. His train of ideas seems to be this. I have proceeded to you with choice *mature, concocted, fermented,* leavened. When Bread is 'leavened', it is left to ferment: a 'leavened' choice is therefore a choice not hasty, but considerate.[29]

The same kind of objection, though not the same terminology (irritatingly, 'harsh' here means unmelodious), occurs in the *Life of Cowley*, in both the general remarks on metaphysical poetry and specific comment on Cowley's practice. The remarks on metaphysical poetry are extremely familiar, and Johnson's hostility is well known. It is worth noting, however, that Johnson's vocabulary of disapproval tends to centre around terms denoting civilisation. Granting that strength of thought was necessary to write metaphysical poetry, Johnson adds:

> genuine wit and useful knowledge may be sometimes found, buried perhaps in grossness of expression, but useful to those who know their value, and such as, when they are expanded to perspicuity and polished to elegance, may give lustre to works which have more propriety though less copiousness of sentiment.[30]

Later on, the charge of being uncivilised stretches to the charge of actual monstrosity: 'Of thoughts so far-fetched as to be not only unexpected but unnatural, all their books are full.'[31] More often, however, it is a question of inelegance.

> Their thoughts and expressions were sometimes grossly absurd. ... They were in very little care to clothe their notions with elegance of dress, and therefore miss the notice and the praise which are often gained by those who think less, but are more diligent to adorn their thoughts.[32]

In the discussion of Cowley himself, Johnson's comments become almost class-ridden. In the *Davideis*, Cowley writes 'in the terms of the mercer and taylor'.[33] He forgets that language is the dress of thought, and a noble thought is 'degraded and obscured by a garb appropriated to the gross employments of rusticks or mechanicks'.[34] Truth is always truth, but 'may be so hidden in unrefined and plebeian words that none but philosophers can distinguish it'.[35] Throughout, the metaphysicals are implicitly measured against the gentlemanly ideal of the easy and the natural, and are found wanting. Instead, they worked in a 'laboured' way;[36] and with violence – 'their fictions were often violent and unnatural'.[37] It is clear, then, that Johnson's complaints about Milton or Cowley have much in common. All offend against elegance and civilisation; pitching their diction or their metaphors into regions remote from the central common stock of refined received usage. Strong though Johnson's respect is for the 'vigorous' in poetry – and it is evident that he has much respect for the qualities of mind of the 'metaphysicals' – vigour is uncomfortably close to 'violence', and violence is without exception abhorred. Hence the famous denunciation of Gray, whose 'language is laboured into harshness. The mind of the writer seems to work with unnatural violence.'[38] Gray, too, is an unlikely barbarian, but this is how Johnson sees him.

This certainly explains Johnson's treatment in the *Lives of the Poets* of such figures as Addison, Denham or Waller. To admire an Addison violates Johnson's strongly-held admiration for vigour in poetry. Addison commands little respect from Johnson on these grounds. He is not a writer who thinks forcefully: he is 'not sufficiently vigorous to attain excellence'. Yet, that part of Johnson which must celebrate civilisation as the highest goal of poetry impels him to celebrate Addison as 'one of our earliest examples of correctness'. As a critic, too, Addison's influence was progressive: thanks to him, 'an emulation of intellectual elegance was excited, and from his time to our own life has been gradually exalted, and conversation purified and enlarged'. As a prose writer, it was Addison's 'principal endeavour to avoid all harshness and severity of diction'. All this compels Johnson's admiration. Amusingly, when the final words of praise are delivered, they sound uncommonly sarcastic:

> Whoever wishes to attain an English style, familiar but not coarse, and elegant but not ostentatious, must give his days and nights to the volumes of Addison.[39]

Nevertheless Addison is established as a model and a landmark on the way to progress. The same is true of Roscommon:

> His versification is smooth, but rarely vigorous, and his rhymes are remarkably exact. He improved taste if he did not enlarge

knowledge, and may be numbered among the benefactors to English literature.[40]

The praise of Denham takes a still more intriguing form:

> He is one of the writers that improved our taste and advanced our language, and whom we ought therefore to read with gratitude, though having done much he left much to do.[41]

The interesting feature here is the explicit link which Johnson makes between correctness of expression and correction of taste. The theme is repeated with Waller:

> it cannot be denied that he added something to our elegance of diction, and something to our propriety of thought.[42]

Elegance of diction is linked, not only to the general question of taste, but to right-thinking. As a man, it is evident that Johnson found Waller despicable; a liar, a coward, an informer and a groveller. Nevertheless, as a writer, he cannot bring himself to deny to Waller the praise of right-thinking. Waller may be 'never pathetick, and very rarely sublime'. Still, in verse at any rate, he thought like a gentleman, and that was enough: 'his thoughts are such as a liberal conversation and large acquaintance with life would easily supply'.[43]

What seems to make absolutely certain Johnson's final declared preference for the civilised in poetry – whatever his instinctive veneration for the vigorous – is his handling of Dryden in the *Life of Dryden* itself. Whereas, in the *Life of Pope*, Dryden is preferred to Pope because of his superior vigour, in the *Life of Dryden*, he is praised in much the same sort of terms as those used for Denham, Roscommon or Waller.

> To him we owe the improvement, perhaps the completion of our metre, the refinement of our language, and much of the correctness of our sentiments. By him we were taught *sapere et fari*, to think naturally and express forcibly.[44]

It is an interesting reversal. In the *Life of Pope* Dryden is praised as a writer who thought forcibly, above all. Pope himself had a genius 'active ambitious and adventurous, always investigating, always aspiring'. Dryden's genius was yet more active. Here, however, he thinks *naturally*, and *expresses* forcibly. And, like Waller, he is celebrated ultimately as a refiner, whose correctness of expression matches the correctness of his sentiments. It would be fair to say that, given Johnson's capacity to celebrate the imagination's inventiveness, such praise is something of a disappointment.

Some compensation is provided when we read the conclusion to the *Life of Ambrose Philips*, where Johnson, with evident relish, crushes mere correctness:

> In his other poems he cannot be denied the praise of lines sometimes elegant; but he has seldom much force or much comprehension. . . . He has added nothing to English poetry.[45]

However, there is no escaping that the final stress of the *Lives of the Poets* lies with the theme of civilised progress (or, in the case of Gray, decline). The praise Johnson accords to originality is at best ambiguous. With Young, the final emphasis is positive: 'he was a man of genius and a poet'. Yet, his exuberant style and powerful thoughts, which are allowed to be 'original', are also too private and idiosyncratic to be accurate. In his tragedy, *Busiris*, 'there are the greatest ebullitions of imagination; but the pride of Busiris is such as no other man can have, and the whole is too remote from known life to raise either grief, terror, or indignation'. The same kind of duality is observable in the comments on Young's poetry: 'it abounds in thought, but without much accuracy or selection'.[46] At least, Young wins *some* approval for his originality. With Swift, originality ('perhaps no writer can be found that has borrowed so little') is linked far more obviously with what is artistically and socially beyond the pale. *Gulliver's Travels* is a book 'written in open defiance of truth and regularity'.[47] Actually, Johnson makes few remarks on Swift's work apart from this. In the section which begins, 'When Swift is considered as an author', Johnson continues to write about Swift's personal peculiarities. Comment tends to be implied rather than stated: for instance in the implied contrast between the 'purity' of his style (and the 'oriental scrupulosity'[48] with which he washed himself) and the loathsomeness of his content. Johnson seems actually unable to bring himself to mention in print what he finds disgusting; and affects to be reluctant to tell the reader what he knows already. With Swift, originality is tantamount to deviancy.

To Milton's originality, Johnson is far kinder, especially in the section where he imagines Milton observing the 'slow sale and tardy reputation' of his great poem in a manner 'calm and confident, little disappointed, not at all dejected, relying on his own merit with steady consciousness, and waiting without impatience the vicissitudes of opinion and the impartiality of a future generation'.[49] This is praise indeed. It sets Milton above the ironies of hope which afflict the vast majority of Johnson's subjects in the *Lives of the Poets*. It is an immunity accorded to him by the originality of his genius: 'of all the borrowers from Homer Milton is perhaps the least indebted. He was naturally a thinker for himself, confident of his own abilities and disdainful of help or hindrance.'[50] Yet, as already seen, originality also produces a remoteness in his great poem from comprehensible life, however noble or instructive its design. When the same self-confidence occurs in an inferior writer, it is far less supportable. Blackmore emerges as a parody-Milton, writing 'not for a livelihood but for fame', and depending 'with great security on his own powers.... The incessant attacks of his enemies, whether serious or merry, are never discovered to have disturbed his quiet, or to have lessened his confidence in himself.'[51] Blackmore ploughed on regardless, producing one epic poem after another, and culminating, with true Miltonic ambition, with *Creation*, a poem of which Johnson approves. However, 'having succeeded so well in his book on *Creation*, by which he established the great principle of all religion, he thought his undertaking imperfect unless he likewise enforced the truth of revelation; and for that purpose added another poem on *Redemption*. He had likewise written, before his *Creation*, three books on the *Nature of Man*.'[52]

Originality, then, tends to be associated with what is perverse, tedious, disgusting or remote, even when found in writers of the highest abilities. The best praise of novelty, for Johnson, is that it is also 'natural'. It is a standard which he offers right at the outset of the sequence, in the *Life of Cowley*, where 'Wit' is defined as that 'which is at once natural and new, that which though not obvious is, upon its first production, acknowledged to be just'.[53] Even though it is the poet who discovers that a consensus of opinion exists, it is still to the concept of 'right-thinking' that Johnson is appealing as his highest standard in poetry.

This is something which specialists in Johnson's criticism seem reluctant to accept. Jean Hagstrum's standard work, *Samuel Johnson's Literary Criticism*, notes Johnson's fear of the imagination, but goes on to say that his tendency to attack the imaginative faculty

> occurs more prominently in his earlier than in his later works. It was in the periodical essays and in *Rasselas* that he was wont to call the imagination 'licentious and vagrant', wild, unrestrained, vehement, and rapid, and to associate it with youth and inexperience, with lyrics and with pastoral verse, to which he was either hostile or indifferent. There is, I think, somewhat less of this in the *Lives of the Poets*, where he praises the inventive genius of Milton and the fiery energy of Dryden and almost regularly places the *mens divinior* above the lower orders of genius; the 'pleasing captivity' and 'allurement' of literary delight above correctness, elegance and refinement.[54]

A similar theory can be found in Leopold Damrosch's recent book, *The Uses of Johnson's Criticism*. Damrosch describes Johnson's apparent hostility to the imagination in the *Preface to Shakespeare*, and of 'the amorality proper to art. In proportion as a writer is brilliant and compelling, Johnson may distrust and even fear his power over the imagination'.[55] He goes on to argue, however, that the format of literary biography in the *Lives of the Poets* enabled Johnson to rehabilitate the imaginative faculty; and that what emerges is that 'Johnson's real interest in literary history was not in the evolution of form and technique, but in the creative leaps of genius.'[56] So strongly expressed a unanimity discourages dissent, yet Hagstrum's account in particular does seem to contain inaccuracies. Indeed, it seems to have missed the point.

One would not by any means dispute the existence in the *Lives of the Poets* of passages in praise of genius. There are passages of praise of Milton, Dryden and for that matter Pope which stand out conspicuously from their context, by the heightened quality of their own writing. However, on examination, what these passages consistently celebrate is imagination as a quality of intellect. It is the ability to 'think forcefully', and to dispose and organise thought to its best advantage. There is nothing beyond this in the description of Pope's poetic mind, 'always investigating, always aspiring'. When, in the case of Milton, the imagination, in its 'unrestrained indulgence', comes close to creativity, Johnson makes it clear that it is precisely here that Milton tends to lose rather than captivate his reader: we 'retire harassed and overburdened, and look elsewhere for recreation; we desert our master, and seek for companions'. The preference for the more accessible and familiar is clear. As to the suggestion that Johnson prefers the *mens divinior* to 'correctness, elegance and refinement', almost all the evidence points the other way. Very occasionally an unguarded comment may betray such an attitude; as when Johnson asserts that Cowley can achieve things which the 'feeble care of Waller never could produce'.[57] Yet Johnson refuses to promote Cowley over Waller. Cowley's 'excellence of this kind is merely fortuitous'. Writers such as Gray or Collins, far from being praised for graces beyond the reach of correctness, are lamented as great and talented men whose abilities were lost in perversity. And with Johnson's paragon, Dryden, strength of thought itself, as the highest virtue, slides quietly into correctness of thought, and strength of expression.

In the *Lives of the Poets*, as Damrosch remarks, there is a 'method of general praise and specific blame'.[58] However, two passages of specific praise come to mind, and both are of interest to the theme of right-thinking. One comes from the *Life of Milton*. It concerns *L'Allegro* and *Il Penseroso*. Johnson describes their theme, which is not 'merely to shew how objects derived their colours from the mind, by representing the operation of the same things upon the gay and the melancholy temper, or upon the same man as he is differently disposed; but rather how, among the successive variety of appearances, every disposition of mind takes hold on those by which it may be gratified'. After a long exploration of these ideas, in which nothing but ideas is discussed, Johnson pronounces the poems to be 'two noble efforts of imagination'.[59] The other passage come from the *Life of Pope*, in which Johnson seizes on the simile of the Alps in the *Essay on Criticism*, to illustrate the 'student's progress in the sciences'. This simile, he says, 'has no useless parts, yet affords a striking picture by itself: it makes the foregoing position better understood, and enables it to take faster hold on the attention; it assists the apprehension, and elevates the fancy'. It is clear how very much subordinate here the fancy is to the understanding, yet to this simile Johnson accords the very highest praise. It is 'perhaps the best that English poetry can shew'.[60] The Shakespeare notes often provide very similar passages when a passage is described as 'exquisitely imagined' or 'exquisitely beautiful'[61] when its paraphraseable meaning seems to Johnson particularly sage and apt.

By comparison, the earlier passages on imagination in *The Rambler* seem altogether different in kind. Their emphasis may not be approving – though this is not the case with the *Macbeth* passage – but they nevertheless acknowledge a constituent in genius which is beyond conscious control. Beside this power, indeed, 'the enclosures of regularity' seem impertinent. Above all, this power is supremely creative. It 'calls new powers into being'.

Johnson moved, in his criticism, not towards a rehabilitation of the imagination, but away from a conception of the imagination as licentious and creative. Even in his most heightened passages, it comes to be defined conservatively, in terms of right-thinking. The turning-point is unquestionably in *Rasselas*, that last production of the creative decade. Imlac does concede that 'no man was ever great by imitation'. Nevertheless, in his 'Dissertation upon Poetry', he believes that, once the ancients have had their say, what is left to future generations is 'elegance and refinement'. He proceeds to describe the training of a poet in terms of gaining knowledge; and the formation of style notable for 'every delicacy of speech and grace of harmony'. Thus equipped, the poet can then pronounce truths, or to be more precise 'general and transcendental truths, which will always be the same. ... He must write as the interpreter of nature, and the legislator of mankind, and consider himself as presiding over the thoughts and manners of future generations.'[62] Even within this 'dissertation', one can observe Johnson's transition from his formerly-held respect for creative invention, towards giving pre-eminence to the power of pronouncement. Yet, as has already been observed, Imlac is a writer who writes nothing. It is fascinating to watch Johnson's retreat from the imagination, in his criticism, coinciding with his own Imlac-like retreat from the life of writing.

11 Levet: 'hope's delusive mine'

On 17 January 1782 died Robert Levet, a man described by Boswell as Johnson's 'humble friend', and by Johnson himself as an 'old and faithful friend'. He had been 'an obscure practiser of physic amongst the lower people', and for the greater part of Johnson's residence in London, Levet 'had an apartment in his house or chambers, and waited upon him every morning, through the whole course of his late and tedious breakfast. He was of a strange, grotesque appearance, stiff and formal in his manner, and seldom said a word while any company was present.'[1] Boswell's tone is patronising. Elsewhere, he humorously notes that Levet used to breakfast on the crusts of Johnson's rolls. Johnson too had been known to find Levet amusing: 'he was, perhaps, the only man who ever became intoxicated through motives of prudence. He reflected, that if he refused the gin or brandy offered him by some of his patients, he could have been no gainer by their cure, as they might have had nothing else to bestow on him. ... He would swallow what he did not like, nay, what he knew would injure him, rather than go home with an idea, that his skill had been exerted without recompense.'[2] His death, however, was a matter of real grief. The previous year, Henry Thrale had died. His widow, Boswell assumed, would marry Johnson. Instead, she determined to be rid of him. By the summer of 1782, she had let the house at Streatham which had been Johnson's second home. She announced that she would travel abroad. What she did not dare to announce for some months more, and then only by letter, was that she had decided to marry Gabriel Piozzi, an Italian musician. In a letter dating from March that year, Johnson revealed his forebodings of painful change, and the reliance he had placed on Levet as a dependable constant. On the night before Levet's death, 'I was musing in my chamber, I thought with uncommon earnestness, that however I might alter my mode of life, or whithersoever I might remove, I would endeavour to retain Levet about me.'³ At the time of Levet's death, Boswell was in Scotland, not returning for over a year. On their reunion, Johnson begged him, 'be with me as much as you can'. He then recited a poem of 36 lines, 'with an emotion which gave them full effect'. The poem was *On the Death of Dr Robert Levet*, his first extended serious poem in English since *The Vanity of Human Wishes*.

The poem is a rough contemporary of *The Lives of the Poets*. Earlier in Johnson's life, as we have seen, there was always a supply of creative work coincident with the great scholarly tasks he undertook as his primary objectives. It could hardly be expected that this should be the case with *The Lives of the Poets*. With his Royal pension, Johnson was no longer required to work in order to live. To write anything at all required what Professor Bate has called an 'Indian Summer' in his life. When he did write, he wrote as a scholar and an encyclopaedist. Nevertheless, there are just a few poems from this period which are not in Latin, and are neither translations, nor parodies, nor humorous occasional pieces. One is the delightful and sprightly satirical sketch on Sir John Lade, 'Long-expected one-and-twenty', of which Johnson said 'it is odd that it should come into any bodies head!'⁴ Then there are two outstanding elegaic pieces. One is a short poem on Hogarth, written for the benefit of Garrick, who had been asked by the widow to provide an epitaph. There are only two stanzas, and even then the second stanza leaves almost intact Garrick's own first effort. The first stanza is one of the most exquisite things Johnson ever wrote:

> The hand of art here torpid lies
>   That traced th'essential form of grace,
> Here death has clos'd the curious eyes
>   That saw the manners in the face.

Johnson achieves so poignant a contrast of life and death by managing to convey a sense of immediate presence. He writes as if Hogarth's body were *visibly* before him; and he himself demonstrating and explaining to the onlooker how this hand and this eye were the centre and epitome of this man's vitality. By creating this sense of himself observing and condensing the 'essential', Johnson comes closer to his subject, to Hogarth's own capacity to observe, and to condense in paint.

Similarly, with *On the Death of Dr Levet*, we become, with Johnson, near-witnesses to Levet's funeral, as we '*see* Levet to the grave descend' (l.6, my italics). In much the same way as with the Hogarth epitaph, Johnson contrives to write a poem in which, even as he directs our attention to the dead man, he himself becomes the indispensable intermediary. More than this, it can be seen that the secret subject of the Levet poem is Johnson himself. The presence of certain Johnsonian key words should warn us at the very least that Levet-as-hero is cast in a specifically Johnsonian heroic mould. The single 'talent' well-employed reminds us of the significance of the parable of the talents to Johnson himself. The breaking of the vital 'chain' recalls to mind all the distressing evidence of Johnson's own 'padlock'.

Such reminders are probably necessary. *On the Death of Dr Levet* is a plain poem. The brisk octosyllabic-lined quatrains, the simple diction innocent of latinism, the elision which urges on the pace, all apparently conspire to deceive the reader as to the emotional charge of the subject for Johnson. Levet's life is delivered in words and phrases so clipped and staccato as to postpone the surprise a reader must feel to hear a man described as not only 'sincere' but 'officious' or 'innocent'. The personal significance actually claimed for Levet at the outset seems minimal. He is one of 'our social comforts', no more. Equally unemphatic is the ending, which departs abruptly, like Levet's soul, 'the nearest way'. Throughout, there is an insistent air of cheerful vigour. The very terms in which Levet is cast act as encouraging prompt-words to our reading of tone: 'His frame was *firm* – his powers were *bright*.' It would be easy, deceived by so modest a manner, to miss the intensity and complexity with which the poem is formed. Not its least interest to the present study is the final development it contributes to Johnson's life-long theme of 'hope and fear, desire and hate'. Unquestionably, its intensity and complexity have to be sought out. The reason is that Johnson had performed a kind of act of concealment. He transposes personal emotions. His poem converts the loss to Johnson of an old and faithful friend into the loss to society of a useful man. A clue to this process is provided in the *Life of Pope*, where Johnson had concluded by examining Pope's epitaphs. He had spent a page or so on each of these thirteen obscure pieces, with particular praise for the one *On Mrs Corbett who died of a Cancer in her Breast*:

> Here rests a Woman, good without pretence,
> Blest with plain Reason, and with sober Sense:
> No Conquest she, but o'er herself desir'd;
> No Arts essay'd, but not to be admir'd.

In all conscience, the poem can only be described as dull. Pope is bored. He lapses into the kind of formulae ('So firm, yet soft, so strong, yet so refin'd') which he had ridiculed in *The Dunciad*[5] ('Tho' stale, not ripe; tho' thin, yet never clear'). The final lines might even be suspected of irony:

> Heav'n, as its purest Gold, by Torture try'd,
> The Saint sustained, but the Woman dy'd.

Johnson, however, is rapturous. 'I have always considered this as the most valuable of all Pope's epitaphs; the subject of it is a character not discriminated by any shining or eminent peculiarities.... Domestic virtue, as it is exerted without great occasions, or conspicuous consequences, in an even tenor, required the genius of Pope to display it in such a manner as might attract attention, and enforce reverence.'[6] The *Levet* poem is, ostensibly, just such another impersonal tribute. Having discreetly introduced, in stanza 1, the framing idea of Levet as one of 'our social comforts', now lost, the author never again uses the first person in the poem. The nearest thing to a reference to personal bereavement is the personification, 'affection's eye', of line 9. Johnson is determined to direct our attention to his friend, not to his own grief at losing him. It is what we might expect, in the light of his severe criticism, in the *Life of Milton*, of the egotism of *Lycidas*. The poem focuses with ever-greater concentration solely on Levet, Levet's energy, Levet's selflessness.

This is an admirably selfless impulse. Yet the effect of Johnson's self-effacement is anything but self-obliterating. The effort of restraint is far more affective than explicit grief. One remembers Boswell recounting, as infinitely moving, Johnson's manner at their final parting: 'When he had got down upon the foot-pavement, he called out, "Fare you well"; and without looking back, sprung away with a kind of pathetic briskness . . . which seemed to indicate a struggle to conceal uneasiness, and impressed me with a foreboding of our long, long separation.'[7] In the *Levet* poem, the 'struggle', being less immediate, is less evident. Its effect is nevertheless emotional. Feeling is actually transmitted by the act of repression.

That this is so is partly the result of Levet's occupation. The professional solicitude of his trade readily lends itself to emotional intensification. Johnson actually ensures that this will happen: that 'care' will become an emotionally loaded term. He surrounds the word with others which unobtrusively but insistently introduce the idea of personal relationship: 'Of ev'ry friendless name the friend', 'affection's eye', 'lonely want'. The result is that the direct emotion of bereavement, which Johnson has apparently excluded from the poem, re-enters it by another route. The poem is hospitable to emotion, but the original emotion is transferred. In place of Johnson's pain of personal loss, there is the pain of the wretches Levet tends. Johnson's care for Levet, as a friend, is transferred to Levet's professional concern for his patients.

The process is at first unsuspected, because the poem so vigorously fends off the sentimental. There is none of the stagnation on which sentimentality thrives. There is significant action. From the fourth stanza, and its sequel in the fifth, we gain the impression of a nightmarish drama, enacted in a gloomy cave; a kind of hospital for terminal cases, but with overtones of persecution. In this scene, where even death is stationary, 'hov'ring', the only active feature is Levet, and the 'power' of his 'vig'rous remedy'. His 'useful care' seems wholly to exempt him from the miseries of others. He may practise medicine in a scene of desolation, but the description of that practice, in the sixth stanza, reveals a daily routine of banal normality. It involves nothing beyond the regular calls of healing. It is a 'round', commercially transacted.

Then, something odd begins to happen. The poem is increasingly invaded by negatives: 'Nor made a pause, nor left a void', 'Unfelt, uncounted', 'No throbbing fiery pain, / No cold gradations of decay'. The invasion seems to constitute a resolute denial that Levet's death, to which the poem now, inevitably, has to turn, is in any way connected with those of the wretches in 'misery's darkest caverns'. Levet is to be differentiated in death as well as in life; not only by function but even by sensation. His immunity from pain must even extend up to the very moment of death. The strain this imposes on the poem shows through, in an unexpected way. With Johnson struggling to portray Levet's stamina as active man; with activity a key virtue; activity itself seems to become vitiated. We see Levet's virtues walking 'a narrow round'. We see death breaking 'the vital chain'. The suggestion of imprisonment cannot be missed, and it is Levet's very virtue that has made the prison. The significance of this is immense. At the last, Levet shares the lot of the mass of humanity, his patients. Like them, he is imprisoned, and it is the repetitive vigour of his life which has itself formed the prison. Unwittingly and paradoxically, Johnson's effort to exempt Levet has convicted him.

It is worth stressing that this last development is inadvertent. Johnson would have denied that his praise of the valour of a useful life, lived in the face of death, was in any way complicated by doubt. He had, after all, attached to Levet a personal dream, of a life uncorrupted, filled with work. The penury which had been Johnson's own early lot is here aggressively embraced, almost as a virtue. It places Levet at a distance from 'arrogance' and 'pride'. Poverty brings 'modest[y]'. It enforces work. Levet, the hardworking, charitable man, is a kind of super-Johnson. Oddly, the poet who hated pastoral has here produced its urban equivalent. Dreams of simplicity have always attracted complicated men. Here, in memory of a friend, Johnson permits himself the pastoral dream; of a life obscure, contented, safe and full. It might be added that in its idealism pastoral almost becomes hagiography. At the very least, Levet's virtues guarantee salvation. The 'Eternal Master' smiles benignly, both before and after Levet's death, on his 'single talent well employ'd'. It is a line which Johnson cannot have written without the sense of his own manifold talents, and the way he had, he believed, squandered and wasted them.

For Levet to become such a heroic figure, there was, on the other hand, a price to be paid. The word in the poem which reveals this is the word 'unfelt' (l. 30). It is not merely that Levet in the end suffers and is imprisoned like the rest of humanity, but that he does not feel his condition. In the end, Johnson seems to suggest, Levet's is a life lived not only without flaw but without consciousness. It is a life without imagination.

This is slightly different from the portrait of virtuous old age in *The Vanity of Human Wishes*. This begins optimistically enough:

> An age that melts with unperceiv'd decay,
> And glides in modest innocence away.

Levet's life also 'glided by'. But, in the earlier poem,

> Yet ev'n on this her load Misfortune flings,
> To press the weary minutes flagging wings. . . .
> Year chases year, decay pursues decay,
> Still drops some joy from with'ring life away;
> New forms arise, and diff'rent views engage,
> Superfluous lags the vet'ran on the stage
> Till pitying Nature signs the last release,
> And bids afflicted worth retire to peace.
> But few there are whom hours like these await,
> Who set unclouded in the gulphs of fate.
>
> (ll. 293–312)

In *Levet*, Johnson specifically immunises his physician subject from such physical misfortune; particularly from the 'cold gradations of decay' which wither the earlier figure. More to the point, Levet is denied the uncomfortably clear vantage point of the unclouded seat above the gulphs of Fate; a vantage point which, in *The Vanity of Human Wishes*, was at least preferable to 'ignorance sedate', rolling 'darkling down the torrent of his fate' (ll. 345–6). By contrast, Levet is unfeeling, not only of physical pain, but of the whole current of his life, benign though it is ('the busy day, the peaceful night'). The impression the Levet portrait finally gives is of an almost relentless automaton-like existence. There are no gulphs here. Levet's perpetual motion fills all available space. His virtues 'Nor made a pause, nor left a void'. The 'Eternal [task-] Master' is well pleased; and though Levet lives condemned under the same sentence in 'Hope's delusive mine', a prisoner like the rest, he is exempted from the torments of hope, desiring nothing beyond 'the modest wants of ev'ry day'. Yet the price is the loss of any intervening intelligence.

Levet is unlike other Johnsonian supermen who have freed themselves of fantasy, from the 'phantoms of hope'. Imlac and the astronomer in *Rasselas* or Milton in *The Lives of the Poets* are intellectual giants, whose achievement of a wise acceptance is the reward of great abilities and long struggle. Levet's achievement is defined less by assets (which are few, though worthily employed) than by negatives. Ultimately his may seem not only an unlikely achievement, but an unenviable one. It is with Levet's triumph, his actual condition, and his impercipience, evenly balanced, that the poem closes. Where everything in Johnson's later years had tended *against* the imagination, in his last great poem he seems to have arrested the trend. Here at last, rather than defining the imagination in terms of intelligence, as in *The Lives of the Poets*, he defines the intelligence in terms of the imagination.

He does so, even where its function is only to perceive the delusiveness of the hope to which all others are condemned; including himself. He sees the cost of its loss.

Appendix: Johnson's 'dramatic sense'

It is possible, on the basis of *Irene*, to conclude that Johnson had no talent for drama. He would not be the last great writer to discover such an incapacity. However, the facts discover the answer to be a little more complex, since Johnson several times proved himself perfectly capable of projecting himself into other men's voices. Some of the best examples admittedly come from much later in his life. There were the occasions, for example, when he put his pen at the service of his friend, the brewer, Henry Thrale, to compose Thrale's election addresses. On these occasions, Johnson had to go some way towards impersonating Thrale, 'the independent representative of independent constituents';[1] particularly on the last occasion, when he had to evoke, in the constituents, the living memory of an earlier fit and thriving Thrale, to redeem the disastrous impression his sick friend had made (his wife called him a 'perfect corpse'[2]) at an election meeting in 1880. Then there was the affair of the Rev. Dr Dodd. Dodd was a fashionable preacher, and at one stage Royal Chaplain; but, living beyond his means, tried to stave off his debts by forging a bond in the name of a former pupil of his, Lord Chesterfield. He was discovered, tried, and sentenced to death. Dodd had once tried to gain entry to the Literary Club. He had been refused. Now, he applied to Johnson for help in getting the sentence commuted to deportation. Johnson obliged with a letter to the King, in Dodd's name, arguing the dangers to public order that the execution might provoke. In this piece of impersonation, Johnson amusingly catches – intentionally or otherwise – something of a note of pious humbug, as 'Dodd' begs for life: 'Nor have I the confidence to petition for impunity; but humbly hope that publick security may be established, without the spectacle of a clergyman dragged through the streets, to a death of infamy, amidst the derision of the profligate and profane.'³ Johnson then turned his hand with equal talent to the task of female impersonation, with a letter from 'Mrs Dodd' to the Queen, striking the pathetic note of ruined family.⁴ Unhappily for the real Mrs Dodd, the 'greatest happiness of conjugal union' of which 'she' boasted to the Queen was terminated on 27 June 1777 by Dodd's execution.

These are late examples of Johnson's ventriloquial skills. There is however a much earlier example, dating from before *Irene*'s performance; namely, the Parliamentary Debates.

In the eighteenth century, Parliamentary proceedings were reported by, among others, the *Gentleman's Magazine*. Because of the risk of proceedings for breach of privilege, they were reported long after the event, in the thin disguise of the proceedings of the Senate of Lilliput, with the names of speakers anagrammatised. Cave assigned Johnson to this task in 1741, when public interest became intense in the attempts of the opposition to oust Walpole as Prime Minister, and Johnson continued the task unassisted for three years, writing something over half a millon words. The results are highly impressive. Johnson never actually went to Parliament, and was supplied with 'very slender materials, and often ... none at all – the mere coinage of his own imagination'.⁵ He confessed to Boswell that 'he had nothing more communicated to him than the names of the several speakers, and the part which they had taken in the debate'.⁶ Hawkins is right to 'wonder' that Johnson, 'born to a narrow fortune, of no profession, conversant chiefly with books ... and so great a stranger to senatorial manners that he was never within the walls of either house of parliament ... should be able to frame a system of debate, to compose speeches of such excellence'.⁷ Among the most interesting talents of Johnson the Parliamentary 'reporter' is his capacity to distinguish the speakers from each other. This applies more especially to proceedings in the Commons; the 'characteristic of the [Lords] we know is Dignity; the privilege of the other, Freedom of Expression'.⁸ Consequently, it was probably of the Lords' debates that Johnson was thinking when he described the value of his efforts being that they provided 'orations upon questions of publick importance'.⁹ The Commons debates on the other hand genuinely reproduce the give-and-take of excited partisan bickering, and scholars from Hawkins onwards have professed Johnson's ability to imitate both the typical arguments and idiom of the various speakers.

One of the best samples of what has been called Johnson's 'considerable dramatic skill' in this area is the Commons debate on the Seamen's Bill in 1741.[10] Donald Greene points out Johnson's habit of concentrating his efforts on just a few central issues of each Session,[11] and the Seamen's Bill is one of these. It was a wartime measure, designed to increase the number of available seamen, with a clause which replaced impressment with a form of conscription, the register. The debates, in Johnson's hands, fully reflect the highly-charged nature of the issue itself, and the Opposition's sensing in it an opportunity to assail the Walpole regime. Among the speakers for the Opposition was William Pitt the Elder, still in his early days as a parliamentarian. Pitt (or 'Ptit', as the *Magazine* calls him) made a speech attacking the 'open Cruelty and notorious Oppression' of the proposals. The debate moved on, but this speech left 'the Prime Minister's Brother' (Horatio Walpole) seething with indignation. Johnson sets the scene for the explosion to come, and the passage is notable for its specific allusions to theatre. Horatio Walpole had 'stood up several Times, but was prevented by other members'. Now at last he catches the Speaker's eye, and delivers himself of his indignation against Pitt's demagoguery:

> I do not answer him for any other purpose than to remind him ... how little the Discovery of Truth is promoted and the security of the Nation established by pompous Diction and theatrical Emotions. ... If the heat of his Temper, Sir, would suffer him to attend to those whose Age and long Acquaintance with Business give them an indisputable Right to Deference and Superiority, he would learn, in time, to reason rather than Declaim.

Needless to say, Pitt's response to this shows little of the deference to which his opponent thought himself entitled:

> The atrocious Crime of being a Young Man, which the honourable Gentleman has with such Spirit and Decency charged upon me, I shall neither attempt to palliate nor deny, but content myself with wishing that I may be one of those whose Follies may cease with their Youth, and not of that Number who are ignorant in spite of Experience.
> Whether Youth can be imputed to any Man as a Reproach, I

will not, Sir, assume the Province of determining; but surely Age may become justly contemptible, if the Opportunities which it brings have past away without Improvement, and the Vice appears to prevail when the Passions have subsided. The wretch that, after having seen the Consequences of a thousand Errors, continues still to blunder, and whose Age has only added Obstinacy to Stupidity, is surely the Object of either Abhorrence or Contempt, and deserves not his grey Head should secure him from Insults.

But Youth, Sir, is not my only Crime; I have been accused of acting a theatrical Part – a Theatrical part may imply either some Peculiarities of Gesture, or a dissimulation of my real Sentiments, and an Adoption of the Opinions and Language of another Man.

In the first sense, Sir, the Charge is too trifling to be confuted, and deserves only to be mentioned, that it may be despised. If any man shall by charging me with Theatrical Behaviour imply, that I utter any Sentiments but my own, I shall treat him as a Calumniator and a Villain. . . .

But with Regard, Sir, to those whom I have offended, I am of Opinion, that if I had acted a borrowed Part, I should have avoided their Censure; the Heat that offended them is the ardour of Conviction, and that Zeal for the service of my Country which neither Hope nor Fear shall influence me to suppress.

When the flow eventually is suppressed, it is by 'Wintinnong' (Winnington), who calls him to order, and accuses him of

Expressions dictated only by Resentment, and uttered without any regard to –
PTIT: If this be to preserve Order, there is no danger of Indecency from the most licentious Tongue; for what Calumny can be more atrocious, or what Reproach more severe, than that of speaking with regard to any thing but Truth. . . . Order may sometimes be broken by Passion or Inadvertency, but will hardly be establish'd by Monitors like this, who cannot govern his own Passion, whilst he is restraining the Impetuosity of others. . . . That I may return in some Degree the Favour which he intends me, I will advise him never hereafter to exert himself on the subject of Order.

WINTINNONG: As I was hindered by the Gentleman's Ardour and Impetuosity from concluding my Sentence, none but myself can know the Equity or Partiality of my Intentions, and therefore, as I cannot, justly, be condemn'd, I ought to be supposed innocent. . . . How wide he may extend his Authority, or whom he may proceed to include in the same Sentence I shall not determine; having not yet arrived at the same Degree of Sagacity as himself, not being able to foreknow what another is going to pronounce.

Pitt is effectively silenced. The whole passage is a vivid histrionic scene. The accusations of theatricality are entirely well-founded, and Johnson depicts very astutely the highly synthetic nature of Pitt's patriotic ardour. The Parliamentary *fracas* accurately reflects the vituperativeness of real political debate. The speakers genuinely respond to each other's attacks, and Pitt in particular deliberately seems to stoke up the violence of his own mood. But we have only to look at the day's earlier proceedings on the same topic to see Johnson's careful discrimination between speakers, and between phases of the debate. 'Sir Rub. Walelop' (Walpole) had defended the measure in these terms:

Every Law which extends its Influence to great Numbers in various Relations and Circumstances must produce some Consequences that were never foreseen or intended and is to be censured or applauded as the general Advantages or Inconveniences are found to preponderate. Of this kind is the Law before us, a Law enforced by the Necessity of our Affairs, and drawn up with no other Intention than to secure the publicke Happiness and produce that Success which every Man's interest must prompt him to desire.

The speech conveys something of the pragmatic gifts of Walpole. Its plea is national necessity; a plea which always has the advantage of making opposition seem treasonable: but its tone could be described as quiet and neutral. Whether or not this was Walpole's own tone is disputable, but it is the tone consistently ascribed to the Prime Minister by Johnson; never more so than in the short final speech he gives him at the conclusion of the censure debate of 1741, and which crushes the Opposition. It closes:

> Having now, Sir, with due submission offered my Defence, I shall wait the decision of the House without any other Solicitude than for the Honour of their Counsels, which cannot but be impaired if Passion should precipitate, or Interest pervert them. For my part, that Innocence which has supported me against the Clamour of the Opposition will establish my Happiness in obscurity, not shall I lose by the Censure which is now threatened any other Pleasure than that of serving my Country.

'No man, certainly no politician, seems to have cared less [than Walpole] what people in general, and his enemies in particular thought about him, or sought less to appease them',[12] and the coolness which Johnson ascribes to 'Walelop' accurately catches this trait. Later in life Johnson alluded specifically to Walpole's 'placability of temper': 'Sir Robert was of a temper so calm and equal, and so hard to be provoked, that he was very sure he never felt the bitterest invectives against him for half an hour.'[13]

Staunch but rather turgid support for the party line then comes from 'Yoneg' (Sir William Yonge, Secretary at War, and among Walpole's loyalest supporters):[14]

> This Debate has been protracted ... by a neglect with which almost all the Opponents of the Bill may be justly charged, the Neglect of distinguishing between Measures preferable to Consequences which are apprehended from particular Conjectures; between Laws made only to advance the publick Happiness and Expedients of which the Benefit is merely occasional, and of which the sole Intention is to avert some national Calamity, and which are to cease with the Necessity that produced them.

But the partisan shipping continues, with Fazakerly's[15] blunt work on the bread-and-butter issues:

> Let me suppose, Sir, a merchant urging it as a Charge against a Seaman that he raises his Demand of Wages in Time of War, would not the Sailor readily reply, That harder Labour required larger Pay? Enquire, says he, of the Workmen in the Docks, have not they double Wages for double Labour? And is not their lot safe and easy in Comparison with mine? ... I know not

Appendix: Johnson's 'dramatic sense' 171

why sailors alone should serve their Country to their Disadvantage, and be expected to encounter Danger without the Incitement of a Reward.

On this one issue alone, then, Johnson displays a more than competent grasp of the available ploys and styles of political rhetoric. He dramatises the issues with living voices. Cave astutely promoted the Parliamentary debates to the leading place in the Magazine, and circulation grew by fifty per cent.[16] The debates were widely admired and discussed, being thought to be genuine. On one occasion, a gentleman was particularly rapturous about a speech of Pitt, saying that he had translated Demosthenes but 'he had met with nothing equal to the speech above-mentioned'. Johnson sat quiet, until he saw his time, then said, 'That speech I wrote in a garret in Exeter Street.'[17] In the said garret, Johnson composed the Debates in a state of near-frenzy. 'He never wrote any part of his works with equal velocity. Three columns of the Magazine in an hour was no uncommon effort, which was faster than most persons could have transcribed that quantity.'[18] The speed of composition was partly a matter of necessity. It may also have been a matter of creative intensity. Hawkins tells us the Debates were 'written at those seasons when he was able to raise his imagination to such a pitch of fervour as bordered upon enthusiasm, which, that he might the better do, his practice was to shut himself in a room assigned to him at St John's Gate, to which he would not suffer any one to approach, except the compositor or Cave's boy for matter, which, as fast as he composed it, he tumbled out at the door'.[19]

The contrast with *Irene* could hardly be stronger. Twelve years elapsed between the time when Johnson set off for London with the partly-finished play in his pocket, and the first performance by Garrick's company in 1749. It is clear that, over the whole of this period, the play underwent successive revisions. The recent discovery of a manuscript notebook of Johnson's – now in the Hyde collection – reveals a substantial reworking of Act V: yet this notebook can be dated not earlier than 1746, and possibly later. Even then, the version of Act V which it gives us, though closer to the final version than any previous text of the play, still has only four scenes, compared with a final nine. We could hardly ask for stronger support of Boswell's remark that *Irene* was rapidly conceived, 'but slowly and painfully elaborated'.[20]

It is clearly this process of slow and painful elaboration which so effectively stifles any life in *Irene*'s speeches. It might be supposed that Johnson's conception of tragedy as a venerable literary medium compelled him to petrify his own essay in the form into polished dignity. Garrick, who was induced to perform the play only by his long personal friendship with Johnson, went to desperate lengths to try to inject a little life into the corpse. These included an ill-judged decision to have Irene strangled on stage, which provoked ironic cries of 'Murder'.[21] One's sympathies go out to Garrick, since the task was clearly hopeless. Whatever Johnson had learned about life in the twelve years since he came to London, little of it was allowed to make its impact on the play, which retained to the last the original draft outline almost intact, and many of the early draft speeches; so that revision often consisted of nothing more than reshuffling and polishing. Although appearing in the same year as *The Vanity of Human Wishes*, *Irene* remains the record of a young man's rather priggish mind. Its interest for us is that it testifies to how far back in life goes Johnson's obsession with dreams.

Notes

NOTES TO CHAPTER 1: LIFE: 'VAIN IMAGINATIONS'

1. Bertrand H. Bronson, 'The Double Tradition of Dr Johnson', *ELH*, 1951, pp. 90–106.
2. *Life*, vol. II, p. 257.
3. Bertrand H. Bronson, 'Johnson Agonistes', in *Johnson and Boswell: Three Essays* (Berkeley and Los Angeles, Calif., 1944).
4. *Life*, vol. IV, p. 72.
5. Christopher Hollis, *Dr Johnson* (London, 1928) p. 146.
6. *Life*, vol. II, p. 121.
7. *Anecdotes*, in *Johnsonian Miscellanies*, vol. I, p. 199.
8. Boswell's *Journal of a Tour to the Hebrides*, in *Life*, vol. V, p. 215.
9. *Johnsonian Miscellanies*, vol. II, p. 230.
10. *Life*, vol. II, pp. 118–19.
11. Ibid., vol. II, p. 238.
12. Ibid., vol. III, p. 200.
13. Ibid., vol. I, p. 465.
14. Ibid., vol. I, pp. 244–6.
15. *Anecdotes*, in *Johnsonian Miscellanies*, vol. I, p. 213.
16. *Life*, vol. II, p. 66.
17. Ibid., vol. III, p. 322.
18. Ibid., vol. IV, pp. 183–4.
19. *Anecdotes*, in *Johnsonian Miscellanies*, vol. I, p. 194.
20. *Life*, vol. IV, p. 236.
21. Ibid., vol. V, p. 74.
22. Ibid., vol. III, p. 64.
23. Ibid., vol. V, p. 73.
24. Ibid., vol. V, pp. 264–5.
25. Ibid., vol. III, p. 39.
26. Ibid., vol. II, p. 100.
27. Ibid., vol. II, pp. 330–1.
28. Ibid., vol. II, p. 326.
29. Ibid., vol. II, p. 464.
30. Ibid., vol. I, p. 348.
31. Ibid., vol. I, p. 247.
32. Ibid., vol. I, pp. 483–5.
33. Ibid., vol. I, pp. 145–7.
34. *Johnsonian Miscellanies*, vol. II, pp. 275, 297.

35. *Life*, vol. IV, p. 427.
36. Ibid., vol. IV, p. 373.
37. *Annals (Works*, vol. I) pp. 50, 81, 264.
38. Hawkins, p. 287.
39. *Thraliana: The Diary of Mrs Hester Lynch Thrale (Later Mrs Piozzi), ...1776–1809*, ed. Katherine C. Balderston (Oxford, 1942).
40. Ibid., p. 415, n. 4.
41. *Annals*, p. 140.
42. *Thraliana*, p. 384.
43. *Letters*, vol. I, nos 307.1, 311.1a.
44. *Thraliana*, p. 386 and n.
45. John Wain, *Samuel Johnson* (London, 1974) pp. 289–90.
46. *Letters*, vol. III, no. 972.

NOTES TO CHAPTER 2: WORK: THE 'SCHEME OF LIFE'

1. Paul Fussell, *Samuel Johnson and the Life of Writing* (London, 1972) p. 9.
2. Ibid., pp. 15, 25.
3. Ibid., p. 7; see also W. J. Bate, *Samuel Johnson* (London, 1978) pp. 62–3; and J. P. Hardy, *Samuel Johnson: A Critical Study* (London, 1979) p. 35.
4. *Annals*, p. 14.
5. *Life*, vol. I, p. 47.
6. Ibid., vol. I, p. 57.
7. Ibid., vol. I, p. 50.
8. Hawkins, p. 9.
9. *Life*, vol. I, p. 441.
10. Ibid., vol. I, p. 74.
11. J. L. Clifford, *Young Samuel Johnson* (London, 1955) p. 188.
12. *Life*, vol. I, p. 102.
13. *Johnsonian Gleanings*, ed. A. L. Reade, 11 vols (privately printed, 1909–52) vol. VI, pp. 29–30.
14. From *Life of Father Paul*, reproduced in J. D. Fleeman, *Early Biographical Writings of Dr Johnson* (Farnborough, Surrey, 1973) p. 22.
15. *Life*, vol. III, p. 7.
16. Ibid., vol. I, p. 182.
17. Bate, *Samuel Johnson*, p. 240. For a full account of the writing of the *Dictionary*, see J. H. Sledd and G. J. Kolb, *Dr Johnson's Dictionary: Essays in the Biography of a Book* (Chicago, 1955). See also Scott Elledge, 'The Naked Science of Language, 1747–1786', in Howard Anderson and John S. Shea (eds), *Studies in Criticism and Aesthetics 1660–1800: Essays in Honor of Samuel Holt Monk* (Minneapolis, Minn., 1967).
18. Bate, *Samuel Johnson*, pp. 115–27.
19. Thomas Tyers, *A Biographical Sketch of Dr Samuel Johnson*, in *Johnsonian Miscellanies*, vol. II, p. 350; and Hawkins, p. 363.
20. Bate, *Samuel Johnson*, p. 277.
21. *Thraliana*, p. 211, and *Anecdotes*, in *Johnsonian Miscellanies*, vol. I, p. 260.
22. *Life*, vol. I, p. 192.
23. Ibid., vol. I, p. 193.

Notes

24. Ibid., vol. IV, p. 384.
25. *Johnsonian Miscellanies*, vol. II, pp. 153–4.
26. *Life*, vol. IV, p. 230.
27. *Annals*, p. 58.
28. Ibid., p. 50.
29. Ibid., p. 43.

NOTES TO CHAPTER 3: *IRENE*

1. *Poems (Works*, vol. VI), p.140, n.2.
2. *The Vanity of Human Wishes*, l. 5.
3. *Poems*, p. 189, n.
4. Ibid., p. 238.

NOTES TO CHAPTER 4: *LONDON*

1. T. S. Eliot, 'Johnson as Critic and Poet', in *On Poetry and Poets* (London, 1957) p. 179.
2. *Life*, vol. III, p. 178.
3. Fussell, *Samuel Johnson and the Life of Writing*, p.19.
4. *Life of Pope*, in *Johnson's Lives of the English Poets*, ed. G. B. Hill (Oxford, 1905; reprinted New York, 1967) vol. III, p. 176.
5. *Life*, vol. I, p. 122.
6. Ibid., vol I, p. 127.
7. Hawkins, pp. 60–1.
8. *Life*, vol. I, p. 164.
9. Ibid., vol. I, p. 125, n.
10. D. J. Greene, *The Politics of Samuel Johnson* (New Haven, Conn., 1960) p. 91.
11. *Life*, vol. II, p. 348.
12. J. P. Hardy, *Reinterpretations* (London, 1971) p. 112.
13. Ian Donaldson, 'The Satirists' London', *EIC*, vol. 25 (1975) p. 103.
14. See W. J. Bate, *The Achievement of Samuel Johnson* (New York, 1955) pp. 103–7 and *passim*.
15. D. V. Boyd, 'Vanity and Vacuity: a Reading of Johnson's Verse Satires', *ELH*, vol. 39 (1972) p. 395.
16. Donaldson, *EIC*, vol. 25, p. 104.
17. Boyd, *ELH*, vol. 39, p. 394.
18. Greene, *The Politics of Samuel Johnson*, p. 139.
19. G. S. Fraser, 'Johnson and Goldsmith: the Mid-Augustan Norm', *ES* (1970) pp. 51–70.

NOTES TO CHAPTER 5: *THE VANITY OF HUMAN WISHES*

1. Andrew Marvell, *Second Advice to a Painter* (1666) l. 165.
2. Boyd, *ELH*, vol. 39, p. 399.
3. Perceived by Boyd, ibid.

4. See MacDonald Emslie, 'Johnson's Satires and the Proper Wit of Poetry', *Cambridge Journal*, vol. 7 (1953–4) p. 348.
5. *Life*, vol. III, p. 358.
6. C. B. Tinker (ed.), *Dr Johnson and Fanny Burney* (New York, 1911) p. 61.
7. *Life*, vol. II, pp. 261–2. For an analysis of Johnson's humour, see W. B. C. Watkins, *Perilous Balance* (Princeton, N.J., 1939); and Bate, *The Achievement of Samuel Johnson*, pp. 115–28.
8. Arieh Sachs, *Passionate Intelligence: Imagination and Reason in the Work of Samuel Johnson* (Baltimore, Md., 1967) p. 79.
9. Boyd, *ELH*, vol. 39, p. 403.
10. *Works*, vol. VI, p. XIX.

NOTES TO CHAPTER 6: *THE RAMBLER*

1. *Life*, vol. I, p. 246.
2. John Wain, *Samuel Johnson* (London, 1974), see especially Chapter 7.
3. Austin Dobson (ed.), *Diaries and Letters of Madame D'Arblay* (London, 1904) vol. I, p. 69.
4. *Life*, vol. IV, p. 111. The phrase is William Gerard Hamilton's.
5. W. K. Wimsatt, Jr, *Philosophic Words: A Study of Style and Meaning in 'The Rambler' and 'Dictionary' of Samuel Johnson* (New Haven, Conn., 1948) p. 54.
6. *Life*, vol. IV, p. 386.
7. Fussell, *Samuel Johnson and the Life of Writing*, pp. 157–8.
8. *The Idler*, no. 74.
9. Random examples might include Northrop Frye ('its chief interest is in human character as it manifests itself in a society'); Edwin Muir ('on the one hand we see characters living in a society; on the other, figures moving from a beginning to an end'); or Malcolm Bradbury ('a dynamic action about persons in a society').
10. J. P. Hardy, *Samuel Johnson: A Critical Study*, p. 148, comments interestingly on the Nile as symbol in *Rasselas*.
11. *Works*, vol. II, ed. W. J. Bate, J. M. Bullitt, L. F. Powell, pp. xix–xx, n. 7.
12. W. J. Bate, *The Achievement of Samuel Johnson*, chapter 2, end; repeated *Works*, vol. III, p. xxix; and again in *Samuel Johnson*, p. 295.
13. *Anecdotes*, in *Johnsonian Miscellanies*, vol. I, pp. 253–4.
14. *Johnsonian Miscellanies*, vol. II, p. 274 (Miss Reynolds).

NOTES TO CHAPTER 7: *THE IDLER*

1. *Annals*, p. 92. See also pp. 77–8: 'a kind of strange oblivion has overspread me, so that I know what has become of the last year, and perceive that incidents and intelligence pass over me without leaving any impression'.
2. The review is conveniently reprinted in R. B. Schwartz, *Samuel Johnson and the Problem of Evil* (Wisconsin, 1975). This extract comes from the penultimate paragraph.
3. Stuart Gerry Brown, 'Dr Johnson and the Old Order', *Marxist Quarterly*, vol. I (1937) pp. 418–30; reprinted in *Samuel Johnson*, ed. D. J. Greene (Engle-

wood Cliffs, N.J., 1965) (*Twentieth Century Views* series).
4. Arieh Sachs, *Passionate Intelligence*.
5. He bracketed Hume and Hobbes together as atheists. Hume has 'no principle. If he is any thing, he is a Hobbist' (*Life*, vol. v, p. 272).
6. David Hume, *Treatise of Human Nature*, in *The Philosophical Works of David Hume*, 4 vols, ed. T. H. Green and T. H. Grose (London, 1874) vol. I, p. 417.
7. *Life*, vol. v, p. 30.
8. Quoted in E. C. Mossner, *The Forgotten Hume; le bon David* (New York, 1943) pp. 206–7.
9. *Annals*, p. 269.
10. Kathleen Grange, 'Samuel Johnson's Account of Certain Psychoanalytic Concepts', *Journal of Nervous and Mental Disease*, vol. 135 (August 1962) pp. 93–8; reprinted in *Samuel Johnson*, ed. D. J. Greene.
11. *Works*, vol. II, p. xx.

NOTES TO CHAPTER 8 : *RASSELAS*

1. *Life*, vol. I, p. 341.
2. John Wain, *Samuel Johnson*, p. 207.
3. Hawkins, p. 366.
4. *Letters*, I, no. 124. The other letters in the correspondence may conveniently be found in *Life*, vol. I, appendix B.
5. Bate, *Samuel Johnson*, p. 337.
6. *Life*, vol. I, appendix B, p. 514, n. 2.
7. *Johnsonian Miscellanies*, vol. I, p. 416.
8. *Annals*, p. 69.
9. Hawkins, p. 368.
10. *Life*, vol. I, p. 343.
11. Bate, *Samuel Johnson*, p. 340.
12. *Thraliana*, p. 179, quoted in Bate, *Samuel Johnson*, p. 299.

NOTES TO CHAPTER 9: *A JOURNEY TO THE WESTERN ISLANDS*

1. *Boswell's Journal of a Tour to the Hebrides*, edited from the original manuscript by F. A. Pottle and C. H. Bennett (London and New Haven, Conn., 1936) pp. 208–9
2. Ibid., p. 175.
3. Ibid., p. 152.
4. Ibid., p. 91.
5. *Life*, vol. III, p. 398.
6. *Annals*, pp. 118–19.
7. Ibid., pp. 278 and 297.
8. Ibid., p. 362.
9. Ibid., pp. 243–4.
10. *Life*, vol. IV, p. 199.
11. Ibid., vol. II, p. 304.
12. *Boswell's Journal*, p. 309.

13. *A Journey to the Western Islands*, ed. Mary Lascelles (1971) (*Works*, vol. IX), pp. 146–7.
14. On Raasay (ibid., pp. 63–4); and again on Col (ibid., p. 126).
15. Ibid., p. 74.
16. Ibid., p. 152.
17. Ibid., p. 50.
18. Ibid., pp. 111–12.
19. Ibid., p. 28.
20. *Boswell's Journal*, pp. 215–16.
21. Ibid., p. 41.
22. *A Journey*, p. 9.
23. Ibid., p. 144.
24. Ibid., p. 152.
25. Ibid., p. 6.
26. Ibid., p. 65.
27. Ibid., p. 111.
28. Ibid., p. 117.
29. Ibid., p. 51.
30. *Boswell's Journal*, p. 59.
31. *A Journey*, p. 28.
32. Ibid., p. 84.
33. Ibid., p. 116.
34. Ibid., pp. 110 and 119.
35. *Thraliana*, p. 345.
36. *Life*, vol. III, pp. 228–9.
37. *A Journey*, p. 22.
38. Thomas Jeremielty, 'Dr Johnson and the Uses of Travel'. *PQ*, vol. 51 (1972) p. 458. For an account of Johnson as empiricist, see R. B. Schwartz, 'Johnson's Journey', *JEGPh*, vol. 69 (1970) pp. 292–303.
39. *A Journey*, p. 84.
40. *Life*, vol. I, pp. 450 and 409.
41. *Boswell's Journal*, p. 103.
42. Ibid., p. 371.
43. *A Journey*, pp. 40–1.
44. Ibid., p. 19.
45. Ibid., p. 34.
46. Ibid., p. 39.
47. Ibid., p. 20.
48. Ibid., p. xx.
49. Ibid., p. 47.
50. Ibid., p. xx.
51. George H. Savage, ' "Roving Among the Hebrides": the Odyssey of Samuel Johnson', *SEL*, vol. 17 (1977) p. 494.
52. For example, R. K. Kaul, '*A Journey to the Western Islands* Reconsidered', *EIC*, vol. 13 (1963) pp. 341–50.
53. Jeffrey Hart, 'Johnson's *A Journey to the Western Islands*: History as Art', *EIC*, vol. 10 (1960) p. 51.
54. *A Journey*, p. 91.
55. Ibid., pp. 90–1.

56. Ibid., p. 92.
57. Ibid., p. 94.
58. Ibid., p. 94.
59. Ibid., p. 97.
60. Ibid., p. 97.
61. Ibid., p. 94.
62. Ibid., p. 97.
63. Ibid., pp. 96–7.
64. Ibid., pp. 128 and 152.
65. Ibid., p. 89.
66. Ibid., pp. 131–2
67. Ibid., p. 37.
68. Ibid., p. 53.
69. Ibid., p. 59.
70. Ibid., p. 77.
71. Ibid., p. 71.
72. Ibid., p. 68.
73. *Boswell's Journal*, p. 135.
74. *A Journey*, p. 60.
75. Ibid., p. 66.
76. Ibid., p. 136.
77. Ibid., p. 136.
78. Ibid., pp. 10–11.
79. Ibid., pp. 139–40.
80. Ibid., p. 138.
81. Ibid., p. 22.
82. Ibid., p. 138.
83. Ibid., p. 58.
84. Ibid., p. 157.
85. Ibid., p. 40.
86. *Life*, vol. III, p. 196.
87. *A Journey*, p. 147.
88. *Works*, vol. II, p. 298.
89. *Life*, vol. v, p. 199.
90. *Letters*, vol. II, no. 528.
91. *Boswell's Journal*, p. 211.
92. *A Journey*, p. 26.
93. Ibid., p. 148.
94. Ibid., p. 153.
95. *Boswell's Journal*; not in original manuscript, but in 1785 edition, see *Life*, vol v, p. 334.

NOTES TO CHAPTER 10: THE LITERARY CRITICISM

1. *Johnson's Lives of the English Poets*, vol. I, pp. 13–17.
2. Ibid., vol. I, p. 314.
3. Ibid., vol. I, p. 75.

4. Ibid., vol. I, pp. 248, 246, 247.
5. Ibid., vol. II, pp. 272, 281.
6. Ibid., vol. II, pp. 259, 260, 261, 262.
7. Ibid., vol. I, pp. 390–1.
8. Ibid., vol. II, p. 47.
9. *The Rambler*, no. 125; *Works*, vol. IV, p. 300.
10. *The Rambler*, no. 155; *Works*, vol. V, p. 59.
11. *The Rambler*, no. 168; *Works*, vol. V, pp. 127–8.
12. *Lives of the Poets*, vol. I, p. 469.
13. Ibid., vol. I, pp. 464–5.
14. Leopold Damrosch, *The Uses of Johnson's Criticism* (Charlottesville, Va., 1976) pp. 214–15: Jean H. Hagstrum, *Samuel Johnson's Literary Criticism* (Minneapolis, Minn., 1952) Chapter VII.
15. *Lives of the Poets*, vol. III, p. 222 (*Life of Pope*).
16. Ibid., vol. III, p. 243.
17. *Preface to Shakespeare, Works*, vol. VII (*Johnson on Shakespeare*) p. 91.
18. *Works*, vol. VIII, p. 1011.
19. Ibid., vol. VIII, p. 704.
20. *Lives of the Poets*, vol. I, p. 177.
21. Ibid., vol. I, p. 170.
22. Ibid., vol. I, p. 178.
23. Ibid., vol. I, p. 178.
24. Ibid., vol. I. pp. 180–2.
25. Ibid., vol. I. pp. 190–1.
26. Ibid., vol. I, p. 188.
27. Ibid., vol. I, p. 181.
28. Warren Fleischauer, 'Johnson, *Lycidas* and the Norms of Criticism', in *Johnsonian Studies*, ed. M. Wahba (Cairo, 1962) pp. 235–56, esp. pp. 243–7.
29. *Works*, vol. VII, p. 177.
30. *Lives of the Poets*, vol. I, p. 22.
31. Ibid., vol. I, p. 24.
32. Ibid., vol. I, pp. 30–1.
33. Ibid., vol. I, p. 53.
34. Ibid., vol. I, p. 58.
35. Ibid., vol. I, p. 59.
36. Ibid., vol. I, p. 21.
37. Ibid., vol. I, p. 28.
38. Ibid., vol. III, p. 440.
39. Ibid., vol. II, pp. 145–6, 149–50.
40. Ibid., vol. I, pp. 239–40.
41. Ibid., vol. I, p. 82.
42. Ibid., vol. I, p. 296.
43. Ibid., vol. I, p. 294.
44. Ibid., vol. I, p. 469.
45. Ibid., vol. III, pp. 324–5.
46. Ibid., vol. III, pp. 399, 395, 397–8.
47. Ibid., vol. III, p. 38.
48. Ibid., vol. III, pp. 51, 55.

49. Ibid., vol. I, p. 144.
50. Ibid., vol. I, p. 194.
51. Ibid., vol. II, pp. 237, 253.
52. Ibid., vol. II, p. 249.
53. Ibid., vol. I, p. 20.
54. Hagstrum, *Samuel Johnson's Literary Criticism*, p. 90.
55. Damrosch, *Uses of Johnson's Criticism*, p. 119.
56. Ibid., p. 161.
57. *Lives of the Poets*, vol. I, pp. 59–60.
58. Damrosch, *Uses of Johnson's Criticism*, p. 146.
59. *Lives of the Poets*, vol. I, pp. 165–6, 167.
60. Ibid., vol. III, pp. 229–30.
61. *Works*, vol. VII, p. 193; vol. VIII, p. 591.
62. *Rasselas*, Chapter x.

NOTES TO CHAPTER 11: LEVET

1. *Life*, vol. I, p. 243.
2. Hawkins, pp. 399–400.
3. *Letters*, vol. II, no. 770.
4. Ibid., vol. II, no. 691.
5. *Dunciad Variorum* (1729) Bk III, l. 164. The immediate target is Welsted, but the formula parodies Denham. The epitaph on Mrs Corbet dates from 1730.
6. *Lives of the Poets*, vol. III, p. 262.
7. *Life*, vol. IV, p. 339.

NOTES TO THE APPENDIX: JOHNSON'S 'DRAMATIC SENSE'

1. *Life*, vol. III, p. 440.
2. *Thraliana*, pp. 453–4.
3. *Life*, vol. III, pp. 144–5.
4. Hawkins, p. 526.
5. *Life*, vol. IV, pp. 408–9.
6. Ibid., vol. I, p. 118.
7. Hawkins, p. 122.
8. Ibid., p. 100.
9. *Life*, vol. I, p. 152.
10. *The Gentleman's Magazine*, vol. XI, pp. 451–586. Quotations here are taken from pp. 562–71.
11. Greene, *The Politics of Samuel Johnson*, p. 114.
12. Ibid., p. 84.
13. Hawkins, p. 514.
14. Yonge subsequently composed the Epilogue for *Irene*.
15. Nicholas Fazakerley was a lawyer and Tory politician; subsequently Recorder for Preston. It is amusing that he had a personal reputation for

stinginess.
16. Hawkins, p. 123.
17. *Johnsonian Miscellanies,* vol. I, p. 378 (the anecdote is Murphy's).
18. *Life,* vol. IV, p. 409.
19. Hawkins, p. 99.
20. *Life,* vol. I, p. 107.
21. *Life,* vol. I, p. 197.

Select Bibliography

COLLECTED WORKS

Of the early editions, the most complete (though not the most textually reliable) is *The Works of Samuel Johnson, LL.D.*, 9 vols, later 11 vols (Oxford, 1825).

The modern standard text is *The Yale Edition of the Works of Samuel Johnson*, gen. ed., vols I, II and VI, A. T. Hazen; subsequently J. H. Middendorf (New Haven, Conn., 1958–). The following volumes have so far appeared:

I	*Diaries, Prayers and Annals*, ed. E. L. McAdam Jr, with Donald and Mary Hyde (1958);
II	*'The Idler' and 'The Adventurer'*, ed. W. J. Bate, J. M. Bullitt and L. F. Powell (1963);
III–V	*The Rambler*, ed. W. J. Bate and A. B. Strauss (1969);
VI	*Poems*, ed. E. L. McAdam Jr, with George Milne (1964);
VII–VIII	*Johnson on Shakespeare*, ed. Arthur Sherbo, with an introduction by B. H. Bronson (1968);
IX	*A Journey to the Western Islands of Scotland*, ed. Mary Lascelles (1971);
X	*Political Writings*, ed. D. J. Greene (1977);
XIV	*Sermons*, ed. Jean Hagstrum and James Gray (1978).

INDIVIDUAL WORKS AND GROUPS OF WORKS

The Critical Opinions of Samuel Johnson, ed. J. E. Brown (Princeton, N.J., 1926; re-issued New York, 1961).

Johnson's Dictionary: A Modern Selection, ed. E. L. McAdam Jr and George Milne (New York, 1963).

Johnson's Journey to the Western Islands of Scotland, and Boswell's Journal of a Tour to the Hebrides with Samuel Johnson, LL.D., ed. R. W. Chapman (London, 1924, 1930, 1970).

Johnson's Lives of the English Poets, ed. G. B. Hill, 3 vols (Oxford, 1905; reprinted New York, 1967).

The Letters of Samuel Johnson, ed. R. W. Chapman, 3 vols (Oxford, 1952).

The Poems of Samuel Johnson, ed. D. Nichol Smith and E. L. McAdam Jr (Oxford, 1941; re-issued 1951); 2nd edn, ed. J. D. Fleeman (Oxford, 1974).

The Political Writings of Dr Johnson: A Selection, ed. J. P. Hardy (London, 1968).
The Rambler (selection), ed. S. C. Roberts (London, 1953).
Rasselas, ed. G. B. Hill (Oxford, 1887; reprinted 1958).
Samuel Johnson's Early Biographies, ed. R. E. Kelley (Iowa, 1971).
Samuel Johnson's Prefaces and Dedications, ed. A. T. Hazen (New Haven, Conn., 1937).

BIOGRAPHICAL SOURCES

Boswell, James, *Journal of a Tour to the Hebrides*, edited from the original manuscript by F. A. Pottle and C. H. Bennett (London and New Haven, Conn., 1936).
Boswell, James, *The Life of Samuel Johnson, LL.D.*, ed. G. B. Hill, rev. L. F. Powell, 6 vols (Oxford, 1934–50; 2nd rev. edns of vols V–VI, 1964).
Hawkins, Sir John, *The Life of Samuel Johnson, LL.D.* (London, 1787).
Dr Johnson and Fanny Burney, ed. C. B. Tinker (New York, 1911).
Johnsonian Gleanings, ed. A. L. Reade, 11 vols (privately printed, 1909–52).
Johnsonian Miscellanies, ed. G. B. Hill, 2 vols (Oxford, 1897).
Shaw, William, *Memoirs of the Life and Writings of the late Dr Samuel Johnson*, and Hester Lynch Piozzi, *Anecdotes of the late Samuel Johnson, LL.D.*, ed. A. Sherbo (London, 1974).
Thraliana: The Diary of Mrs Hester Lynch Thrale (later Mrs Piozzi) ... 1776–1809, ed. K. C. Balderston, 2 vols (Oxford, 1942).

BIOGRAPHICAL STUDIES

Bailey, J., *Dr Johnson and his Circle* (London, 1913).
Bate, W. J., *Samuel Johnson* (London, 1978).
Clifford, J. L., *Young Samuel Johnson* (London, 1955).
Krutch, J. W., *Samuel Johnson* (New York, 1955).
Stephen, L., *Samuel Johnson* (London, 1909).
Wain, John, *Samuel Johnson* (London, 1974).

CRITICAL AND OTHER STUDIES

Bate, W. J., *The Achievement of Samuel Johnson* (New York, 1955).
Bloom, E. A., *Samuel Johnson in Grub Street* (Providence, R.I., 1957).
Bronson, B. H., *Johnson and Boswell: Three Essays* (Berkeley and Los Angeles, Calif., 1944).
Bronson, B. H., *Johnson Agonistes and Other Essays* (Cambridge, 1946).
Chapin, C. F., *The Religious Thought of Samuel Johnson* (Ann Arbor, Mich., 1968).
Damrosch, L., *The Uses of Johnson's Criticism* (Charlottesville, Va., 1976).
Fussell, Paul, *Samuel Johnson and the Life of Writing* (London, 1971).
Greene, D. J., *The Politics of Samuel Johnson* (New Haven, Conn., 1960).
Greene, D. J. (ed.), *Samuel Johnson: A Collection of Critical Essays* (Englewood Cliffs, N.J., 1965).
Greene, D. J. *Samuel Johnson* (New York, 1970).

Select Bibliography

Hagstrum, J. H., *Samuel Johnson's Literary Criticism* (Minneapolis, 1952; rev. edn Chicago, 1967).
Hardy, J. P., *'Dictionary' Johnson* (Armidale, 1967).
Hardy, J. P. *Samuel Johnson: A Critical Study* (London, 1979).
Hilles, F. W. (ed.), *New Light on Dr Johnson* (New Haven, Conn., 1959).
Hoover, B. B., *Samuel Johnson's Parliamentary Reporting: Debates in the Senate of Lilliput* (Berkeley and Los Angeles, Calif., 1953).
Lascelles, M. M., Clifford, J. M., Fleeman, J. D., Hardy, J. P. (eds), *Johnson, Boswell and their Circle: Essays Presented to Lawrence Fitzroy Powell* (Oxford, 1965).
McIntosh, Carey, *The Choice of Life: Samuel Johnson and the World of Fiction* (New Haven, Conn., 1973).
Raleigh, Walter, *Six Essays on Johnson* (Oxford, 1910).
Sachs, Arieh, *Passionate Intelligence: Imagination and Reason in the Work of Samuel Johnson* (Baltimore, Md., 1967).
Sledd, J. H. and Kolb, G. J., *Dr Johnson's Dictionary: Essays in the Biography of a Book* (Chicago, 1955).
Schwartz, R. B., *Samuel Johnson and the Problem of Evil* (Wisconsin, 1975).
Voitle, Robert, *Samuel Johnson the Moralist* (Cambridge, Mass., 1961).
Wahba, Magdi (ed.), *Bicentenary Essays on 'Rasselas'* (Cairo, 1959).
Wahba, Magdi (ed.), *Johnsonian Studies* (Cairo, 1962).
Wain, John, *Johnson on Johnson* (London, 1976).
Walker, Robert, *Eighteenth Century Arguments for Immortality*, English Literary Studies series, gen. ed. Samuel Macy, no. 9 (University of Victoria, 1977).
Wimsatt, W. K., Jr, *The Prose Style of Samuel Johnson* (New Haven, Conn., 1941).
Wimsatt, W. K., Jr, *Philosophic Words: A Study of Style and Meaning in 'The Rambler' and 'Dictionary' of Samuel Johnson* (New Haven, Conn., 1948).

Index

Ad Ricardum Savage, 31
Adams, Dr, 12
Adison, Joseph, 150
Adversaria, 14
Age, comforts of, 114–15
Ambition, theme of, *see* Power
Annals
  on early perception, 12
  record of self-reproach, 8
Authorship
  hopes mocked, 139
  Johnson's views on, 57–8
  perils, 58
  public apathy towards, 58–9
  Rambler essays on, 67, 72

Bate, Walter Jackson, 15, 16, 64, 69, 87, 92, 117, 158
Bereavement
  imagery of, 96–7
  process in *Rasselas* 104–5
Blackmore, Richard Doddridge, 153
Boswell, James
  Journal of a Tour to the Hebrides, 119, 122, 124, 126, 137–8
  on circumstances of writing *Rasselas*, 89
  on Johnson's poetry, 16–17
  on Johnson's precision in use of words, 136–7
  on Johnson's wide-ranging curiosity, 119–20
  on Levet, 157
  on parting from Johnson, 160–1
  on *Vanity of Human Wishes* revisions, 49
  role in promoting Johnson's reputation, 4–5
Boyd, D. V., 36n., 45, 55
Bronson, Bertrand, 1

Brown, Stuart Gerry, 84
Burney, Fanny, 52–3, 59
Burton, Robert, 2, 53

Cave, Edmund, 13, 31, 166, 171
Choice, in *Rasselas*, 112–14
Clan system, view of, in *Journey to the Western Isles*, 131
Clarification of thought, as Johnson's aim, 3, 4
Classical imitation, 29, 34
  also by Pope, 30
  see also Juvenal
Competition, in appearance of success, 65–6
A Complete Vindication of Licensers of the Stage, 13
Conspiracy theory, in *London*, 37
Conversation, clarity of thought in, 4
Cowley, Abraham, 153, 155
  Johnson's discussion of language of, 149–50
  Johnson's treatment in *Lives of the Poets*, 139–40
  on his metaphysical poetry, 149
The Craftsman, 30, 32
Creativity
  defining quality of, 147
  source of urge, 116–17

Damrosch, Leopold, 144
  on Johnson's attacks on imagination, 154–5
Death, imagery of, 96–7
Denham, Sir John, 141, 150, 151
Dictionary of the English Language, 15–16
  initiating creative period, 15–16
Dodd, Rev. Mr, 165–6
Donaldson, Ian, 36
Dramatic ability, 165–72

Index

in letters and speeches written for others, 165–6
in Parliamentary Debates, 166–7
see also *Irene*
Dreams
in *The Idler*, 79–80
in *Rasselas*, 112–14
Dryden, John, 142, 154
Johnson's celebration of, 144–5, 151–2

Eliot, T. S., 29
Enlightenment, philosophy of, 83
Envy
attached to others' attainments, 64–5
of talent, 67, 71–2
of the virtuous, 66
theme of evils of, 36–7
Epigrams, 1
Erse language, 124
Esteem, ways of achieving
catalogued in *The Rambler*, 62–3
competitive aspect, 65
Evil
enforcement of morality, 84
explanation, in *The Idler*, 83

Fantasy
combination with metaphor, in *The Idler*, 77–8
in *Irene*, 20, 21–3; abjured by the good, 26
in Johnson's life and work, 2, 9–10
of leisure, in *London*, 39–40
religion as area of, 27, 84–7
Farce, Johnson's sense of, 52–3, 54, 56
Fear, phantom of, in *Irene*, 27–8
Fenton, Elijah, 141–2
Fleischauer, Warren, 148
Ford, Cornelius, 12
Fraser, George, 42
Friendships, basis of, 61–2
Fussell, Paul, 11, 29n., 60

Garrick, David, 13
performance of *Irene*, 171–2
Gay, John, 141
Gentleman's Magazine, 13, 14

Parliamentary Debates, 14, 166–71
'Glide', Johnson's uses of word, 63–4, 163
Goldsmith, Oliver, 1
Gray, Thomas, 150, 152
Greene, Donald, 29, 32, 41, 167

Habit, power of, 78–9
Hagstrum, Jean, 144, 154
Happiness, counterfeiting, 75–6
Hardy, John, 36, 64n.
Harleian descriptive catalogue, 14
Hector, Mr, 12, 13
Heroic couplets, effect in *London*, 34
Hobbes, Thomas, 85
Hogarth, William, 7
epitaph for, 158–9
Hope
disappointed, theme in *Lives of the Poets*, 140–2
phantom of, in *Irene*, 27–8
theme in *The Rambler*, 57
Human relationships
avoidance, in *Rasselas*, 102–4, 108
exploration in *The Rambler*, 62
see also Solitariness
Hume, David, 85, 86
Hussey, Rev. John, 31

Idleness
aspect in *Rasselas*, 117
denying capacity for reflection, 77
evident in Scotland, 123–4
in period after mother's death, 93
theme, 74–5, 83
The Idler, 2, 15, 16, 78–88, 93, 137
compared with *The Rambler*, 74
philosophical and metaphysical content, 83–5
self-portraits, 87
Imagination
Johnson's apparent fear of, 154
Johnson's description of difficulties of, 143
passages in *The Rambler*, 156
Immortality, dream of, 19
Irene, 11, 13, 20–8, 165
message on states of mind, 20
revisions, 171–2

Jenyns, Soame, 83–4
Johnson, Samuel
   appearance, 6
   as linguist, 17–18
   as schoolteacher, 13
   at Oxford, 12
   behavioural peculiarities, 6–8
   creative period, 11, 158: coinciding with Shakespeare edition, 19; initiated by *Dictionary*, 15
   evidence of generosity, 92
   facets of personality, 1–2
   financial position, 69, 92–3
   gifts recognised at school, 12
   knowledge of wide range of subjects, 119–20
   lack of business acumen, 92
   social awkwardness, 70
Johnson, Sarah, 89–91
Jorden, William, 12
A Journey to the Western Islands, 119–38
   images of progress, 131–3
   record of observations, 120–2
   sociological concerns, 126–30
Juvenal, 30, 34, 55, 97
   theme of victory turned to defeat, 47

Lade, Sir John, 4, 158
Langton, Bennett, 6, 53
Lascelles, Mary, 128
Levet, Dr Robert, 64, 157–64
   death, effect on Johnson, 157–8
   description, 157
   see also On the Death of Dr Robert Levet
The Life of Savage, 59
Linguistic ability, 17–18
Literary criticism, 139–56
   in *Rambler* series, 67
Literature
   detractors of talent, 71–2
   Johnson's wish for greatness, 19, 57
   perils of success, 70
   themes in *The Rambler*, 67
   see also Authorship; Writing
The Lives of the Poets, 19, 59, 60, 139ff.
Lobo, Father Jerome, 13, 94–5
London, Johnson's love of, 29
London, 11, 13, 29–42, 51
   character of Thales, 35–6
   contemporary detail withheld, 34–5
   immediate success, 30
   political comment, 30–1
   problems of interpretation, 33

Macaulay, Thomas Babbington, Lord, 1
Marmor Norfolciense, 13, 33
Marriage
   absurd reasons for, 62
   discussion in *Rasselas*, 106–7, 109, 110–11
Maxwell, Rev. Dr, 3
Melancholy, proximity to hilarity, 53–4
Memory, value of, in *The Idler*, 81–2
Mental illness, Johnson's interest in, 2, 8–9
Metaphysical poets, 149–50
Milton, John, 153–4, 155
   criticism, 147–8
Monboddo, Lord James Burnett, 4
Montague, Charles, Earl of Halifax, 142
Morality
   and peace of mind, in *Irene*, 20
   defended by retreat from world, 73
   in *Rambler* essays, 61
   in reforming bad habits, 78–9
   link with stylistic purity, 60, 151

New English Dictionary, 15
Newberry, John, 93

On the Death of Dr Robert Levet, 158, 159
   repressed emotion, 160–1
   style, 159
   theme of imprisonment, 161–2
   see also Levet, Dr Robert
Oral tradition, deplored by Johnson, 122, 124
Originality, Johnson's views on, in *Lives of the Poets*, 152–3
Otway, Thomas, 141

Parenthood, discussion in *Rasselas*, 105–6, 109
Parliamentary Debates, *see Gentleman's Magazine*

Passions
  status in *The Idler*, 86
  theme in *Irene*, 23–4
Pastoral ideal, in *London*, 36; in *Levet*, 162
Patriotism, 30, 31, 33
Philips, Ambrose, 152
Philips, John, 140–1
Picture-frame metaphor, in *Vanity of Human Wishes*, 43
Piozzi, Gabriel, 157
Pitt, William, the Elder, 167
Pleasure, counterfeiting, 75–6
Poetry
  essential elements, 144
  extempore facility, 16
  less controllable than prose, 42
  pre-eminence of *Vanity of Human Wishes*, 56
Political careers blighted, in *Vanity of Human Wishes*, 43–5
Political comment, in *London*, 30–1
Pope, Alexander, 29, 30, 154, 155
  deficiencies as poet, 144–5
  epitaphs by, 159–60
Porson, Richard, 85, 87
Porter, Lucy, 89–91, 92
Porter, 'Tetty' (Mrs Samuel Johnson), 13
Portrait theme, in *Vanity of Human Wishes*, 43–4
Poverty
  references to, 32
  theme in *London*, 38
Power
  as alternative to possession of money, 130
  competitive urge in man, 65
  dream of, in *Irene*, 24–5
  jealousy between holders of, in *Rasselas*, 103
  overestimated in *Vanity of Human Wishes*, 48
Prayer on Losing the Power of Speech, 18
Predation, concept of, 51
Puns, Johnson's use of, 50, 54

Quest theme in *Rasselas*, 98–100, 111–12

The Rambler, 15, 19, 57–73, 106
  autobiographical element, 70–1
  essential features, 61
  eventual tranquillity of content, 75
  fortnightly essays, 60
  literary criticism, 143
  passages on imagination, 156
  recurrent themes, 66–7
  some parody in *The Idler*, 74
Rasselas, 15, 89–118
  description of the Happy Valley, 95–6
  effect of death of Johnson's mother, 89–94
  episodic structure, 99
  plot, 94
  theme of vain hope, 2
Reformation, effects in Scotland, 122–3
Religion
  as area of fantasy in *Irene*, 27; in *Idler*, 84
  compatibility with concept of evil, 79
  deficiency in Scots learning, 122–3
  in ending of *Vanity of Human Wishes*, 55
  Johnson's scepticism, 85
Reynolds, Sir Joshua, 3–4, 7, 59, 89
Richardson, Samuel, 7
Rudeness in Johnson, 4

Sachs, Arieh, 55, 81, 84
Sarpi, Father Paolo, 13
Savage, George, 128
Savage, Richard, 31–2, 59
Scholarship
  linked with wit, 72
  themes in *The Rambler*, 67
Scotland
  destruction of places of worship and universities, 122–3
  Johnson's view of life in, 122
Secrets, reasons for betrayal, 62–3
Senility, 54; *see also* Age
Shakespeare, Johnson's edition of, 93, 143–4
  coinciding with creative period, 19
  criticism in, 145–7
Society, viciousness of, comments in

The Rambler, 68–9
  see also Vacuity of human mind
Sociological interest, in *Journey to the Western Islands*, 126–30
Solitariness,
  theme in *Rasselas*, 100–1, 105, 107
  turned into self-sufficiency, 115
  see also Human relationships
Speech, Johnson's Midlands accent, 5
Success, scorning of, 65–6
Swift, Jonathan, 152–3

Teacher, Johnson's role as, 3
Thrale, Henry, 157
  election addresses, 165
Thrale, Mrs Hester Lynch
  apologises for poor reporting, 4
  Johnson's poem for birthday, 16
  marriage to Piozzi, 157
  nature of relationship with Johnson, 9–10
  on Johnson's interest in mental illness, 2
  on Johnson's passion for accuracy, 125
  on Johnson's view of vacuity, 117
To a Young Lady on Her Birthday, 98
Translations, verse, 17
Truth, search for, in *Journey to the Western Islands*, 125–6
Tyers, Tom, 15; quoted 5n. 23

Vacuity of mind
  among Highlanders, 123–4
  in *Vanity of Human Wishes*, 52
  Johnson's views, 117
  of wits, 72–3
  satirised in *The Rambler*, 68–9
The Vanity of Human Wishes, 15, 19, 43–56, 61, 69
  greatness of poem, 56
  Johnson's corrections, 49
  and old age, 162–3
  rapid composition, 16–17
  sense of enclosure, 47
  techniques, 43, 47

Wain, John, 9, 59
Waller, Edmund, 150, 151, 155
Walmesley, Gilbert, 12, 13
Walpole, Sir Robert, 30–2, 41, 166–9
Wilkes, John, 5
Wolsey, Thomas, 43, 44, 45, 50–1, 52, 54, 69
Writing
  in 18th century, characteristics, 11
  Johnson's determination at Oxford, 12
  Johnson's list of projects, 14
  theme of literary greatness, 19
  see also Authorship; Literature

Young, Edward, 152
The Young Author, 58, 139
Youth
  age as mentor in *Rasselas*, 98
  detachment from parents, 107–8
  Johnson's regard for, 97–8

GPSR Compliance

The European Union's (EU) General Product Safety Regulation (GPSR) is a set of rules that requires consumer products to be safe and our obligations to ensure this.

If you have any concerns about our products, you can contact us on

ProductSafety@springernature.com

In case Publisher is established outside the EU, the EU authorized representative is:

Springer Nature Customer Service Center GmbH
Europaplatz 3
69115 Heidelberg, Germany

www.ingramcontent.com/pod-product-compliance
Lightning Source LLC
Chambersburg PA
CBHW031521100426
42873CB00013B/153